Microsoft®

Office 2003

VISUAL™

Quick Tips

by Sherry Willard Kinkoph

Wiley Publishing, Inc.

Microsoft® Office 2003 Visual Quick Tips

Published by
Wiley Publishing, Inc.
111 River Street
Hoboken, NJ 07030-5774

Library of Congress Control Number: 2005937795

ISBN-13: 978-0-470-00925-3

ISBN-10: 0-470-00925-X

Manufactured in the United States of America

10 9 8 7 6 5 4 3 2

1K/SQ/RS/QV/IN

Trademark Acknowledgments

Contact Us

For general information on our other products and services contact our Customer Care Department within the U.S. at 800-762-2974, outside the U.S. at 317-572-3993, or fax 317-572-4002.

For technical support please visit www.wiley.com/techsupport.

WILEY

Wiley Publishing, Inc.

Sales

Contact Wiley at (800) 762-2974 or fax (317) 572-4002.

Praise for Visual Books

"I have to praise you and your company on the fine products you turn out. I have twelve Visual books in my house. They were instrumental in helping me pass a difficult computer course. Thank you for creating books that are easy to follow. Keep turning out those quality books."

Gordon Justin (Brielle, NJ)

"What fantastic teaching books you have produced! Congratulations to you and your staff. You deserve the Nobel prize in Education. Thanks for helping me understand computers."

Bruno Tonon (Melbourne, Australia)

"A Picture Is Worth A Thousand Words! If your learning method is by observing or hands-on training, this is the book for you!"

Lorri Pegan-Durastante (Wickliffe, OH)

"Over time, I have bought a number of your 'Read Less - Learn More' books. For me, they are THE way to learn anything easily. I learn easiest using your method of teaching."

José A. Mazón (Cuba, NY)

"You've got a fan for life!! Thanks so much!!"

Kevin P. Quinn (Oakland, CA)

"I have several books from the Visual series and have always found them to be valuable resources."

Stephen P. Miller (Ballston Spa, NY)

"I have several of your Visual books and they are the best I have ever used."

Stanley Clark (Crawfordville, FL)

"Like a lot of other people, I understand things best when I see them visually. Your books really make learning easy and life more fun."

John T. Frey (Cadillac, MI)

"I have quite a few of your Visual books and have been very pleased with all of them. I love the way the lessons are presented!"

Mary Jane Newman (Yorba Linda, CA)

"Thank you, thank you, thank you...for making it so easy for me to break into this high-tech world."

Gay O'Donnell (Calgary, Alberta,Canada)

"I write to extend my thanks and appreciation for your books. They are clear, easy to follow, and straight to the point. Keep up the good work! I bought several of your books and they are just right! No regrets! I will always buy your books because they are the best."

Seward Kollie (Dakar, Senegal)

"I would like to take this time to thank you and your company for producing great and easy-to-learn products. I bought two of your books from a local bookstore, and it was the best investment I've ever made! Thank you for thinking of us ordinary people."

Jeff Eastman (West Des Moines, IA)

"Compliments to the chef!! Your books are extraordinary! Or, simply put, extra-ordinary, meaning way above the rest! THANKYOU THANKYOU THANKYOU! I buy them for friends, family, and colleagues."

Christine J. Manfrin (Castle Rock, CO)

Credits

Project Editor
Robyn Siesky

Acquisitions Editor
Jody Lefevere

Product Development Supervisor
Courtney Allen

Copy Editor
Marylouise Wiack

Technical Editor
Lee Musick

Editorial Manager
Robyn Siesky

Editorial Assistant
Adrienne D. Porter

Manufacturing
Allan Conley
Linda Cook
Paul Gilchrist
Jennifer Guynn

Book Design
Kathie S. Rickard

Production Coordinator
Kristie Rees

Layout
Sean Decker, Jennifer Heleine,
Amanda Spagnuolo

Screen Artists
Steven Amory
Matthew Bell
Jacob Mansfield
Jill Proll

Illustrators
Ronda David-Burroughs

Cover Design
Anthony Bunyan

Proofreaders
Laura Albert, Robert Springer,
Brian Walls

Indexer
Sherry Massey

Vice President and Executive Group Publisher
Richard Swadley

Vice President Publisher
Barry Pruett

Composition Director
Debbie Stailey

About the Author

Sherry Willard Kinkoph has written and edited more than 60 books over the past 10 years covering a variety of computer topics ranging from hardware to software from Microsoft Office programs to the Internet. Her recent titles include *Teach Yourself Visually Premiere 6*, *Master Visually Dreamweaver MX and Flash MX*, and *Teach Yourself Visually Restoration and Retouching with Photoshop Elements 2*. Sherry's ongoing quest is to help users of all levels master ever-changing computer technologies. No matter how many times they — the software manufacturers and hardware conglomerates — throw out a new version or upgrade, Sherry vows to be there to make sense of it all and help computer users get the most out of their machines.

How To Use This Book

Microsoft Office 2003 Visual Quick tips includes tasks that reveal cool secrets, teach timesaving tricks, and explain great tips guaranteed to make you more productive with Office 2003. The easy-to-use layout lets you work through all the tasks from beginning to end or jump in at random.

Who Is This Book For?

You already know Office basics. Now you'd like to go beyond, with shortcuts, tricks and tips that let you work smarter and faster. And because you learn more easily when someone shows you how, this is the book for you.

Conventions Used In This Book

❶ Steps

This book uses step-by-step instructions to guide you easily through each task. Numbered callouts on every screen shot show you exactly how to perform each task, step by step.

❷ Tips

Practical tips provide insights to save you time and trouble, caution you about hazards to avoid, and reveal how to do things in Office that you never thought possible!

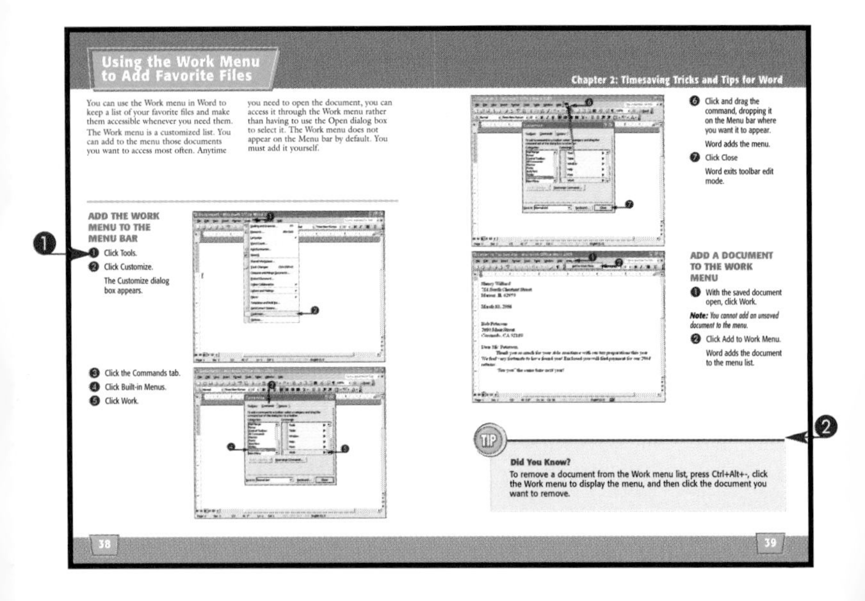

Using the Work Menu to Add Favorite Files

Chapter 2: Timesaving Tricks and Tips for Word

You can use the Work menu in Word to keep a list of your favorite files and make them accessible whenever you need them. The Work menu is a customized list. You can add to the menu those documents you want to access most often. Anytime you need to open the document, you can access it through the Work menu rather than having to use the Open dialog box to select it. The Work menu does not appear on the Menu bar by default. You must add it yourself.

ADD THE WORK MENU TO THE MENU BAR

1. Click Tools.
2. Click Customize.

   The Customize dialog box appears.

3. Click the Commands tab.
4. Click Built-in Menus.
5. Click Work.
6. Click and drag the command, dropping it on the Menu bar where you want it to appear.

   Word adds the menu.

7. Click Close

   Word exits toolbar edit mode.

ADD A DOCUMENT TO THE WORK MENU

1. With the saved document open, click Work.

Note: You cannot add an unsaved document to the menu.

2. Click Add to Work Menu.

   Word adds the document to the menu list.

TIP

Did You Know?

To remove a document from the Work menu list, press Ctrl+Alt+-, click the Work menu to display the menu, and then click the document you want to remove.

38

39

Table of Contents

chapter 1 Lighten Your Workload with General Office Tips and Tricks

chapter 2 Timesaving Tricks and Tips for Word

Increase the Power of Your Spreadsheet with Excel

Enhance Your PowerPoint Presentations

chapter 5

Customize & Optimize Your Outlook Features

Improve Your Database Productivity Using Access

appendix

Appendix

Chapter 1

Lighten Your Workload with General Office Tips and Tricks

Are you looking for ways to speed up your work with the programs in Microsoft Office? This chapter shows you some techniques for customizing programs, and for working smarter and faster in the Microsoft Office applications.

There are literally dozens of techniques that you can apply to speed up your work in the Microsoft Office programs. For example, did you know that you can right-click over screen elements to display a shortcut menu of related commands? If you right-click over text in Word, the shortcut menu lists commands such as Cut, Copy, and Paste. The menu also allows you to access the Font dialog box where you can change the formatting of your text. You can also find commands on the shortcut menu to help you improve your writing skills, such as the Lookup command, which opens Word's Thesaurus where you can look up related synonyms. You can also use the right-click feature in the other Office programs to quickly access a relevant shortcut menu.

Keyboard shortcut keys, which activate common commands and features when you press a few keys, are another overlooked way to speed up your work. The trick to utilizing these shortcuts is to memorize the keyboard selections for the commands you use the most. With a little practice, memorizing keyboard shortcuts becomes second nature.

You can use the techniques in this chapter to customize your Office programs, files, and graphics you use across the Office programs. Customizing the Office programs can really increase your productivity.

Quick Tips

Clear Your Screen of Default Task Panes

You can turn off default task panes so they do not appear when you start an Office program. In most Office programs, task panes appear by default and take up valuable workspace onscreen when you are not using them.

Although you can easily turn them off using the task pane's Close button, you may prefer to keep them from appearing in the first place. Docked on the far right side of the program window, the Getting Started pane offers quick shortcuts that you can use to open files or conduct a search.

DEACTIVATE THE TASK PANE

1. Click Tools.
2. Click Options.

Note: *The task pane feature is not available in Outlook.*

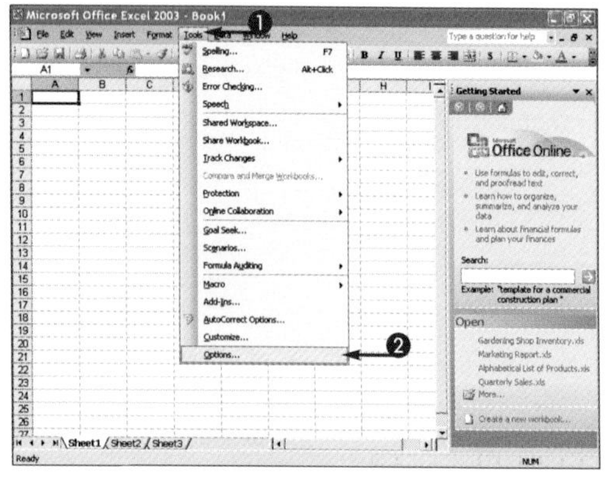

3. Click the View tab.

   The Options dialog box appears.

4. Click the Startup Task Pane option to deselect it.
5. Click OK.

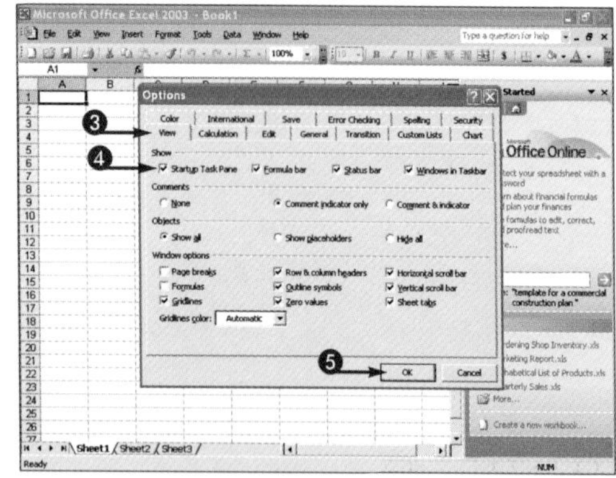

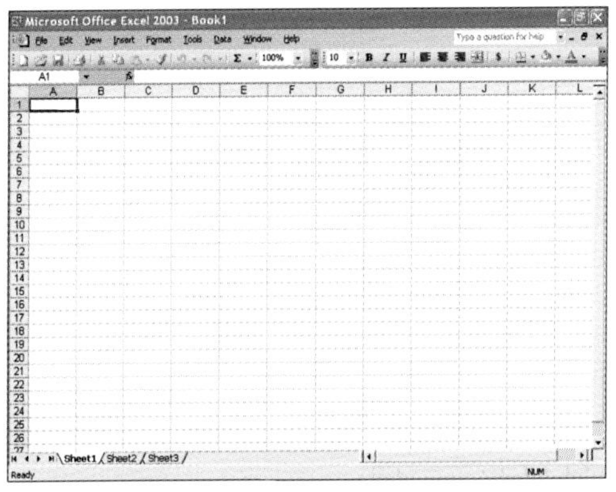

The next time you open the program, the default task pane does not appear.

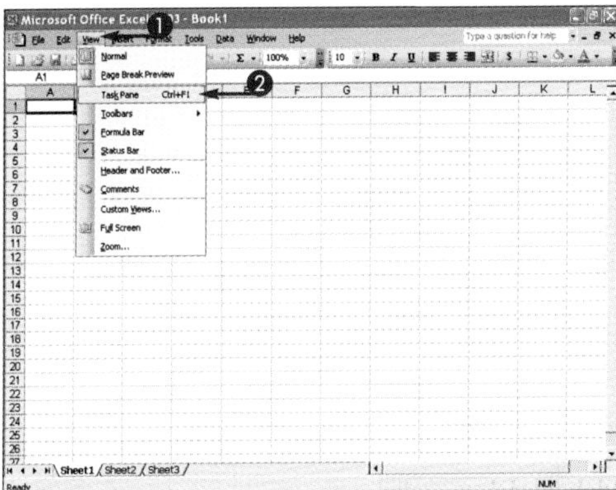

OPEN THE TASK PANE

1. Click View.
2. Click Task Pane.

   Alternatively, you can press Ctrl+F1.

   The Task Pane opens.

TIP

Did You Know?

By default, Microsoft Office task panes dock on the right side of the program window, however, you can move them to another location. To do this, move the mouse pointer over the upper-left corner of the pane until it becomes a four-sided arrow pointer. Click and drag the pane, releasing it at the desired location. To redock the pane, double-click over the upper-left corner of the pane.

Quickly Learn Shortcut Keys

You can use keyboard shortcut keys to greatly speed up your work in a Microsoft Office program. Shortcut keys allow you to quickly activate a command instead of using a mouse.

The Microsoft Office toolbars also allow you to quickly activate commands and features with a click of the mouse, but if you need to access a command while you type in data, you may not want to stop typing to switch to the mouse to click a toolbar button.

You can find shortcut keys listed next to the commands on the drop-down menus. You can also tell a Microsoft Office program to list keyboard shortcut keys along with toolbar button names.

1. Click Tools.
2. Click Customize.

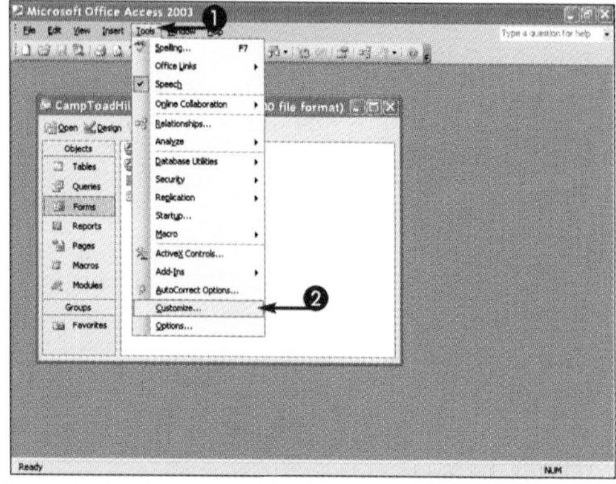

- The Customize dialog box appears.

3. Click the Options tab.
4. Click the Show ScreenTips on toolbars option to select it.

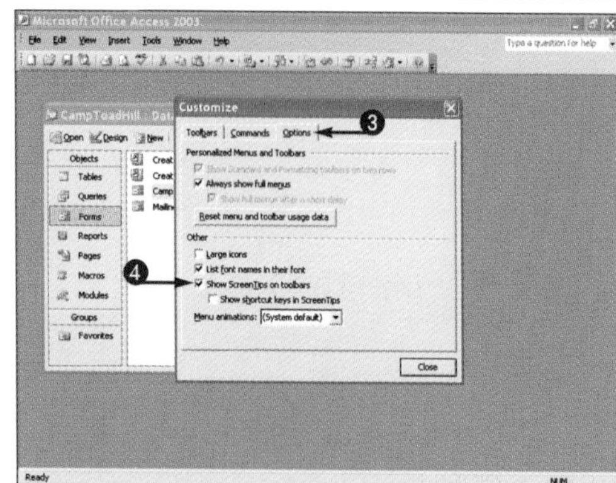

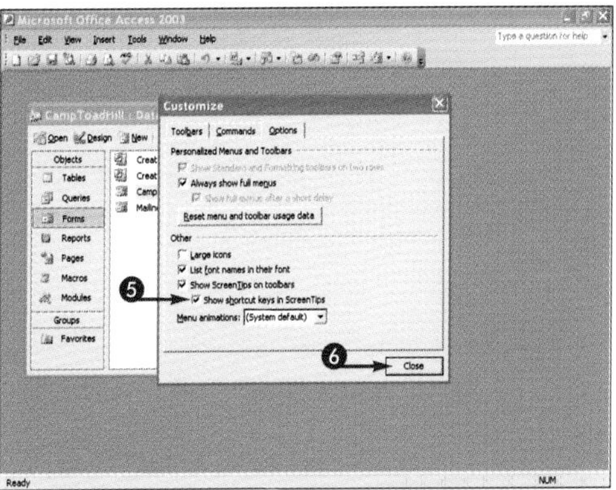

5. Click the Show shortcut keys in ScreenTips option.
6. Click Close.

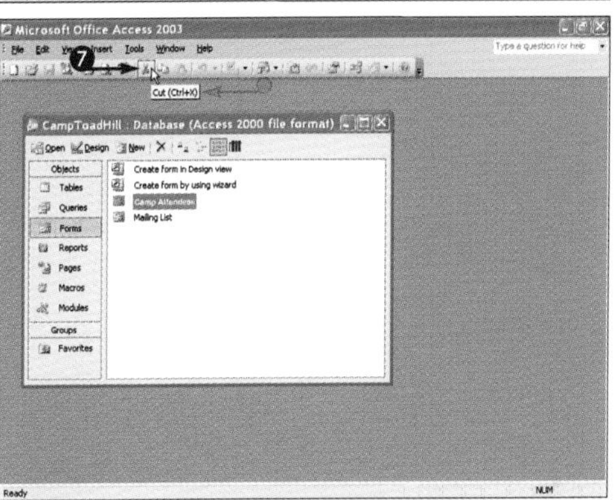

7. Move the mouse pointer over a toolbar button.

- A ScreenTip box appears detailing the button name along with the equivalent shortcut key combination for activating the command.

Did You Know?

You can activate Microsoft Office menu commands without lifting your fingers from the keyboard. Each menu name and command contains an assigned underlined letter. If you press and hold the Alt key and then press the menu's associated letter, you display the menu. After displaying the menu, you then press the underlined letter for the command you want to activate. Or you can press the keyboard up or down arrow keys to highlight the command you want. Press Enter to apply the command.

Simplify Repeated Tasks with Customized Menus

You can create your own customized menu in any of the Microsoft Office programs and tailor it to include just the commands you use most often. The key to personalizing a new menu is to determine what sort of commands you want to list on the menu.

You can use the Customize dialog box to create a new menu and populate it with various commands. You can control the name of the menu and add or subtract commands as needed. When you open the Customize dialog box, you can immediately make changes to the menus onscreen, as well as add new menus.

CREATE A NEW MENU

1. Click Tools.
2. Click Customize.

   The Customize dialog box opens.

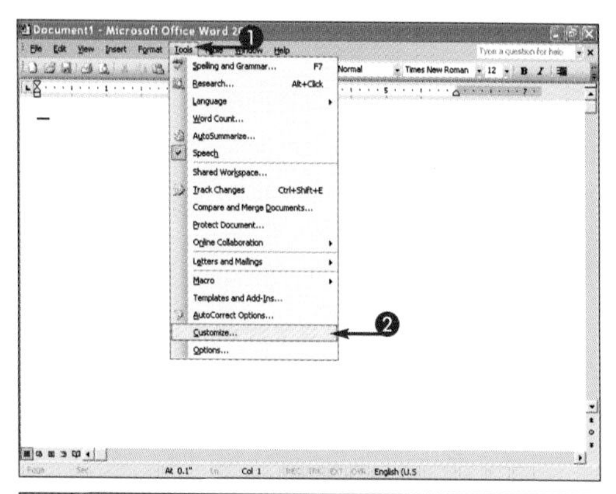

3. Click the Commands tab.
4. Scroll through the Categories list and click New Menu.
5. Click and drag the New Menu label from the Categories list box, dropping it on the menu bar where you want it to appear.

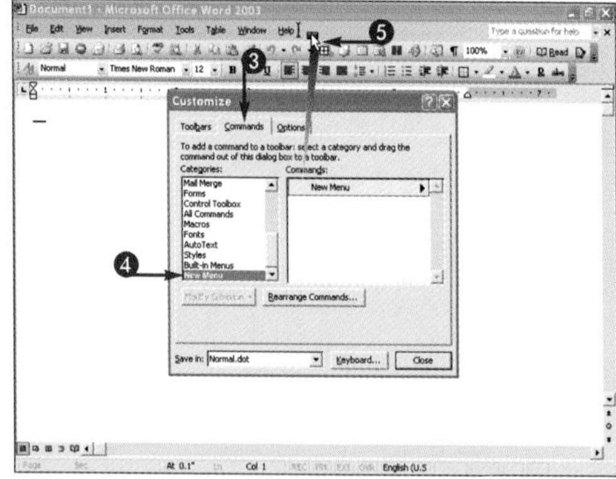

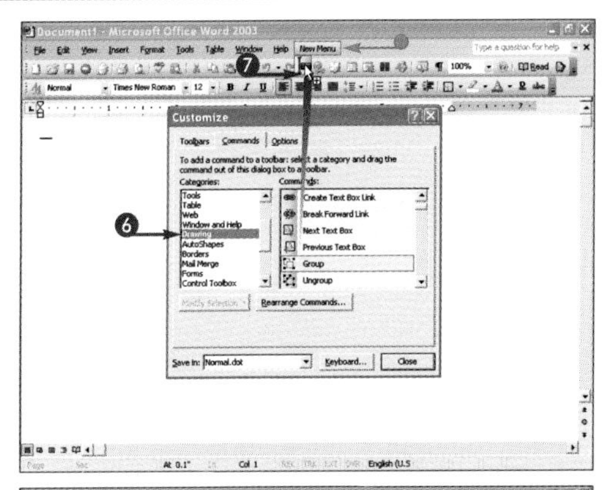

ADD COMMANDS TO A MENU

- The new menu appears on the menu bar.

6. Click a category.
7. Click and drag a command and drop it on the open menu.

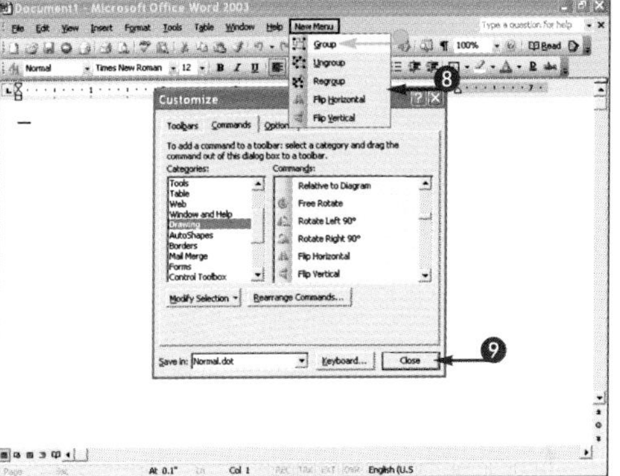

- The command appears on the drop-down menu.

8. Repeat steps **6** and **7** to add more commands to the menu.
9. Click Close.

You can now try out your new menu.

Customize It!

You can assign any name you want to your new menu, preferably a name that best describes the contents of the menu. To rename the custom menu, open the Customize dialog box., right-click the menu on the menu bar, click inside the Name field, and type a new menu name. Press Enter to apply the menu name, and then close the Customize dialog box.

Create a Customized Toolbar

Microsoft Office applications include an assortment of specialized toolbars which give you access to commonly used commands and features.

Using the Customize dialog box, you can build a new toolbar, give it a distinct name, and add a select number of buttons. The Customize dialog box features a library of all the program's commands, plus those that do not appear on the default toolbars. When you open the Customize dialog box, the Office program allows you to make changes to the existing menus and toolbar buttons as well as create new ones. After completing a custom toolbar, Microsoft Office adds it to the list of available toolbars for the program.

CREATE A NEW TOOLBAR

1. Click Tools.
2. Click Customize.

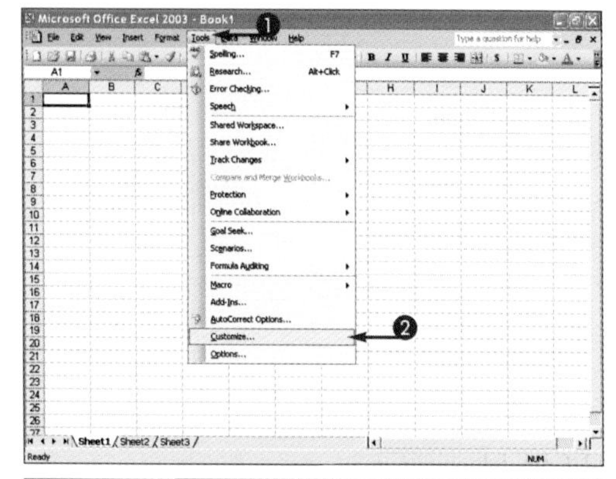

The Customize dialog box appears.

3. Click the Toolbars tab.
4. Click New.

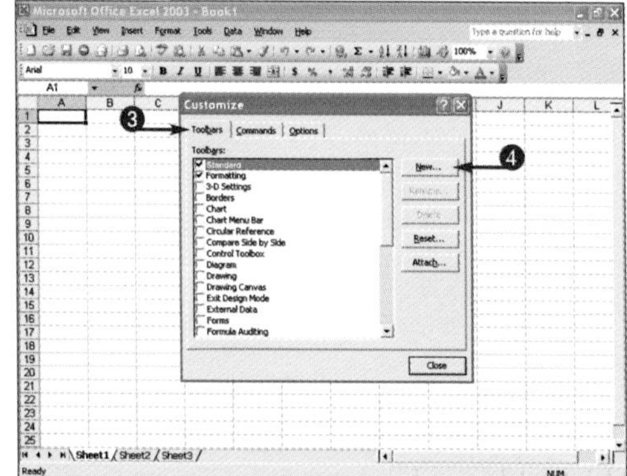

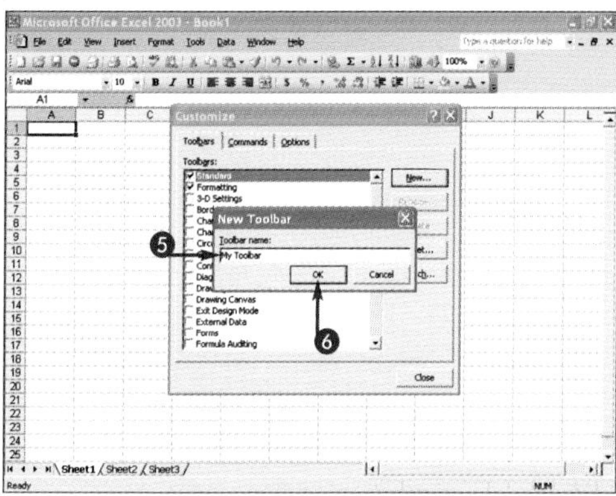

The New Toolbar dialog box opens.

5. Type a unique name for the toolbar.
6. Click OK.

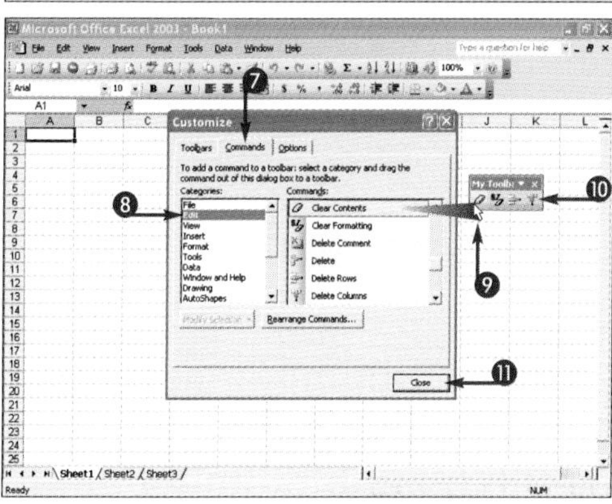

ADD COMMANDS TO THE MENU

A new blank toolbar appears onscreen.

7. Click the Commands tab.
8. Click a category.
9. Click and drag a command and drop it on the empty toolbar.

   Microsoft Office adds the button to the toolbar.

10. Repeat steps **8** and **9** to add more commands.
11. Click Close.

Did You Know?

By default, the Standard and Formatting toolbars share a row at the top of the Word, Excel, and PowerPoint windows. However, you may not see all of the available toolbar buttons for these toolbars. To see both toolbars in their entirety, click (▾) to the right end of the toolbar, and click Show Buttons on Two Rows.

Create a Customized Toolbar Button

You can create your own customized toolbar buttons in any of the Microsoft Office programs to give your work a distinctive look for a button.

While you can create a completely new button icon, you may find it much easier to modify an existing button icon or choose from a variety of pre-made buttons from the Office Button Image Library. You can modify the color and position of a button, and even delete parts you do not want to include, or draw new areas to appear in the button image. You can also give the button a unique name that appears in a ScreenTip when you hover the mouse over the button.

CUSTOMIZE A BUTTON

1. Click Tools.
2. Click Customize.

   The Customize dialog box opens.

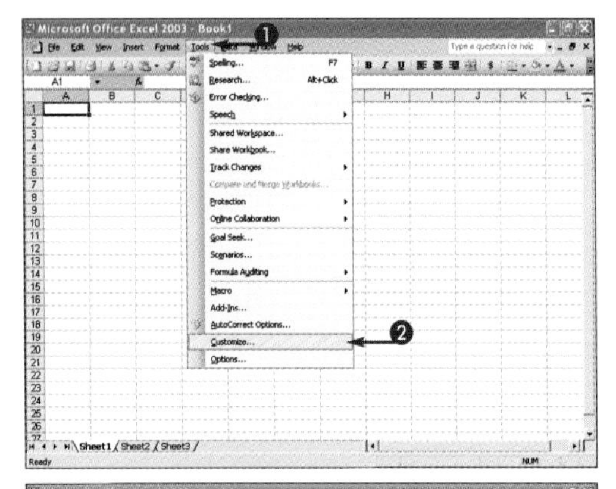

3. Right-click the button you want to edit on the toolbar.
4. Click Edit Button Image.

   The Button Editor dialog box opens.

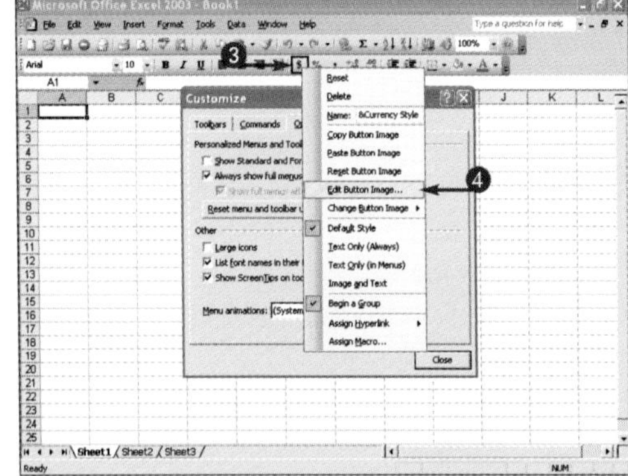

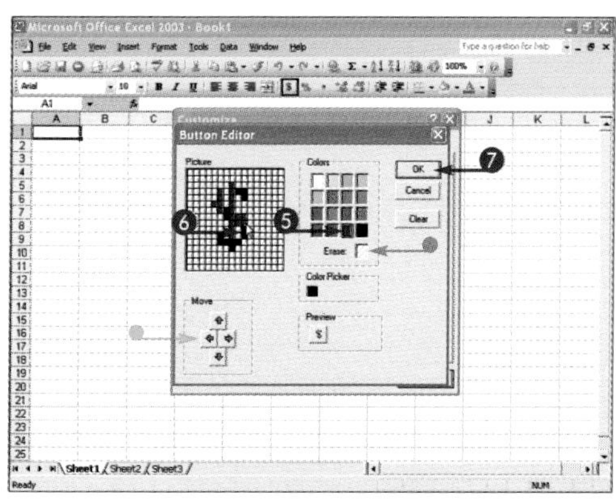

5. Click a color from the Colors palette.
6. Drag the mouse over areas of the graphic where you want to edit the color of the graphic.

- To erase a part of an image, click the Erase option and drag over the image.
- To reposition the image, click the arrow buttons.

7. Click OK.

The changes appear on the button icon.

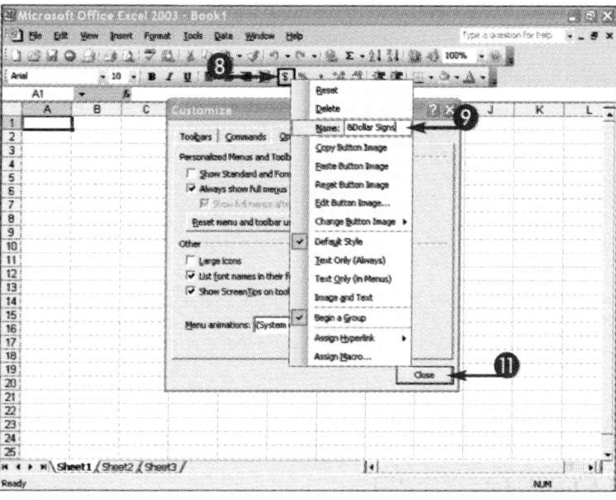

NAME A CUSTOM BUTTON

8. Right-click the button.
9. Click inside the Name field, and type an ampersand symbol followed by a new name.
10. Press Enter.
11. Click Close.

Microsoft Office applies the new name to your button.

Customize It!

You can assign a completely new image icon to a button using any of the available images in the Button Image Library. Click Tools, and then Customize to open the Customize dialog box. Right-click the button you want to edit on the toolbar, click Change Button Image, and then click a new icon to apply it. When you finish editing a button, click Close on the Customize dialog box.

Assign a Hyperlink to a Button

You can assign a hyperlink to a button that takes you to another file on your computer or network, or links you to a Web page on the Internet. A hyperlink button is a great way to speed up your access to other files or Web pages.

The Microsoft Office programs include a library of buttons you can use for many purposes, such as assigning a particular command or feature, a macro, or a hyperlink. For best results, consider creating a new toolbar button for the hyperlink button feature.

ASSIGN A LINK

1. Click Tools.
2. Click Customize.

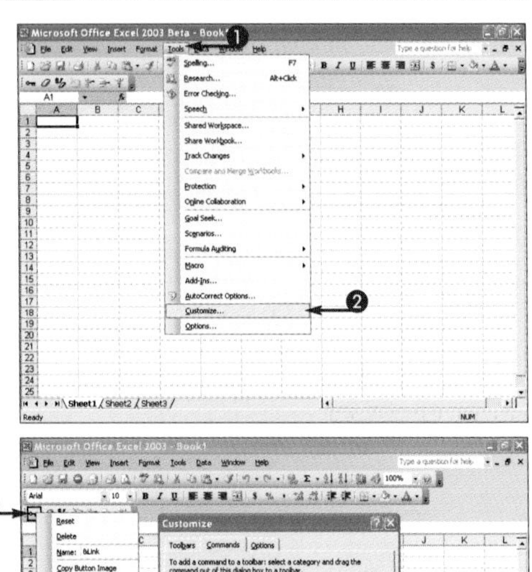

- The Customize dialog box appears.

3. Right-click the button to which you want to assign a hyperlink.
4. Click Assign Hyperlink.
5. Click Open.

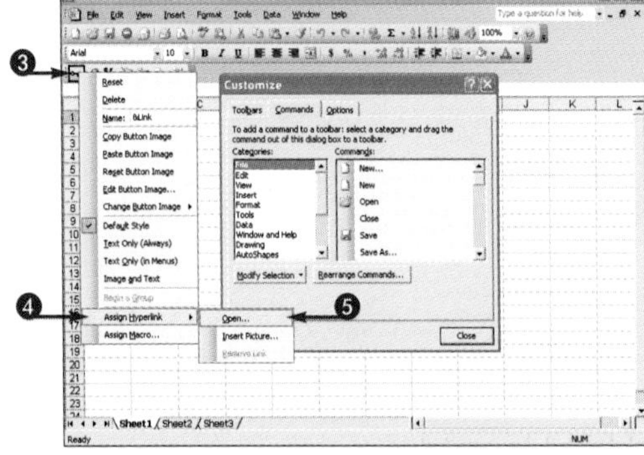

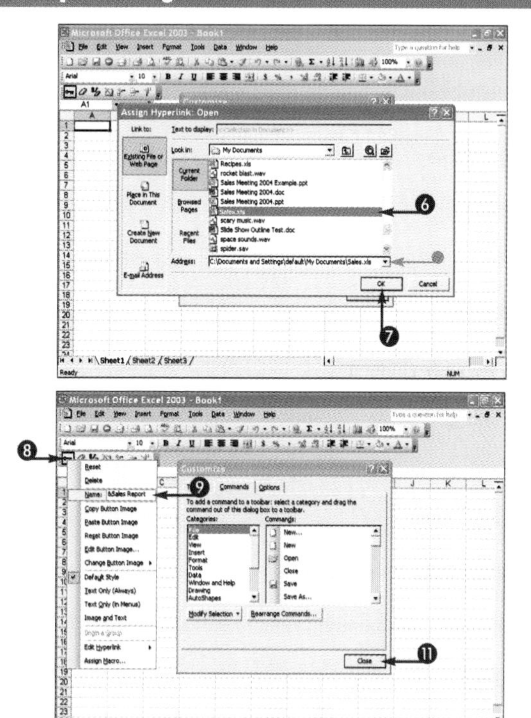

The Assign Hyperlink: Open dialog box appears

6. Click the file to which you want to link.
   - Alternatively, you can type in the Web page address.
7. Click OK.

NAME THE LINK BUTTON

8. Right-click the button.
9. Click inside the Name field, and type an ampersand symbol followed by a new name.
10. Press Enter.

    Microsoft Office applies the new name to your button.
11. Click Close.

    You can now click the button to test the hyperlink.

Customize It!

To reassign a different hyperlink to a button, first display the toolbar containing the button you want to edit. Click Tools, and then click Customize. Right-click the button, click Edit Hyperlink and then click Open to open the Edit Hyperlink: Open dialog box. Type a new Web page address or select another file for the link, then click OK. Close out of the dialog boxes. To remove a link, right-click the button with the Customize dialog box opened, click Edit Hyperlink, and then click Remove Link.

Using an Office Program to Manage Computer Files

You can manage your computer files from within any Microsoft Office program.

For example, you may want to save a new Word file to a new folder in the My Documents folder. You can create the new folder in the Save As dialog box and then save the file to the new folder. You can also edit folder names, delete folders and files, and move files to other folders. In addition, you can view the contents of your computer hard drive or other disk drives and conduct a search for a specific file. You can perform the same procedures in the Open dialog box.

CREATE A NEW FOLDER

1. Click the Open button.

   You can also click the File menu and click open.

   The Open dialog box appears.

***Note:** Microsoft Outlook includes different features for managing files and messages. See your Outlook documentation for more information.*

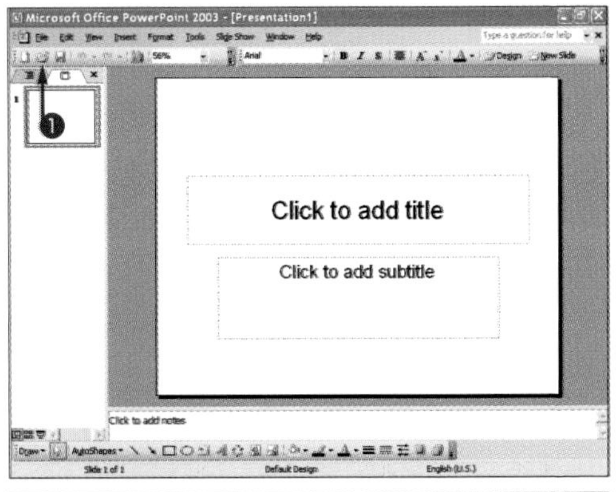

2. Click the Create a New Folder button.

   The New Folder dialog box appears.

3. Type a new folder name.
4. Click OK.

   The program adds the new folder and opens it in the list box.

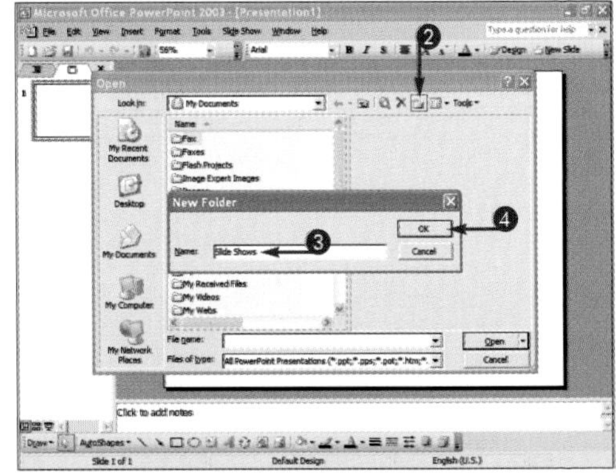

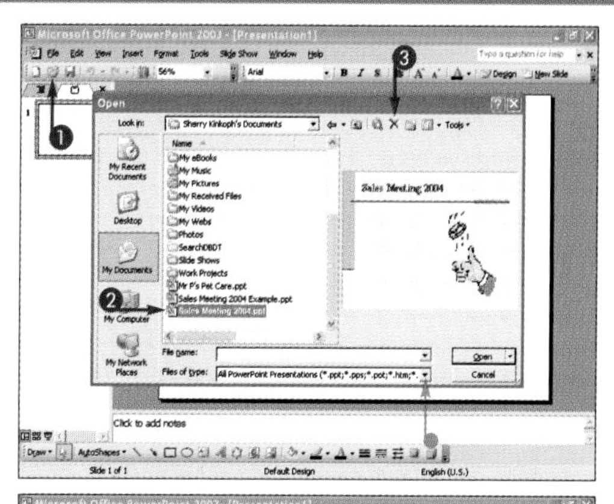

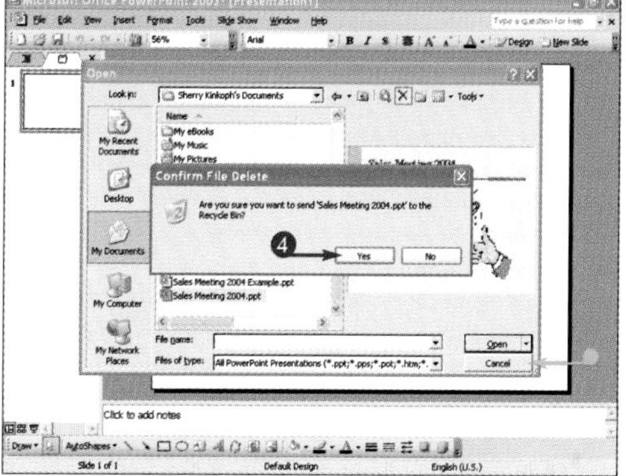

DELETE A FILE

1. Click the Open button.

   The Open dialog box appears.

2. Click the file you want to delete.

   - To see all the files listed, click here and then click All Files (*.*).

3. Click the Delete button.

   You can also press the Delete key on the keyboard.

   A confirmation prompt window appears.

4. Click Yes.

   Office deletes the file.

   - You can click Cancel to exit the Open dialog box without opening a file.

TIP

Did You Know?

You can use shortcut menus within the Open and Save As dialog boxes. For example, right-clicking a filename activates a shortcut menu that lists related commands, such as Open and Print. Clicking the Print command prints the file without opening the program window.

Store Files in a Different Default Location

You can tell Microsoft Office where to store the files that you create. When you open the Save As dialog box to save a file in Word, Excel, PowerPoint, and Access, these programs select the My Documents folder as the default working folder.

Rather than manually selecting a different folder from the My Documents folder each time you save, you can tell Microsoft Office to save your files to a default folder of your choosing.

Word is the only Office program that allows you to browse through drives and folders in the Options dialog box to set a new default working folder.

SET EXCEL, POWERPOINT, OR ACCESS FOLDERS

1. Click Tools.
2. Click Options.

   The Options dialog box appears.

Note: *Microsoft Outlook does not include an option for changing the default working folder.*

3. In Excel or Access, click the General tab.

   In PowerPoint, click the Save tab.

4. Inside the Default file location field, select the My Documents text and type the desired name of the folder.

   In Access, click inside the Default database folder field to select the text, and type a folder name.

5. Click OK.

   Office assigns the new default folder.

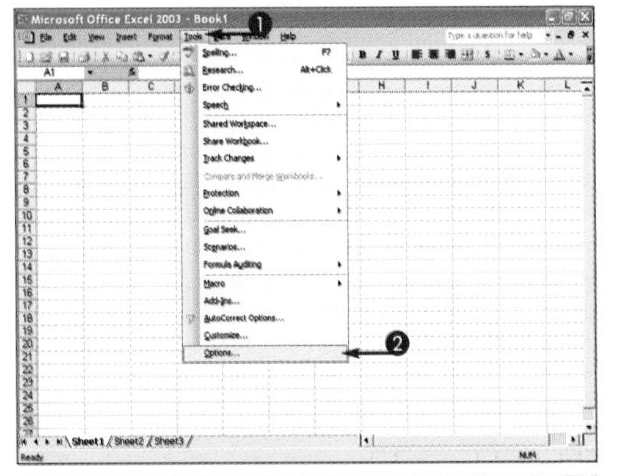

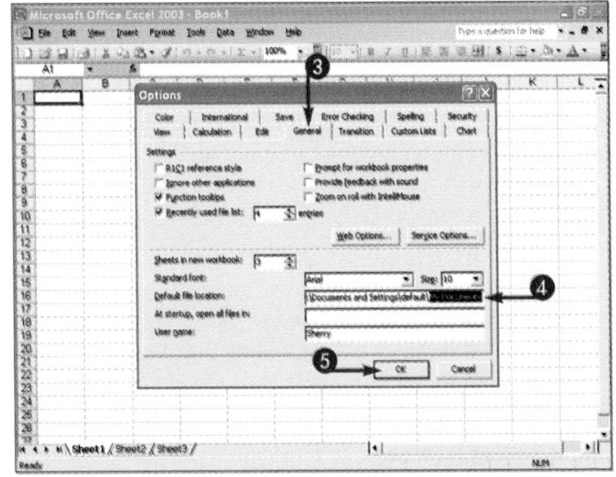

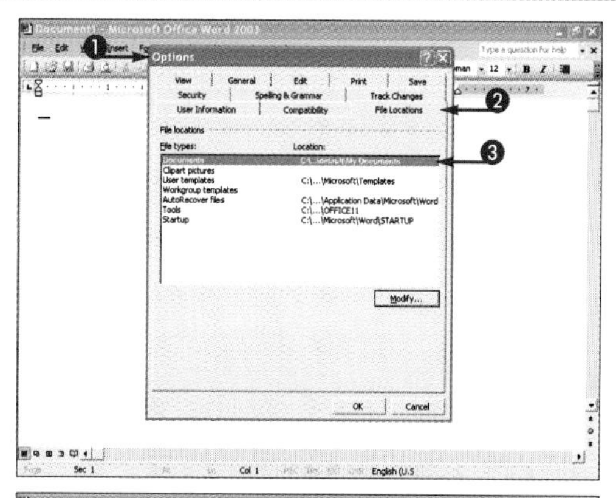

SET THE DEFAULT FOLDER IN WORD

1. Open the Options dialog box again.
2. Click the File Locations tab.
3. Double-click the Documents file type.

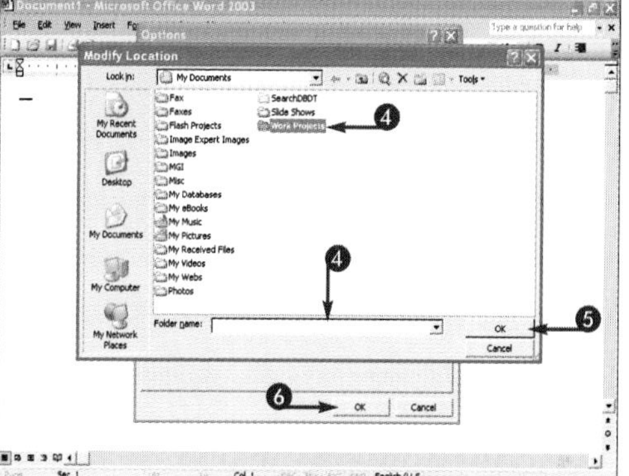

The Modify Location dialog box appears.

4. Type the name of a new folder to use as the default folder, or click the folder you want to use.
5. Click OK.
6. Click OK.

Office assigns the new default folder.

Customize It!

You can rename the My Documents folder within the My Computer window. In Windows XP, the My Documents folder utilizes the following path: C:\Documents and Settings\default\My Documents. Click the folder name twice to highlight it, then type a new folder name and press Enter. Depending on how Office installed, your Office setup may use a different folder location.

Change File Properties to Make Documents Private

You can add security features to make your document information private. When you save a file in Word, Excel, or PowerPoint, the programs automatically include additional details about the file.

If you plan to share your files with others, you may not want to show these details in the file.

The Options dialog box includes a tab with options for setting file security features. You can view file properties by opening the Properties dialog box, which includes several tabs containing file details.

VIEW THE PROPERTIES DIALOG BOX

1. Click File.
2. Click Properties.

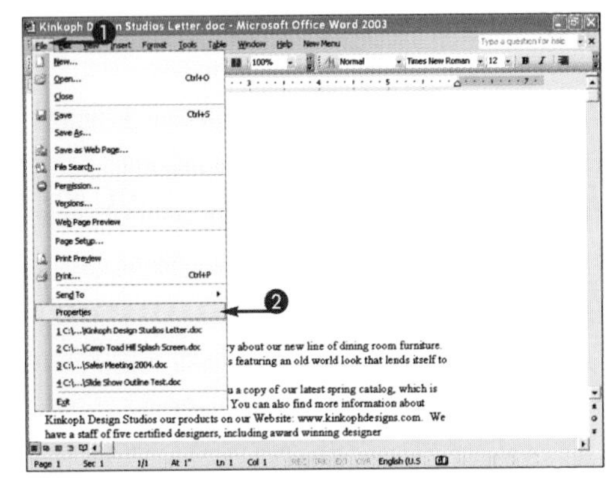

The Properties dialog box appears for the file.

3. Click the Summary tab.

- Personal information about the author and company appear in these fields.
- You can click the General tab to view file size and location properties.

4. Click OK to close the dialog box.

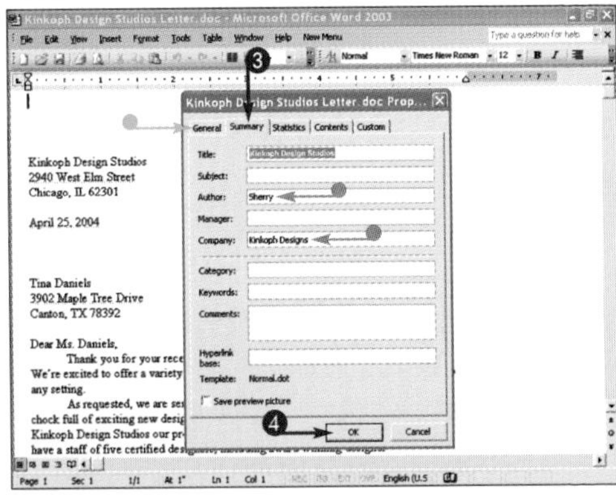

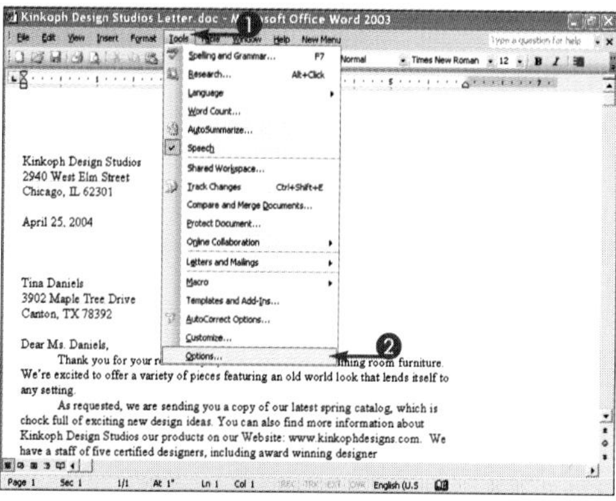

REMOVE PERSONAL INFORMATION

1. Click Tools.
2. Click Options.

   The Options dialog box appears.

***Note:** Microsoft Outlook does not include an option for changing the default working folder.*

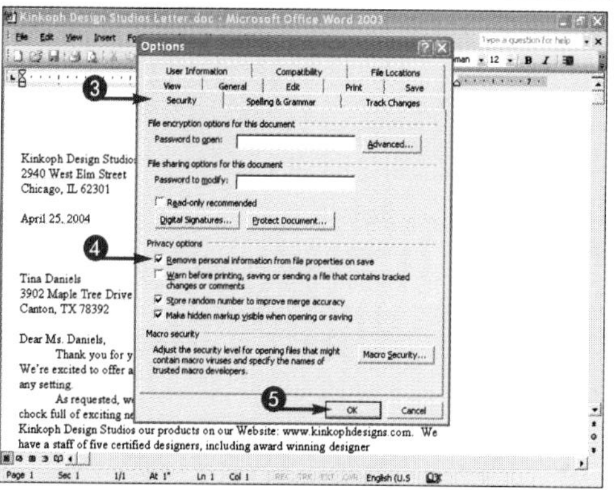

3. Click the Security tab.
4. Click the Remove personal information from file properties on save option.
5. Click OK.

   To verify that the personal information no longer appears, follow the steps on the previous page.

Did You Know?

You can assign a password to make your files private. In Word, Excel, and PowerPoint, you use the Options dialog box. Click Tools, Options, and then click the Security tab. In Access, you can click Tools, Security, and then Set Database Password. Be sure to record the password because without it, you cannot open the file again.

Recover a File After a Systems Failure

You can recover a file that you lost during a system freeze or crash. System freezes and crashes can cause you to lose valuable data if they occur while you have an opened file.

With the Office Application Recovery tool, you can exit an Office application when it appears to stall, rather than using the Windows Task Manager or any other Windows tools. The Application Recovery tool saves the last version of the file that existed before the glitch occurred. When you restart the application, the Office Document Recovery task pane lists the most recent versions of the file. You can choose a version to reopen and continue working.

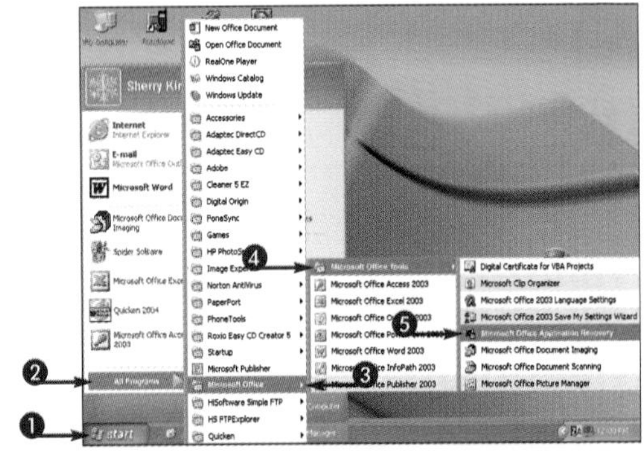

1. Click the Windows Start button.
2. Click All Programs.
3. Click Microsoft Office.
4. Click Microsoft Office Tools.
5. Click Microsoft Office Application Recovery.

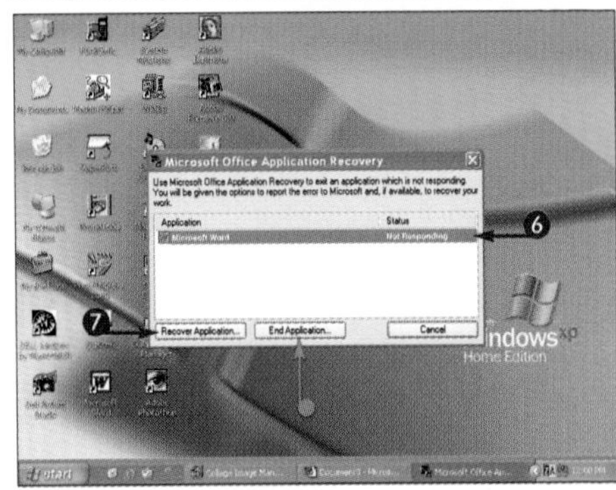

The Microsoft Office Application Recovery dialog box appears.

6. Click the program or file that is not responding.
7. Click Recover Application.

- You can click End Application to close the program without recovering any files.

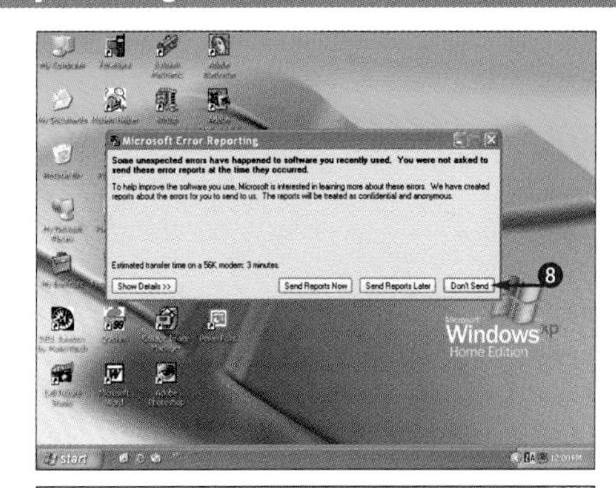

A prompt window appears, asking if you want to report the error to Microsoft.

Note: *Your prompt window may vary in appearance and wording, depending on the type of error.*

8. Click Don't Send.
9. Relaunch the application.

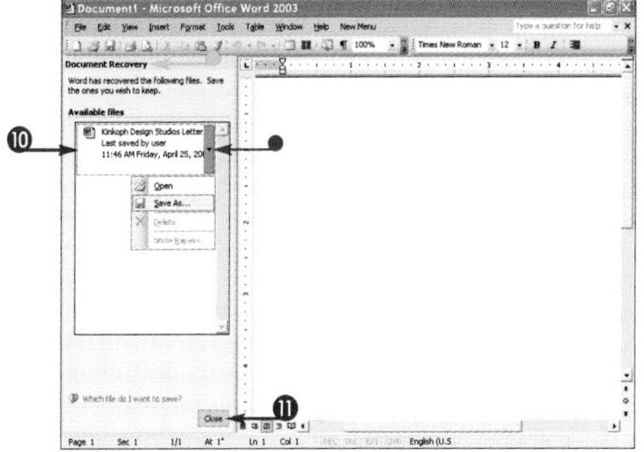

- The Document Recovery pane appears.

10. Click the recovered version you want to keep.

    Office opens the selected file.

- To save files to compare later, you can click here, then click Save As, repeating this step for each file you want to save.

11. Click Close to exit the pane.

Did You Know?

Word offers an option for creating backup files in case of a system crash or program glitch. Click Tools and then Options to open the Options dialog box. Click the Save tab and click the Always create backup copy option (☐ changes to ☑). Word now saves a backup copy of the existing file.

Convert Scanned Documents into Text Files

You can use the Optical Character Recognition, or OCR, capabilities in Microsoft Office to convert a scanned document into text. You can then import this text into Word and edit it.

If you have a scanner hooked up to your computer, you can activate the Office Document Scanning program and convert the document into a TIFF, or Tagged Image File Format, file, which is a common graphics file format. You can view the file in the Office Document Imaging program and export it to Word as a document file.

The Document Scanning program offers you several presets for scanning your document.

1. Click the Windows Start button.
2. Click All Programs.
3. Click Microsoft Office.
4. Click Microsoft Office Tools.
5. Click Microsoft Office Document Scanning.

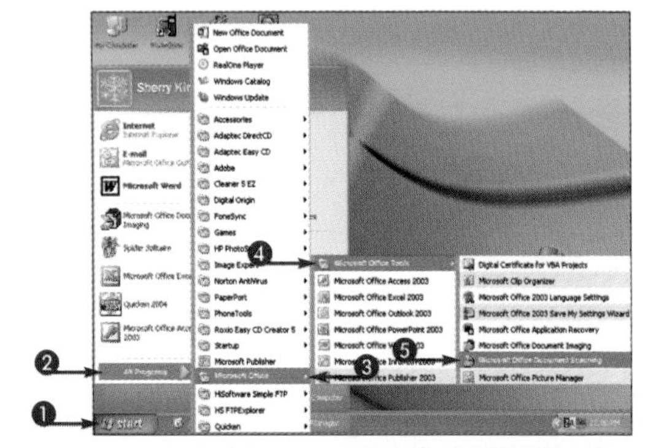

The Scan New Document dialog box appears.

6. Click a preset option.

   The default, Black and white, works best for scanning text.

   You can click the Color preset for artwork.

- If you need to specify a scanner, click Scanner and choose a scanner.

7. Click Scan.

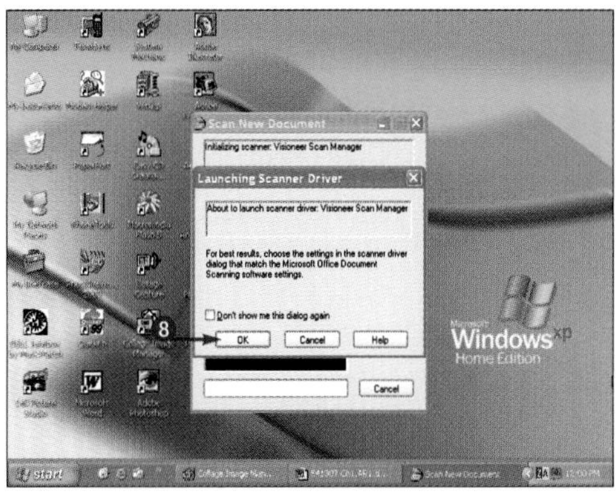

The Launching Scanner Driver prompt window appears.

8. Click OK.

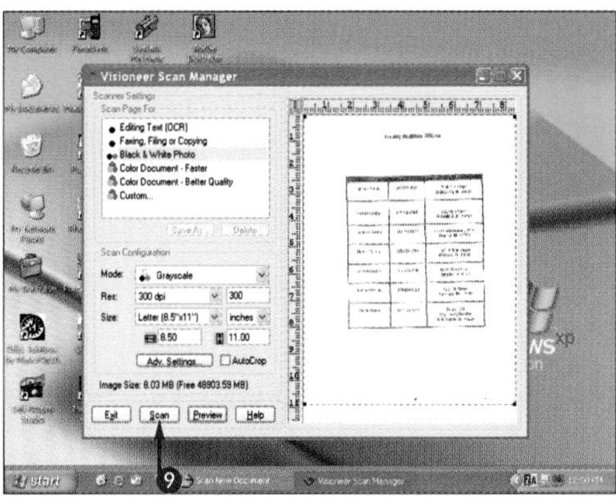

The Image Manager or Scan Manager window appears for your scanner.

9. Click Scan.

Note: *See your scanner's documentation to learn more about your own scanner's settings and how to scan a document.*

Did You Know?

With the Document Imaging program, you can convert e-mail attachments and faxes into editable documents. For example, you may exchange important faxed documents with a mortgage company. Using the OCR capabilities in the Document Imaging program, you can convert these faxes from TIFFs into editable data in Word or Excel.

continued

Convert Scanned Documents into Text Files *(continued)*

You can export scanned text from the Microsoft Document Imaging program into other Office programs. Optical Character Recognition (OCR), also called *text recognition*, is software that analyzes a scanned page and attempts to convert it into editable text characters.

If you want to export the scanned document text into another Office application besides Word, you can copy the text from the Document Imaging window and paste it into another file.

Once you convert a scanned document into text, you can use the Document Imaging program window to search for text within the document, annotate the document, fill out form fields, and more.

The Document Imaging window opens and displays the newly created TIFF of the scanned document.

⑩ Click the Send Text To Word button.

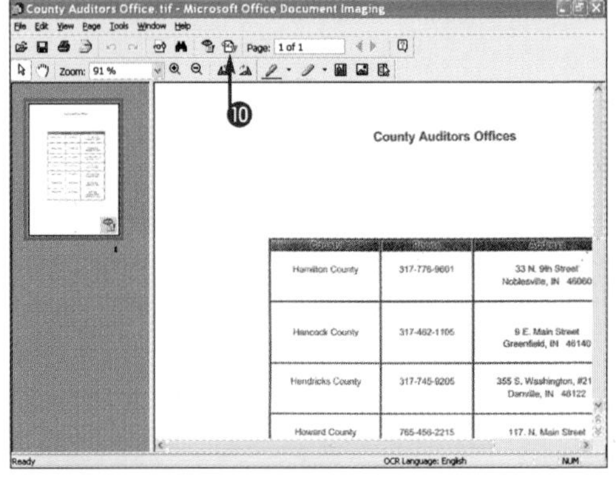

The Send Text To Word dialog box appears.

- If you prefer not to include any images from the original document, leave this box unchecked.

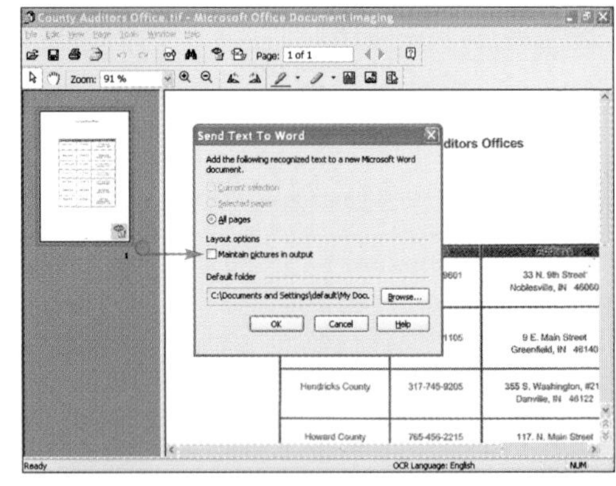

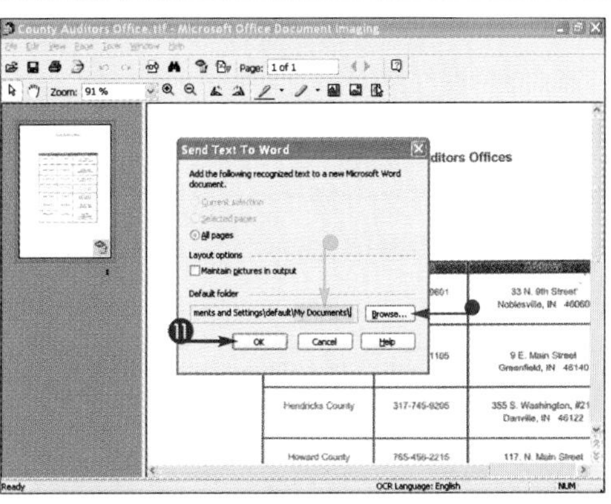

- By default, the program sends the text to the My Documents folder.
- To indicate another folder, click Browse and specify another folder.

⑪ Click OK.

County Auditors Office.htm - Microsoft Office Word 2003

County Auditors Offices

Hamilton County 317-776-9601 33 N. 9th Street
Noblesville, IN 46060

Hancock County	317-462-1105	9 E. Main Street Greenfield, IN 46140
Hendricks County	317-745-9205	355 S. Washington, #215 Danville, IN 46122
Howard County	765-456-2215	117 N. Main Street Kokomo, IN 46901
Johnson County	317-736-3745	86 W. Court Street Franklin, IN 46131
Madison County	765-641-9420	16 E. 9th Street

Microsoft Word opens and displays the scanned document as text in HTML file format.

You can now edit the text as needed.

The Microsoft Office Document Scanning and Document Imaging program windows remain open onscreen until you close them.

Apply It!

You can tell the Document Imaging program to export only portions of a scanned document to another program. Click the Select button ( ) on the View toolbar in the Document Imaging program window. Select the text or graphics you want to copy. Click Edit and then Copy. Open the destination program and file, and paste your selected item.

Print Placeholders in Place of Graphics

If your Word or Excel document contains numerous graphics, you may not want the graphics to appear when printing out draft copies of the document. Microsoft Word includes an option for hiding graphics and substituting them with placeholders. A placeholder is simply an empty box that appears in the document in place of the original graphic. When you are ready to print the final document with the graphics, you can turn off the placeholder option.

In Word, you can turn the Picture Placeholders option on or off in the Options dialog box. In Excel, you can turn graphics on or off using the Show All and Hide All options.

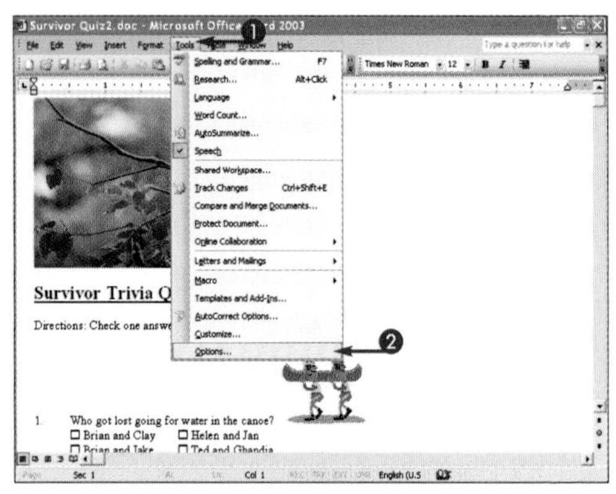

1. Click Tools.
2. Click Options.

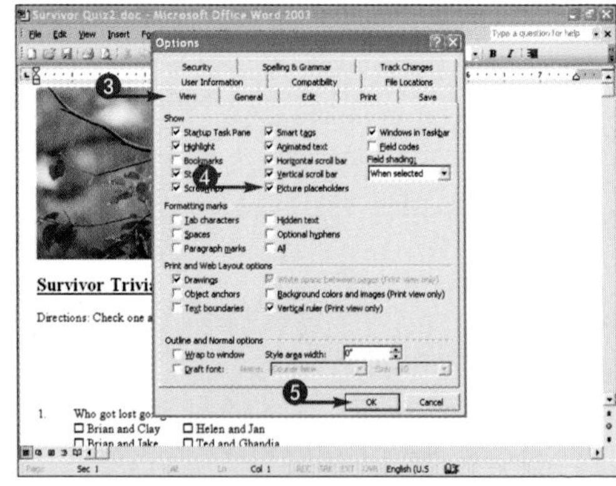

The Options dialog box appears.

3. Click the View tab.
4. Click the Picture placeholders option.
5. Click OK.

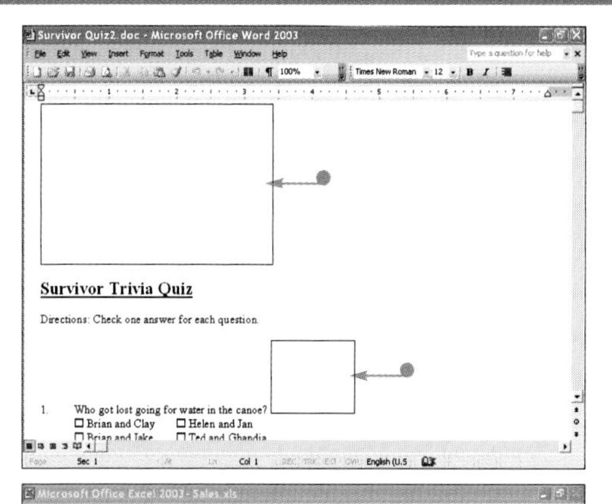

- Placeholder boxes replace the graphics in the document.

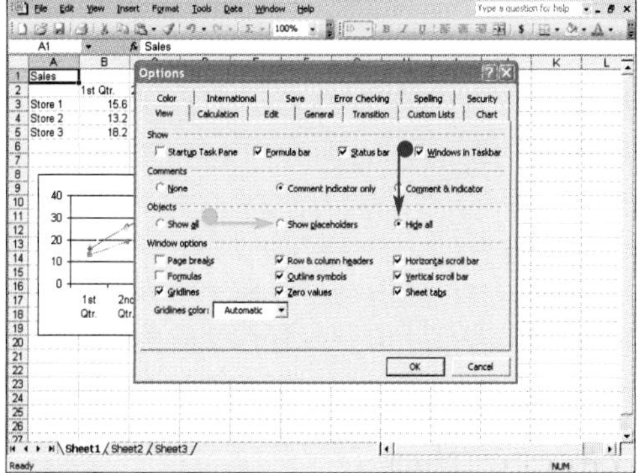

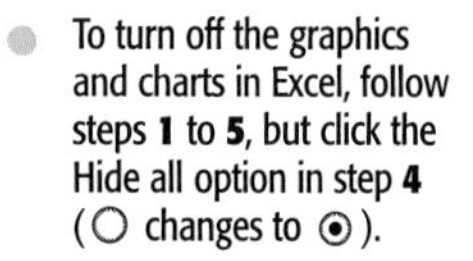

- To turn off the graphics and charts in Excel, follow steps **1** to **5**, but click the Hide all option in step **4** (○ changes to ◉).

Note: *Placeholder boxes do not appear on printouts when you hide graphics in Excel.*

- To turn charts into placeholders, but leave clip art showing, follow steps **1** to **5**, but click the Show placeholders option in step **4** (○ changes to ◉).

Did You Know?

You can reduce the file size of a graphic from within Word or Excel. Double-click the graphic to open the Format Picture dialog box. Click the Picture tab and click Compress. In the Compress Pictures dialog box, click a Change resolution option. Click the Compress Pictures option (☐ changes to ☑) and click OK. A prompt appears, warning you the compression may affect picture quality. Click Apply and OK to exit the dialog box.

Using the Ungroup Command to Customize Clip Art

You can customize clip art and other illustrations you insert into your Word, Excel, or PowerPoint files using the Ungroup command.

To edit a picture, you must first convert the image into a Microsoft Office drawing object. You can then use the Draw menu commands in the Drawing toolbar to ungroup the picture. You can then select a specific part of the picture to modify. You can also edit a picture element by changing the color or size. When you finish editing the picture, you can apply the Group command to reassemble the separate components into one picture again.

1. With the Drawing toolbar on display, click the clip art or picture you want to edit.

***Note:** To display the Drawing toolbar, click View, then Toolbars, and then Drawing.*

2. Click Draw.
3. Click Ungroup.

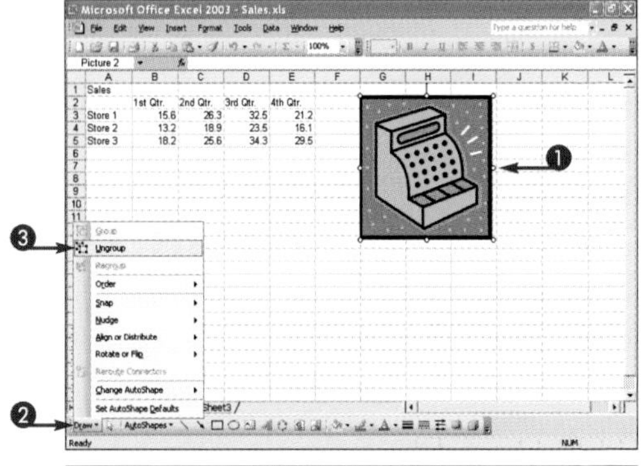

A prompt window appears.

4. Click Yes to convert the image to a drawing object.

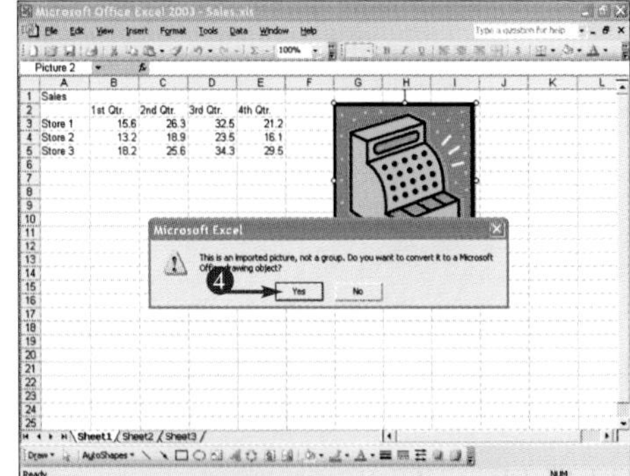

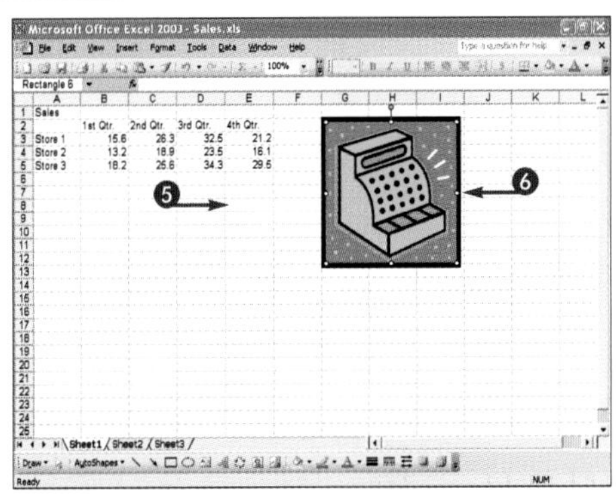

Note: *You may need to activate the Ungroup command again for a complex image.*

All the parts, or elements, of the object are selected by default.

5. Click outside the object to deselect the elements.
6. Click a part of the object you want to remove.
7. Press Delete.

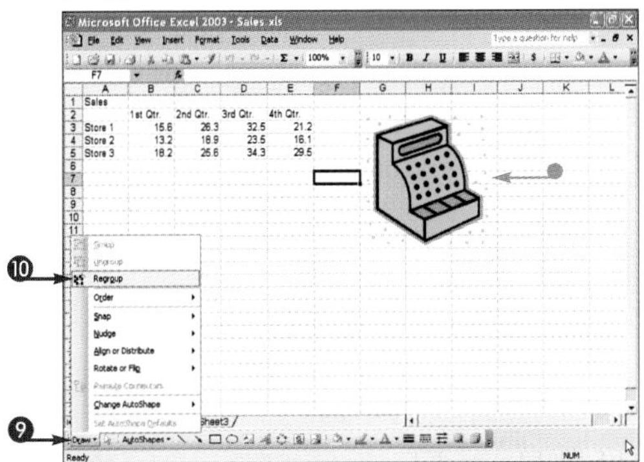

- Office removes the element from the object.

8. Repeat steps **6** and **7** to continue editing parts of the object as needed.
9. Click Draw.
10. Click Regroup.

Office regroups the image again as one object.

Customize It!

You can remove the white background of a placed picture or bitmap image. Select the image, and then click View, Toolbars, and then Picture. In the Picture toolbar that appears, click the Set Transparent Color button ( ) and then click the background to make it transparent. For best results, change the background color of the document. This technique does not work on regular clip art images.

Using Text Boxes to Position Clip Art

You can use text boxes to position clip art and other graphics in a document. Text boxes are ordinarily used as containers for text that you want to set apart from the regular document text.

Placing graphics in a document without text boxes is not always an easy procedure. But by placing your clip art in a text box, you have greater control over the position and size of the graphic on the page.

You can also apply the options found on the Drawing toolbar to change the box fill color, or add a border. By default, text boxes include a border.

1. Display the Drawing toolbar.

Note: To display the Drawing toolbar, click View, then Toolbars, and then Drawing.

2. Click the Text Box button.

*Note: The Drawing Canvas may appear by default. Ignore it and continue to step **3**.*

3. Click and drag where you want the text box to appear.

   A text box appears.

4. Click the Insert Clip Art button.

   The Clip Art task pane appears.

5. Click the art you want to use.

- The clip art appears in the text box, and the text box resizes itself to fit the new art.

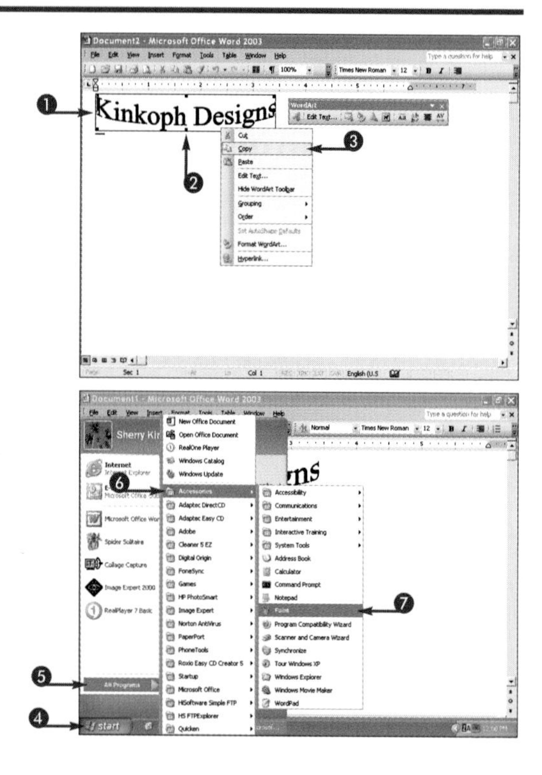

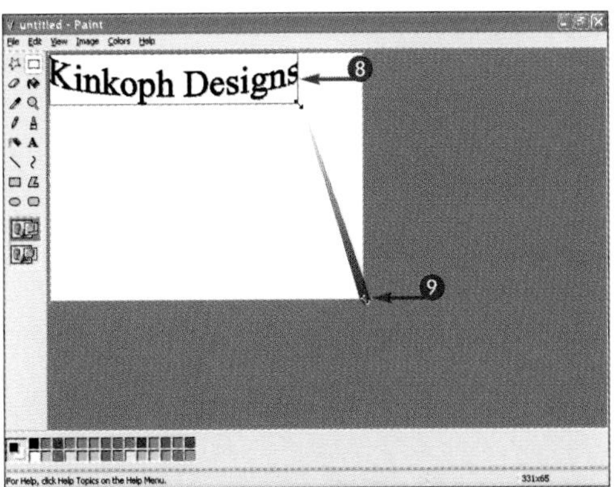

6. Click and drag the text box to reposition it in the document (↖ changes to ✥).
7. Release the mouse button.

The text box appears in the new location.

You can move a text box over existing text or graphics, if desired.

- You can resize a text box by dragging any corner of the box.

Resizing the box does not resize the clip art within.

To resize the clipart, you must click the clip art and then drag the border.

Customize It!

To remove the default border of a text box, first click the text box, then double-click it to open the Format Text Box dialog box. Be careful to double-click the text box instead of the clip art inside it. Click the Colors and Lines tab, then click the Color (▾). This displays a palette of color options. Click No Line, then click OK to apply your changes.

Chapter 2

Timesaving Tricks and Tips for Word

Microsoft Word is the workhorse of the Office suite. Not only can you use Word to produce all kinds of written communication, but also to easily integrate data from other Office programs. You can bring in Excel data, PowerPoint slides and Access tables to create dynamic reports, research papers, letters, newsletters, and more.

Word offers an impressive abundance of commands and features. Each new version brings more features and techniques for improving and building your documents. You can quickly access these features through shortcuts, tricks, and tips that make your use of Word more productive and speedy.

A great way to make Word work more effectively for you is to customize the basic program features; for example, by revising the toolbars to include the buttons you use frequently. You can use the Word Options dialog box to turn on features you use the most and turn off features you rarely need. For example, you may want Word to check your grammar as you type, so you can activate this feature in the Spelling & Grammar tab.

In addition to acclimating yourself to Word program options, you can also take advantage of the AutoCorrect features. The AutoCorrect dialog box contains options for controlling AutoText, AutoCorrect, AutoComplete, AutoFormat, and smart tags. All of the auto-features can help you speed up your text entry, whether it is correcting misspellings as you type, or saving you from repeatedly typing out the same phrase.

Quick Tips

Utilize Status Bar Shortcuts

You can use the status bar to quickly access several useful features to speed up your work.

Word divides the status bar into sections. The far left section of the bar displays page information. The next section displays the current cursor or insertion point position.

The next section displays the status of features. Activating these features makes their names appear in black instead of gray on the status bar.

The next section shows the current language selection. You can activate it to change which language you type.

The next section displays a Spelling and Grammar check shortcut for your document.

ACTIVATE FIND AND REPLACE

1. Double-click anywhere on these sections of the status bar.

   Word opens the Find and Replace dialog box.

- You can use the Go To tab to jump around to specific areas in a document and the Find and Replace tabs to look up and replace words in your document.

***Note:** See your Word documentation to learn more.*

ACTIVATE OVERTYPE MODE

1. Double-click OVR.

   OVR turns from gray to black in the status bar, indicating the feature is on.

- As you type, Word types over any existing characters that fall to the right of the cursor.

***Note:** You can use this same technique to activate the Record Macro, Track Changes, and Extend Selection shortcuts.*

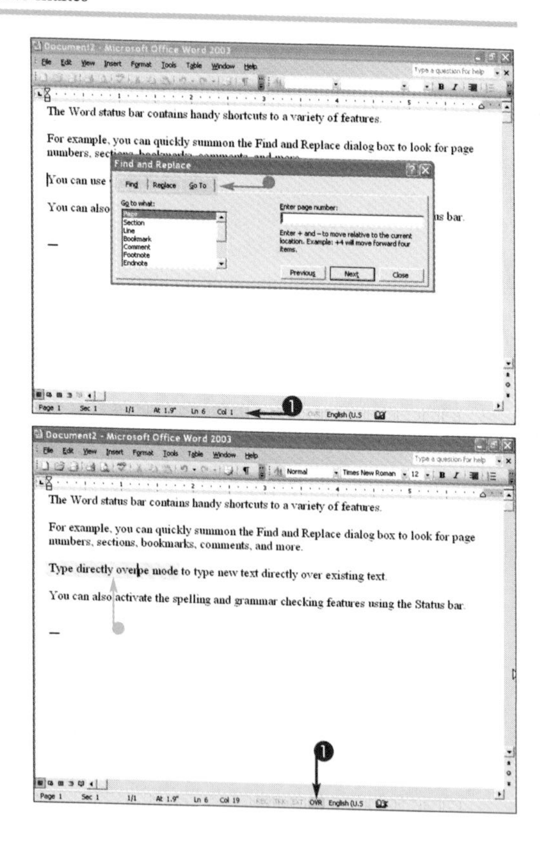

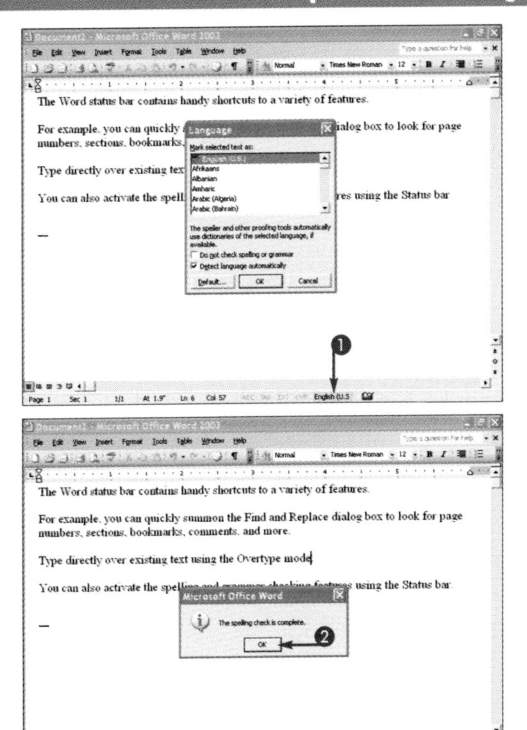

ACTIVATE THE LANGUAGE FEATURE

1. Double-click the Language status section.

Note: *The feature is only active if you install the Word language dictionaries.*

The Language dialog box appears, allowing you to select another language or to activate a proofing tool.

Note: *See your Word documentation to learn more about this feature.*

ACTIVATE THE SPELL CHECKER

1. Double-click the Spelling and Grammar Status icon.

   Word performs a spelling and grammar check on your document.

   A prompt window appears to tell you that the check is complete.

2. Click OK.

Note: *See your Word documentation to learn more about this feature.*

Did You Know?

The Extend Selection mode, which you toggle on or off in the status bar, lets you select a section of text by clicking at the beginning and end of the section. With the mode off, clicking a word simply inserts the cursor. With the mode on, you can select characters and words by clicking your mouse.

Using the Work Menu to Add Favorite Files

You can use the Work menu in Word to keep a list of your favorite files and make them accessible whenever you need them.

The Work menu is a customized list. You can add to the menu those documents you want to access most often. Anytime you need to open the document, you can access it through the Work menu rather than having to use the Open dialog box to select it. The Work menu does not appear on the Menu bar by default. You must add it yourself.

ADD THE WORK MENU TO THE MENU BAR

1. Click Tools.
2. Click Customize.

   The Customize dialog box appears.

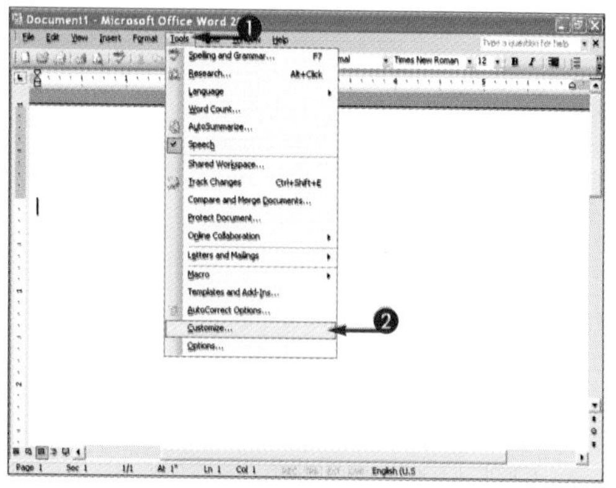

3. Click the Commands tab.
4. Click Built-in Menus.
5. Click Work.

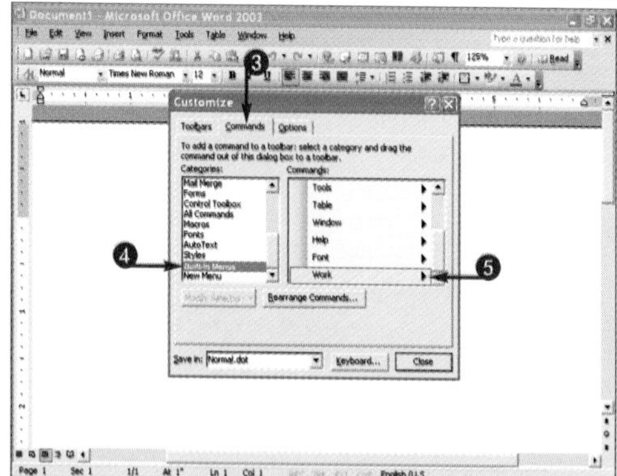

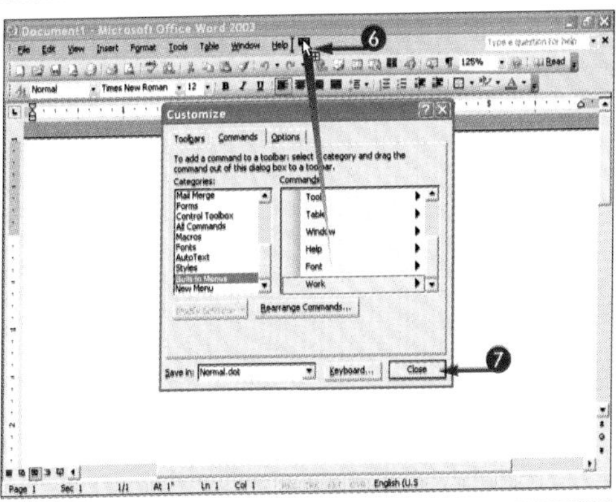

6. Click and drag the command, dropping it on the Menu bar where you want it to appear.

   Word adds the menu.

7. Click Close.

   Word exits toolbar edit mode.

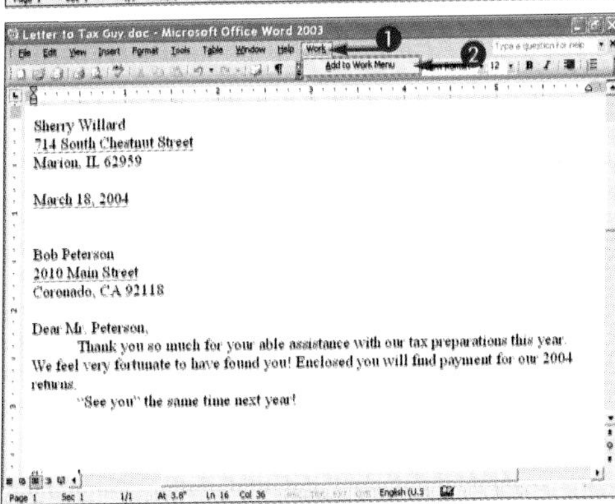

ADD A DOCUMENT TO THE WORK MENU

1. With the saved document open, click Work.

Note: *You cannot add an unsaved document to the menu.*

2. Click Add to Work Menu.

   Word adds the document to the menu list.

Did You Know?

To remove a document from the Work menu list, press Ctrl+Alt+-, click the Work menu to display the menu, and then click the document you want to remove.

Remove a File from the Recent Files List

By default, Word keeps track of the files you work with and lists the four most-recently used files at the bottom of the File menu. The recent files list offers a convenient way to quickly open your most recent files. Unless you password-protect a file, other users can also easily open and view this file if it appears on the recent files list.

Fortunately, there is a method you can use to remove a document from the Word recent files list. Using a keyboard shortcut in conjunction with a mouse click, you can make a file disappear from the list. However, the results of this method are not permanent.

1. Press Ctrl+Alt+-.

- The mouse pointer takes the shape of a minus sign.

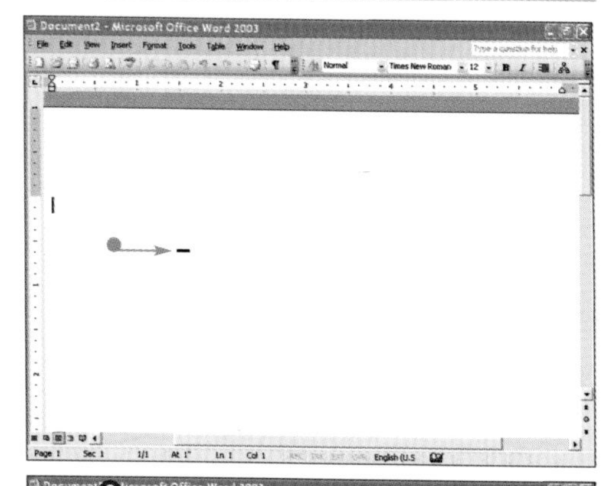

2. Click File.
3. Click the file you want to remove from the list.

   Word removes the file from the list.

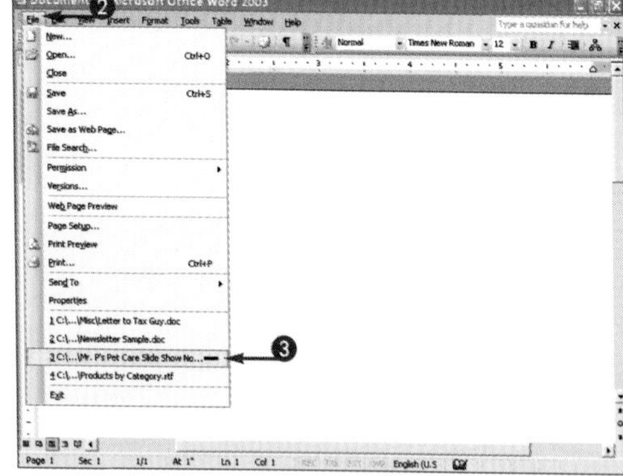

Using the Zoom Options to Conserve Paper when Printing

As any Word user knows, you can waste a lot of paper when printing out documents during editing. You can use the Zoom options found in the Print dialog box to help conserve paper consumption by printing out multiple pages on a single sheet of paper.

By default, the Print dialog box sets the Pages Per Sheet option to 1 page, which means one document page uses one sheet of printer paper. You can change this setting to print 2 pages per sheet, 4 pages per sheet, and so on, up to 16 pages per single sheet.

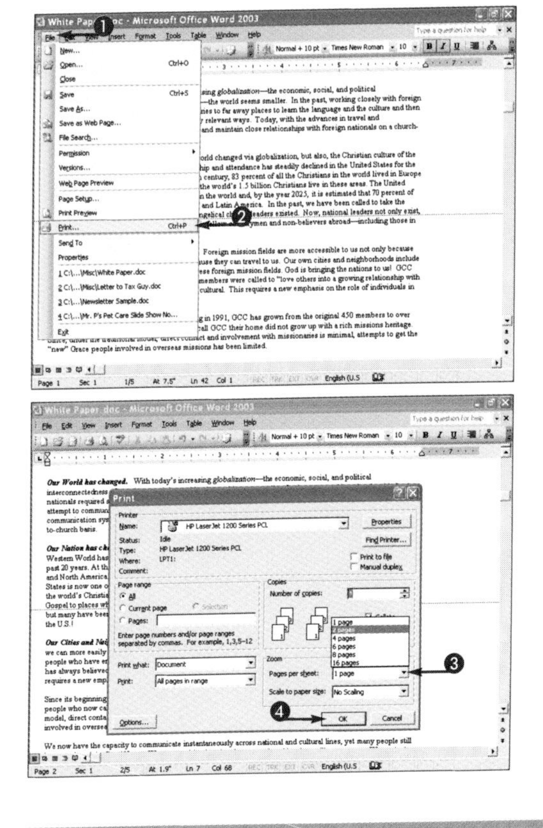

1. Click File.
2. Click Print.

The Print dialog box appears.

3. Click here and select the desired number of pages per sheet.
4. Click OK.

Word prints out the document based on your new settings.

Navigate Long Documents with a Table of Contents

You can use a temporary table of contents, also called a TOC, to help you move around a long document. The TOC works by creating links to headings throughout your document. Styles are pre-selected formatting that you can apply to document text, such as headings and body text.

When you activate the TOC feature, Word attempts to build a table of contents by searching your document for headings and then sorting the headings based on heading levels. By default, Word includes page numbers along with the TOC headings and aligns them to the right of the heading text.

1. Click in the document where you want to insert the TOC.
2. Click Insert.
3. Click Reference.
4. Click Index and Tables.

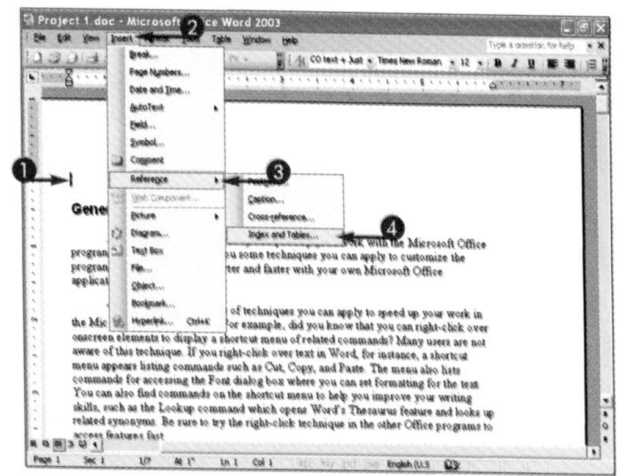

The Index and Tables dialog box appears.

5. Click the Table of Contents tab.
6. Click here and select a format.

- The Print Preview area shows the TOC format.

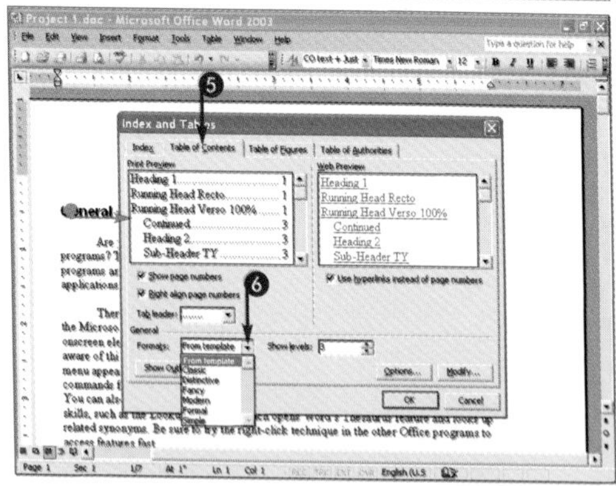

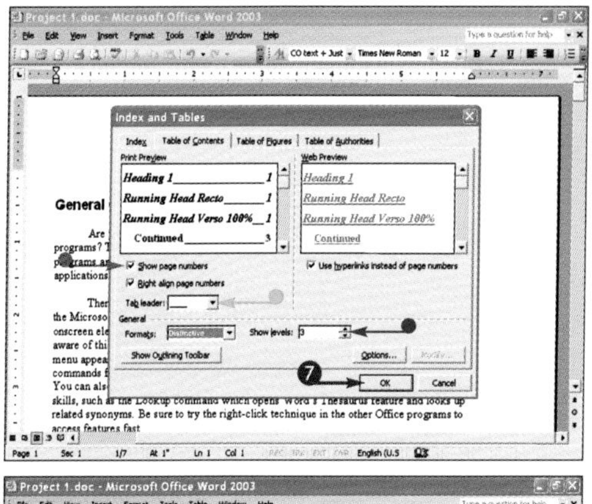

- If you want page numbers, click here to select a type of leader character.
- If you use custom headings, click here to select the number of heading levels.
- Deselect the Show page numbers option if you do not want page numbers to appear in the TOC.

7 Click OK.

Word adds the TOC to the document.

- To jump to a heading, click the heading in the TOC.

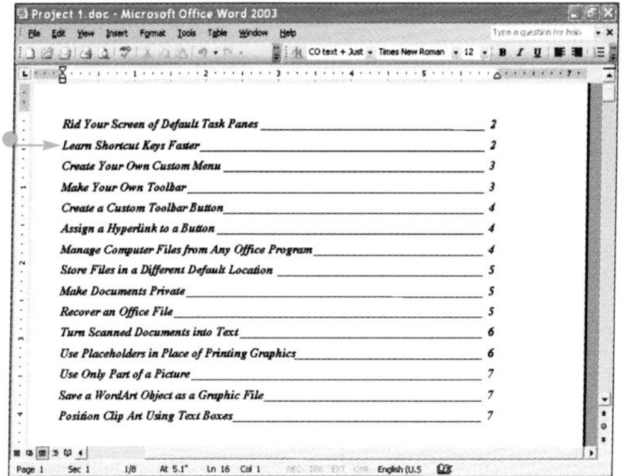

Did You Know?

To create a table of contents from custom styles that you create in Word, follow the steps **1** to **4** in this task to open the Table of Contents tab of the Index and Tables dialog box. Click Options to open the Table of Contents Options dialog box, and select the custom headings you want to use in the TOC.

Navigate Long Documents Using Bookmarks

Long documents can be difficult to navigate, especially when you are trying to locate a specific section of text. You can use a bookmark to tag a location or section of text for quick future access.

Bookmarks in Word are similar to those you use in a Web browser to mark your favorite Web pages. The bookmark identifies a location or section of text, and by giving a bookmark a distinct name, you can use the bookmark at any time to quickly jump to that location in the document.

You can only begin a bookmark name with a letter, not a number. Also, you cannot use spaces in bookmark names.

INSERT A BOOKMARK

1. Select the text or click where you want to insert a bookmark.
2. Click Insert.
3. Click Bookmark.

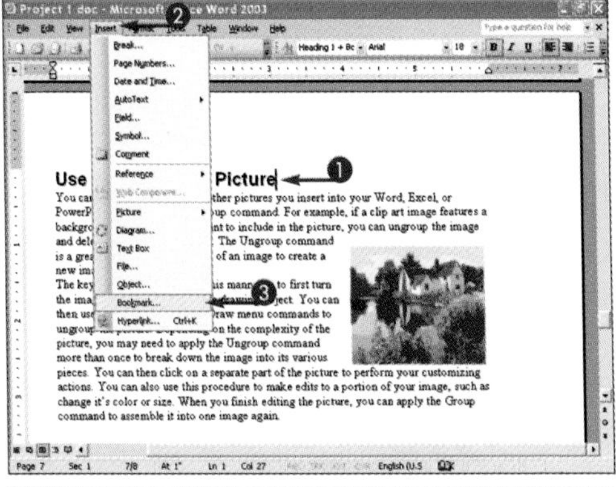

The Bookmark dialog box appears.

4. Type a name for the bookmark.
5. Click Add.

Word adds the bookmark.

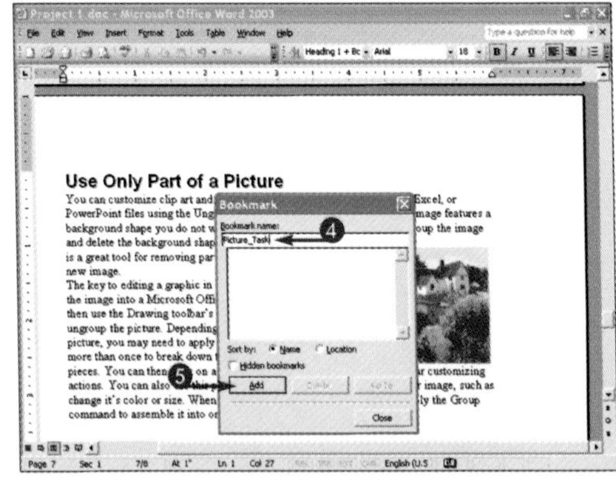

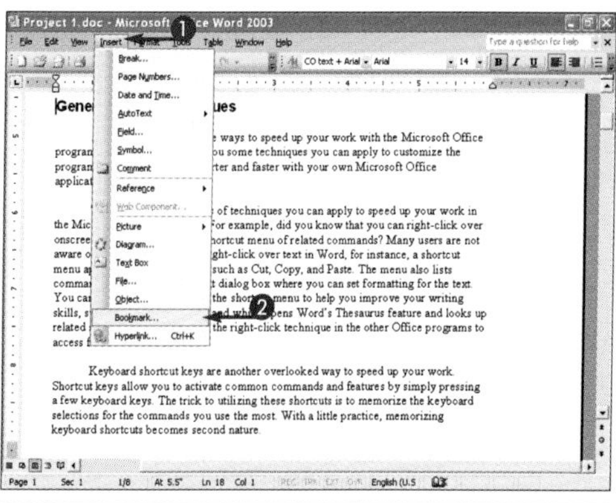

LOCATE A BOOKMARK

1. Click Insert.
2. Click Bookmark.

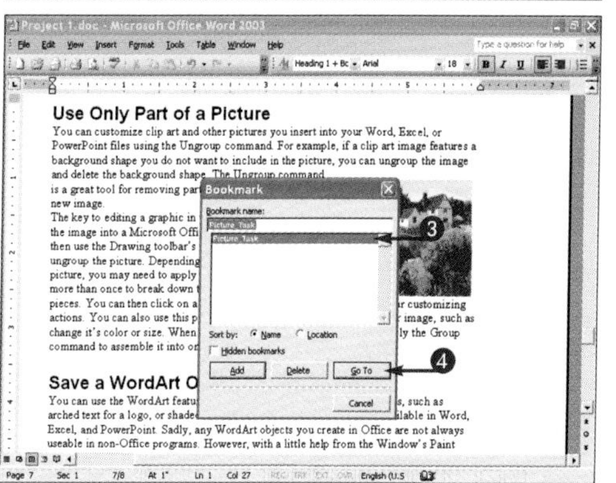

The Bookmark dialog box appears.

3. Click the bookmark to which you want to jump.
4. Click Go To.

Word displays the page containing the bookmarks.

Did You Know?

You can use the Go To command to jump to various locations in a document. Click the Select Browse Object button (◎) at the bottom of the vertical scroll bar, then click the Go To icon (→). In the Find and Replace dialog box, click the Go To tab, and click Bookmark in the Go To What box. Click (▾) and select the desired bookmark. Click Go To, and Word jumps to that location.

Using AutoText to Automate Repetitive Typing

If you consistently retype the same text over and over again, Word allows you to add the text to the AutoText entries. Instead of typing out the whole string of words each time, AutoText lets you type just the first few letters and offers to fill in the rest for you.

Word includes AutoText as a part of the AutoCorrect features. Your entry must contain at least four characters. You can also use AutoText to insert a graphic into your document.

ADD AN AUTOTEXT ENTRY

1. Type and select the text you want to store as an AutoText entry.
2. Click Insert.
3. Click AutoText.
4. Click AutoText.

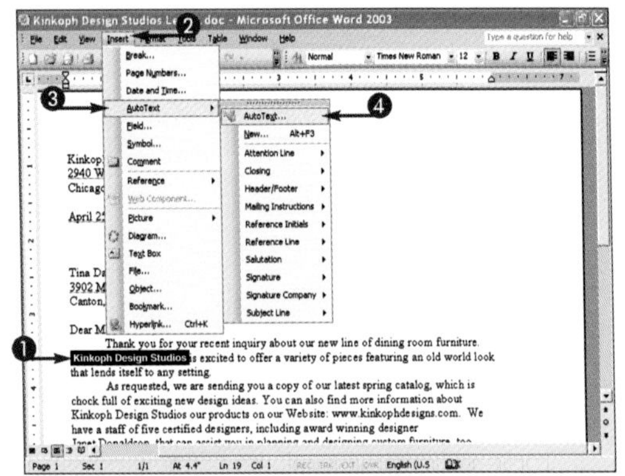

The AutoCorrect dialog box appears.

- Word displays your entry.

5. Click Add.

   Word adds your entry to the list.

6. Click OK.

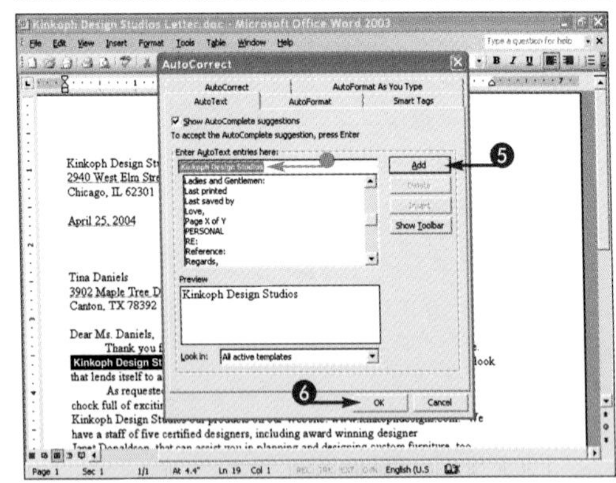

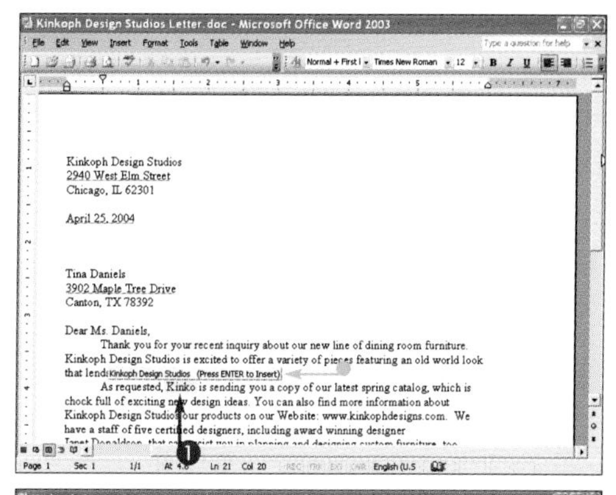

ACTIVATE AN AUTOTEXT ENTRY

1. Type the first few letters of the entry.
   - AutoText displays the entire word or phrase.
2. Press Enter.

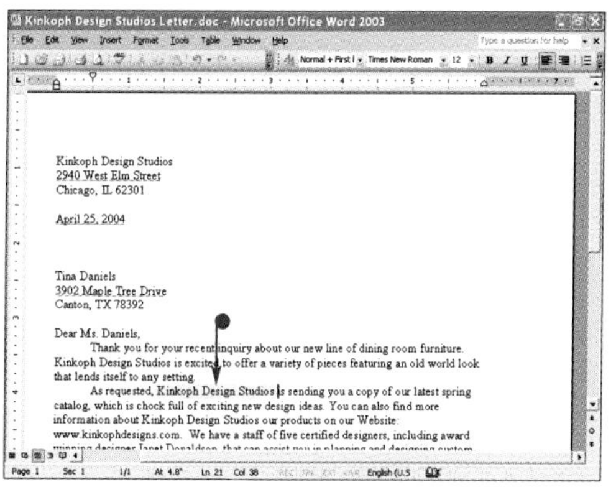

- AutoText inserts the word or phrase.

Did You Know?

If you type text that is similar to an AutoText entry, and the AutoText box pops up, you can ignore the suggestion and keep typing.

Remove a Text Hyperlink

Every time you type a Web page address into a document, the text takes on the appearance of a Web link, indicating that you can click the link to jump to the designated Web page. However, you can tell Word to undo any hyperlink formatting and return the text to regular text. This removes the link entirely. If you want to create the hyperlink again, you must reassign the hyperlink or type the address again.

1. Right-click over the hyperlink text.
2. Click Remove Hyperlink.

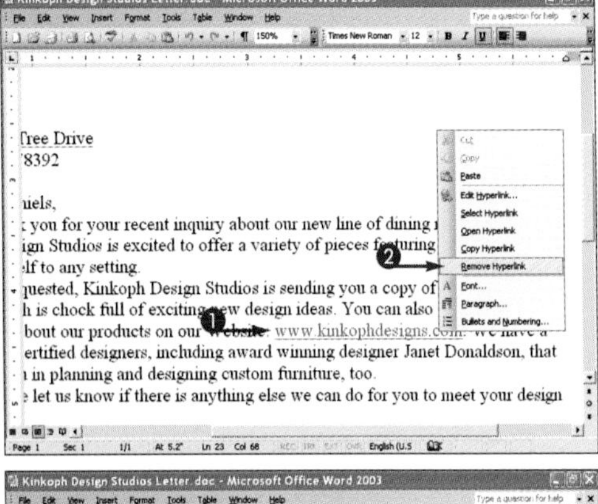

- Word restores the text to regular format.

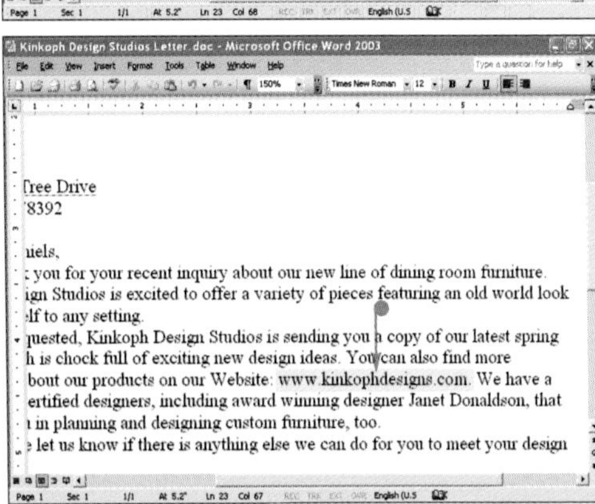

Keep Words Together with a Non-Breaking Space

By default, Word automatically wraps a line of text to the next line once you reach the right margin. However, this may result in an awkward break up of a multiword phrase or proper names. For example, if you type the name John Smith at the end of the line, Word may wrap the last name to the next line of text. Thankfully, you can apply a non-breaking space to keep names and other multiword phrases together and Word breaks before or after the phrase or name rather than in the middle.

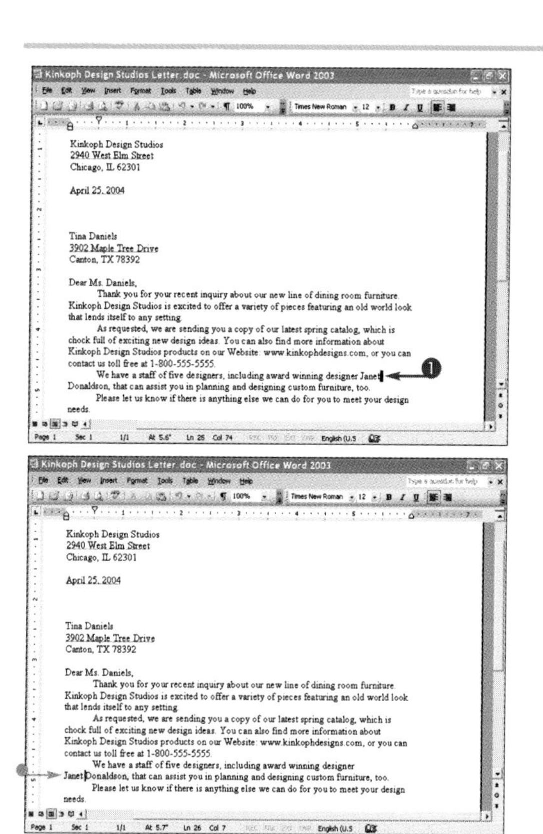

1. Select the space after the first word in the phrase or name.
2. Press Ctrl+Shift+Spacebar.

- Word adds a non-breaking space.

Repeat steps **1** and **2** for each additional space in the phrase or name.

Note: *You do not need to apply a non-breaking space to the space immediately following the last word in the phrase or name.*

Control Sentence Spacing

You can control the spacing between sentences as you type. Ordinarily, you press the Spacebar once to create a space between sentences. However, some types of documents, such as research and term papers, commonly require double spaces between sentences. If you activate the double-space rule in the Word Grammar and Style options, you can achieve the effect of a double space between sentences without having to press the Spacebar twice. Word inserts the double space for you. This reduces your typing time and ensures consistency throughout the document.

1. Click Tools.
2. Click Options.

   The Options dialog box appears.

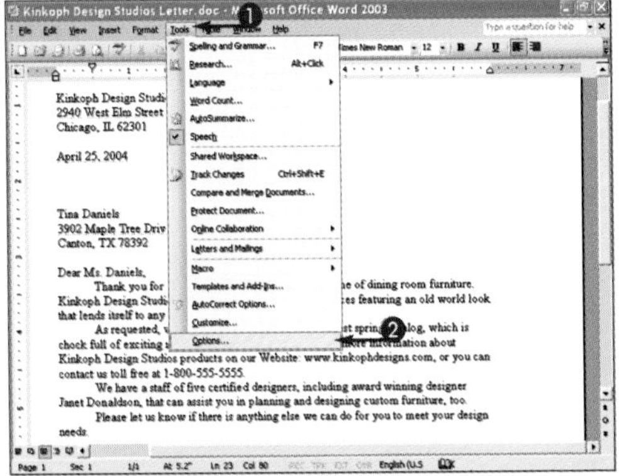

3. Click the Spelling & Grammar tab.
4. Click Settings.

   The Grammar Settings dialog box opens.
5. Click here and select 2.
6. Click OK twice to close out of the dialog boxes.

   Word inserts a double space after every sentence.

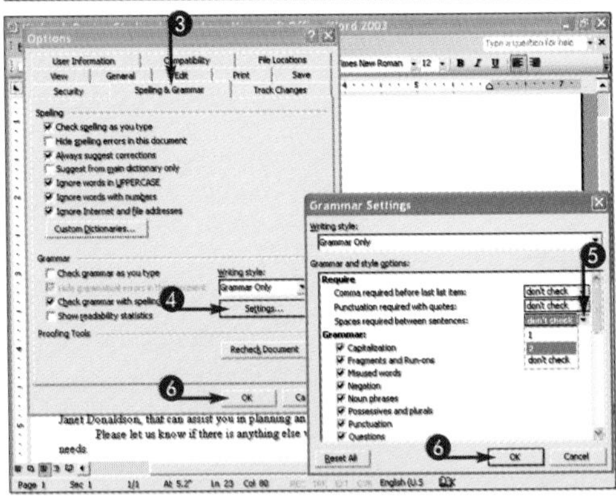

Track Word Count

You can use the Word Count toolbar to speed up the process of counting words, characters, lines, paragraphs, and pages. This feature is handy for users who need to track the number of words for research papers, reports, and more. You may want to keep the toolbar onscreen for quick access. Any time you need a word count, you can check the total word count for the document with a mouse click.

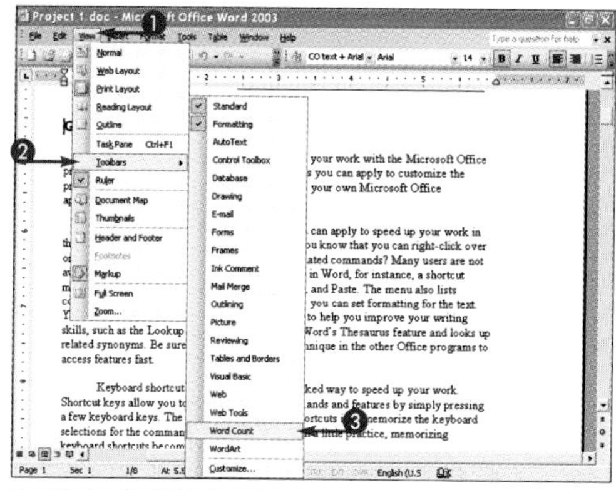

1. Click View.
2. Click Toolbars.
3. Click Word Count.

The Word Count toolbar appears.

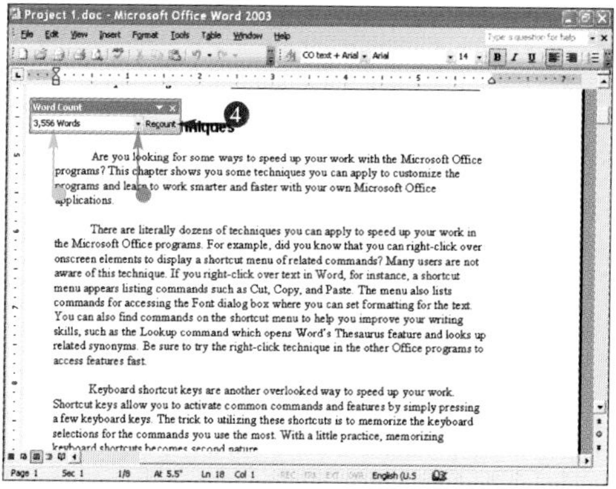

- To count parts of the document other than words, click here and select an item.

4. Click Recount.

- Word counts the number of items you select.

If you did not select any items, Word tallies all the words in the document.

Check Your Document for Clichéd Text

You can use the Grammar feature in Word to proofread your document for many kinds of style issues.

As long as the Grammar checker is active, whenever you type a cliché, Word displays a green wavy line under the clichéd text. You can open the Grammar dialog box to display an explanation about the text in question. You can then choose to edit the text, or resume with your typing.

The Word proofing tools, including Spell checker and Grammar checker, do a very good job of pointing out problems with your writing. However, they cannot catch every mistake.

1. Click Tools.
2. Click Options.

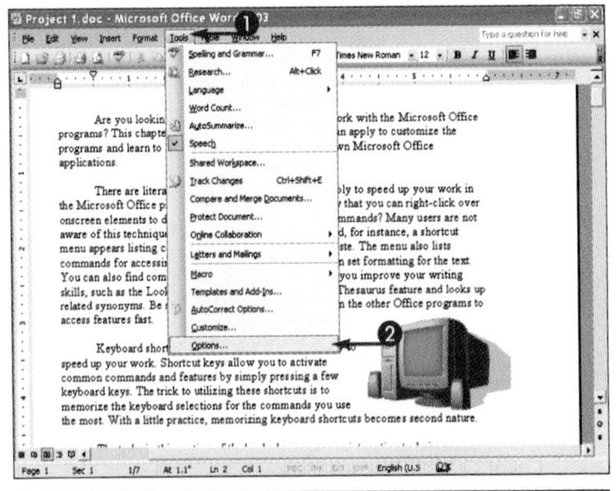

The Options dialog box appears.

3. Click the Spelling & Grammar tab.
4. Click the Check grammar as you type option.
5. Click Settings.

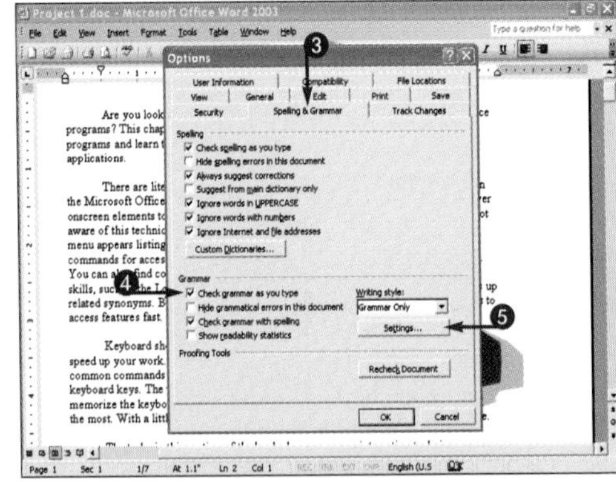

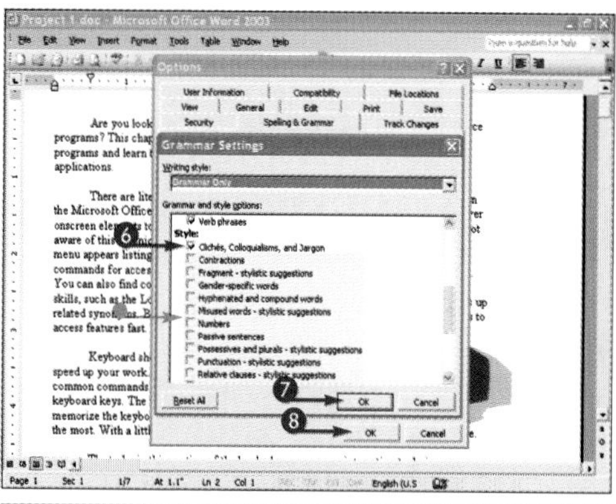

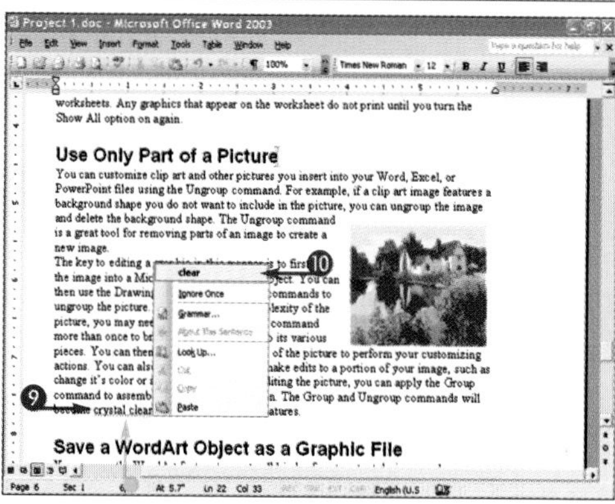

The grammar Settings dialog box appears.

6. Scroll down to the Style check boxes and select the Clichés, Colloquialisms, and Jargon option.

- You can also check for other style issues by selecting these options.

7. Click OK.
8. Click OK to exit the Options dialog box.

- When you type in clichéd text, Word underlines it with a green wavy line.

9. Right-click over the green wavy text.
10. Click a suggestion.

Word corrects the clichéd text.

Did You Know?

To see a full explanation about a grammar problem that Word identifies with a green wavy line, right-click over the text and select Grammar from the shortcut menu. The Grammar dialog box appears and more thoroughly identifies the problem, along with suggestions for fixing it. Click Change to make a correction, or click Ignore Once to ignore the grammar problem and continue checking the document.

Using the Research Pane to Translate Text

You can use the Research task pane in Word to translate a single word, a phrase, or your entire document to another language.

You can use the bilingual dictionaries that install with Word to translate single words or short phrases. For larger amounts of text, you can use machine translation on the Web. You need an Internet connection to access the Web and utilize the machine translation services of Microsoft. When translating larger amounts of text, your Web browser opens to display the results.

1. Select the word or phrase you want to translate.
2. Click Tools.
3. Click Research.

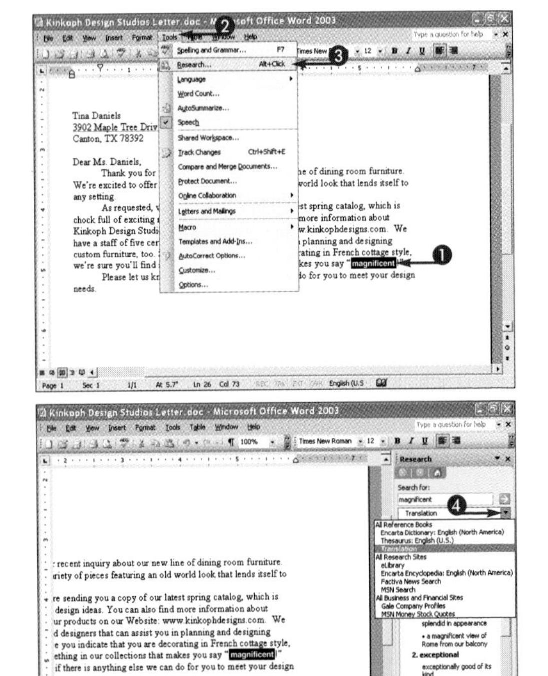

The Research task pane appears.

4. Click here and select Translation.

Note: *The first time you use the translation services, you must install the bilingual dictionaries to enable the service. Insert your Office CD-ROM and click OK to install the features.*

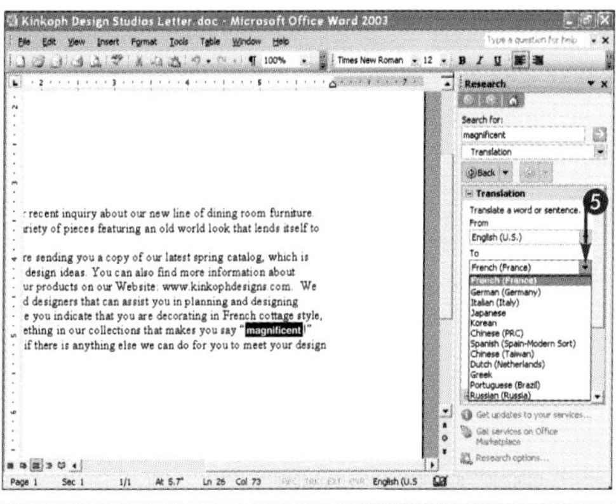

❺ Click here and select the language to which you want to translate.

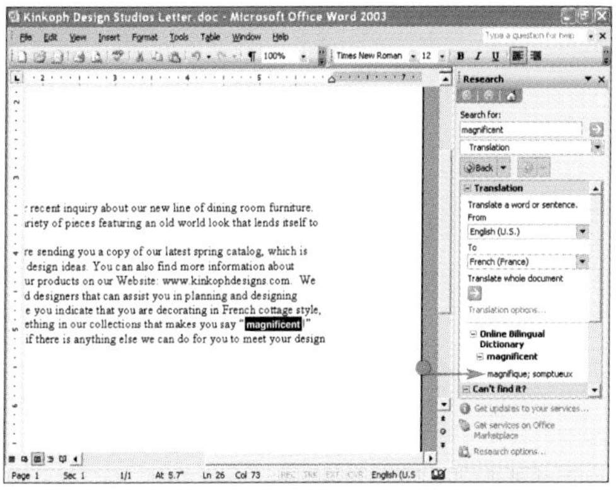

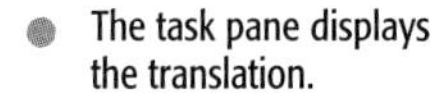

- The task pane displays the translation.

You can copy and paste translated items from the task pane to your document by selecting the word or words in the pane and using the Copy and Paste commands to insert them into your text.

Did You Know?

To quickly translate a specific word in your document, open the Research task pane and display the translation options, setting the language to which you want to translate. Press Alt and click the word you want to translate. The Research task pane immediately shows the results.

Add Line Numbers in the Document Margin

You can add line numbers that appear in the margins of your Word documents. This is particularly helpful if you use Word in an office environment.

When you turn on the line-numbering feature, Word displays line numbers in the left margin for every line of text in the document. You can tell Word to start at a certain number, restart numbering for different pages and sections in your document, or to apply continuous line numbering throughout the entire document.

Word automatically renumbers for you. Because the line numbers appear in the margin, you cannot select the line numbers for editing.

1. Click File.
2. Click Page Setup.

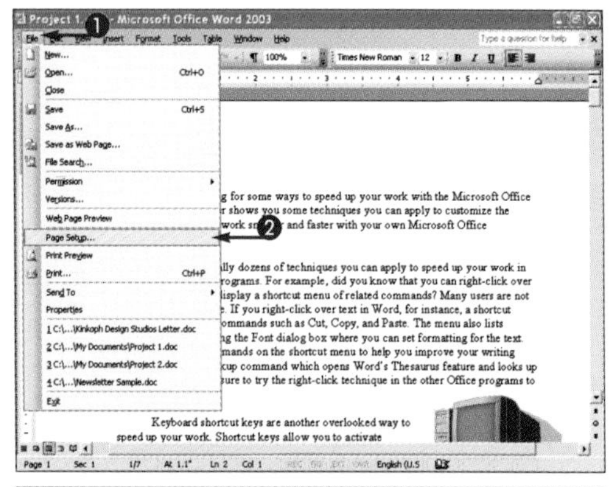

The Page Setup dialog box appears.

3. Click the Layout tab.
4. Click Line Numbers.

The Line Numbers dialog box appears.

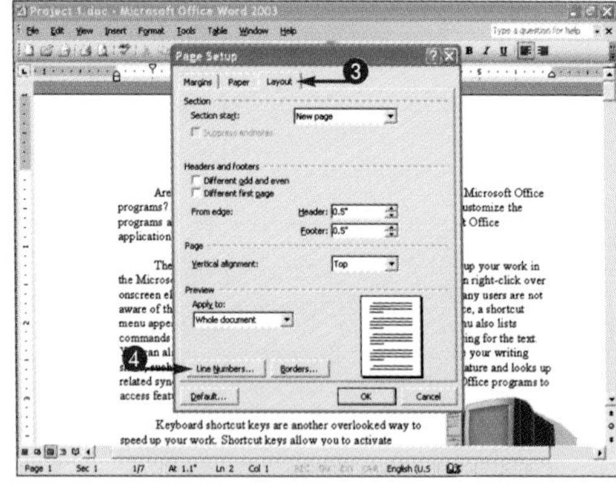

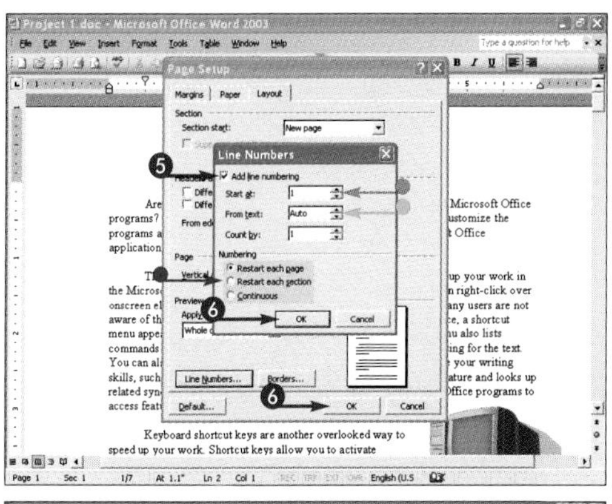

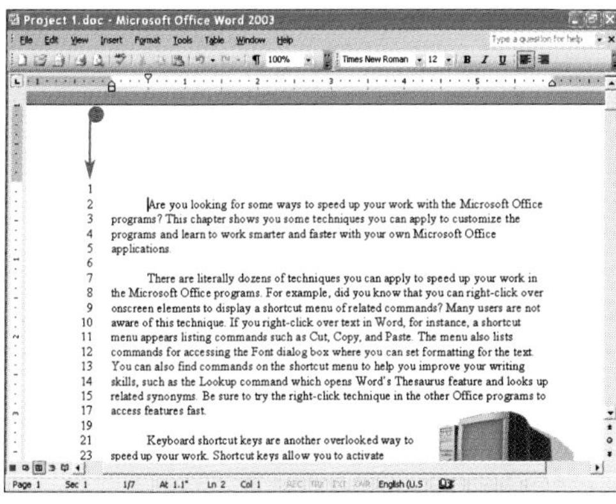

5. Click the Add line numbering option.
   - You can select a starting number.
   - You can select the spacing between the text and the line numbers.
   - You can select an option to restart numbering for each page or section, or to set continuous numbering.
6. Click OK twice to exit the dialog boxes.
   - Word adds line numbers to the margin of the document.

Note: *To view the line numbers, you can switch to Print Layout view.*

Did You Know?

To apply line numbers to a portion of the document, first select the text, and then open the Page Setup dialog box as shown on this task. Click the Layout tab, click the Apply to (▾), and select Selected text. You can now open the Line Numbers dialog box and apply the line options.

Set Off a Paragraph with a Border

You can use partial or full borders to set off a paragraph within your document.

You can also set off an entire paragraph with a border, drawing attention to the text or message.

You can use the Borders and Shading dialog box to control how a border appears around a paragraph, as well as the style of the line borders. You can choose from a variety of line styles and thicknesses, and control the color of the line borders. You can preview your border selections before applying them to the actual paragraph.

1. Click inside of, or select a paragraph to which, you want to add a border.
2. Click Format.
3. Click Borders and Shading.

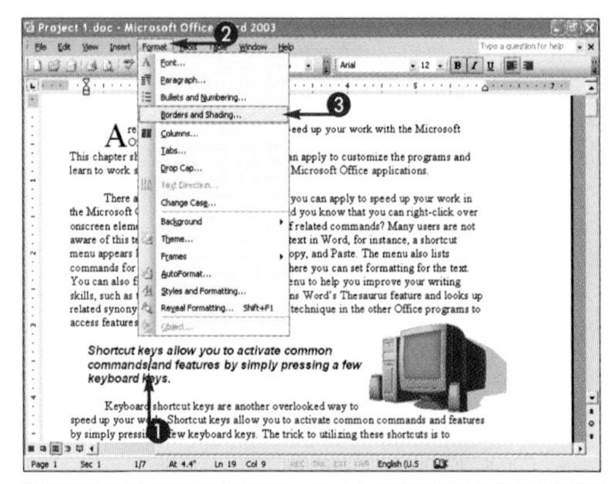

The Borders and Shading dialog box appears.

4. Click the Borders tab.
5. Click Box.

- You can click here to select a line style.
- You can click here to select a color.
- You can click here to select a line width.

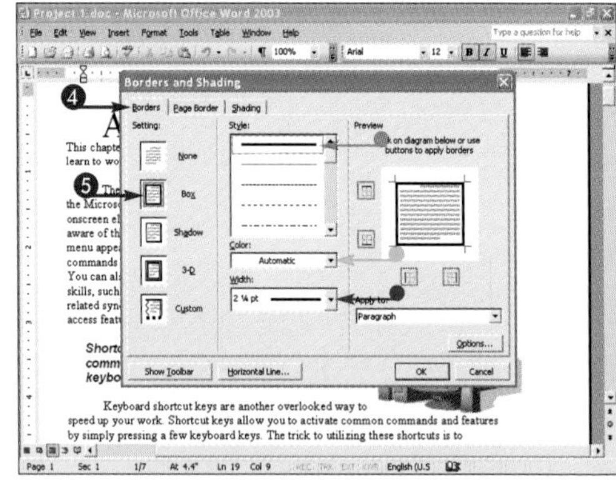

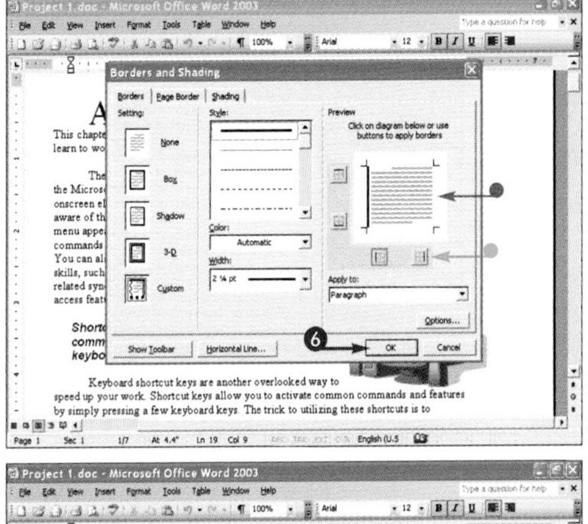

- The Preview shows your current setting and styles.
- To remove any sides of the border, you can click a border button.

6. Click OK.

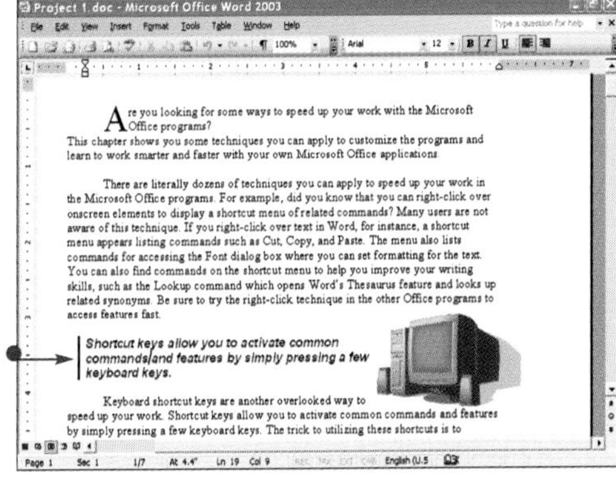

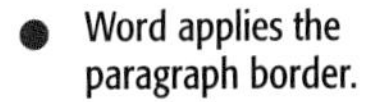

- Word applies the paragraph border.

In this example, Word applied a partial paragraph border and indented the paragraph to create a pull-quote effect.

Did You Know?

You can apply shading to a paragraph. Shading is a color or pattern that appears behind the paragraph text. To apply shading, click the Shading tab in the Borders and Shading dialog box. Select a fill color from the palette, or click More Colors to select another color. Click the Style (☐) to change the color intensity or select a fill pattern.

Resume Numbering in an Interrupted Numbered List

When you use numbered lists in your Word document, you may sometimes need to interrupt the numbered list with a paragraph, and then resume the list. The smart tags in Word can help you pick up where you left off. When the smart tag options are active, which they are by default, a smart tag icon appears next to the paragraph. When clicked, the smart tag, which looks like a lightening bolt, displays several options that relate to your work. In the case of numbered lists, the smart tag displays AutoCorrect options that create numbered lists.

1. When you start a new paragraph to continue the numbered list, click the Numbering button.

   A smart tag appears next to the first number.

2. Click the smart tag.
3. Click Continue Numbering.

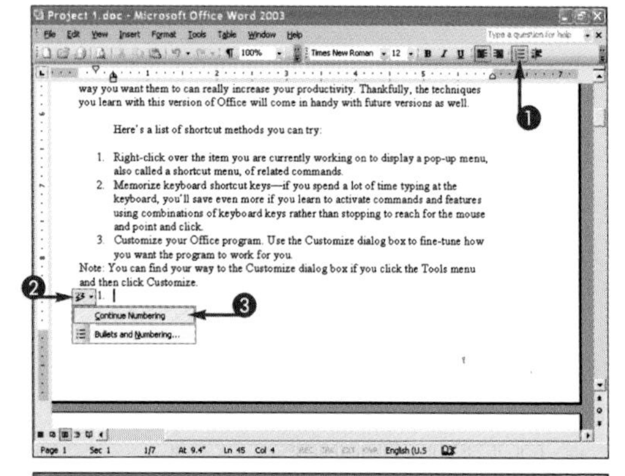

- Word resumes the numbering sequence of the previous numbered list.

  To change the formatting of your numbers in a numbered list, double-click over a number to open the Bullets and Numbering dialog box, and select another number style.

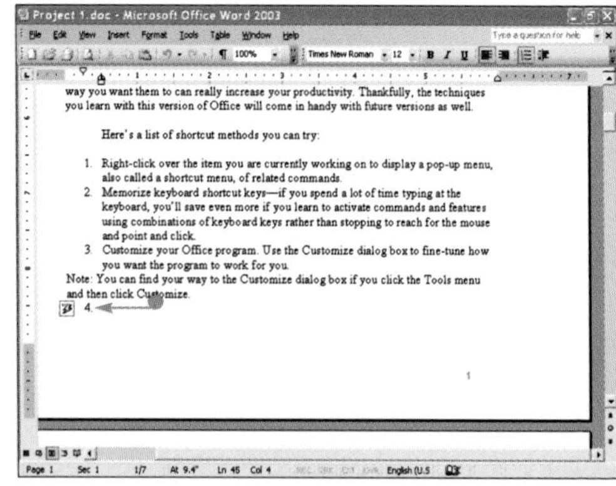

Quickly Insert Horizontal Lines

You can quickly insert a horizontal line across your document page using a keyboard shortcut in Word. For example, you can insert a horizontal line between two sections to act as a divider.

Ordinarily, you must go through the Borders and Shading dialog box to get to the Horizontal Line dialog box, and then specify a line type to apply. However, for a simple line, you can use a keyboard shortcut by typing three special characters. If you enter three special characters but do not want to create a line, simply activate the Undo command.

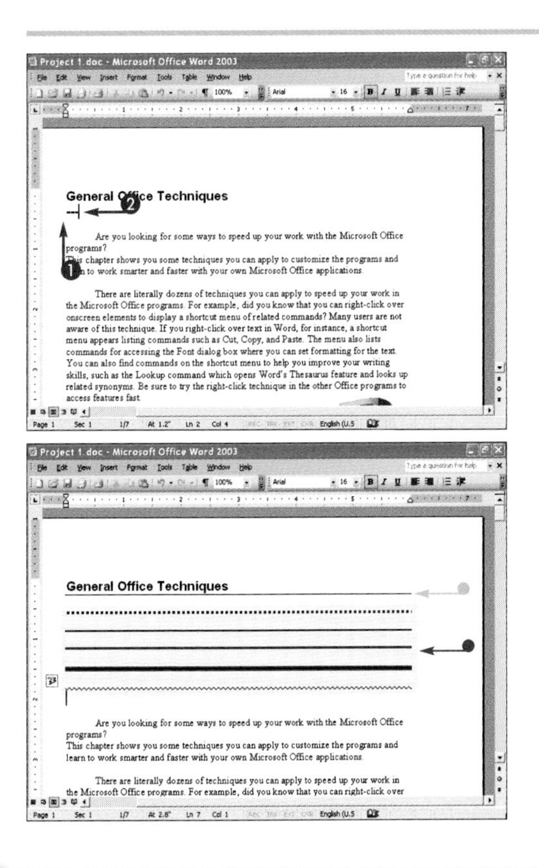

1. Click in the document where you want to insert a line.
2. Type three dashes.

   For a different effect, type three asterisks, underscores, equal signs, pound signs, or tildes.
3. Press Enter.

- Word inserts the line.
- You can also insert other types of lines using the keyboard shortcut.

Emphasize Paragraphs with Drop Caps

You can use drop caps to add emphasis to your text or to create a dramatic effect. A drop cap is a large initial or capital letter that appears at the beginning of a paragraph.

By default, a drop cap is set up to drop three lines. This means that the height of the drop cap is equivalent to three lines of text. You can specify how many lines down to set the drop cap. You can also specify a distance from the text. By default, the drop cap appears at zero distance from, or directly next to, the paragraph text.

The Drop Cap dialog box also allows you to change the font of the drop-cap.

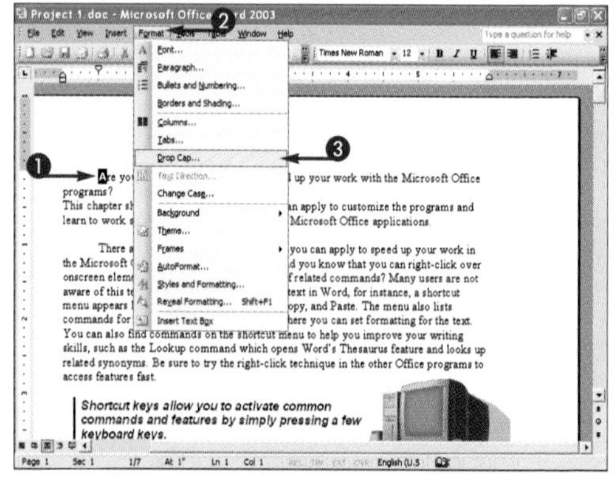

1. Select the character you want to turn into a drop cap.

***Note:** This feature works only on the first letter of a paragraph.*

2. Click Format.
3. Click Drop Cap.

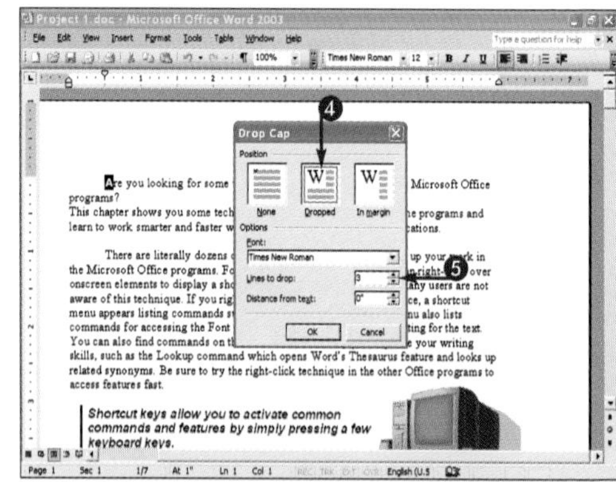

The Drop Cap dialog box appears.

4. Click the type of drop cap position you want to apply.
5. Click the up or down arrows, or type the number of lines you want the character to drop.

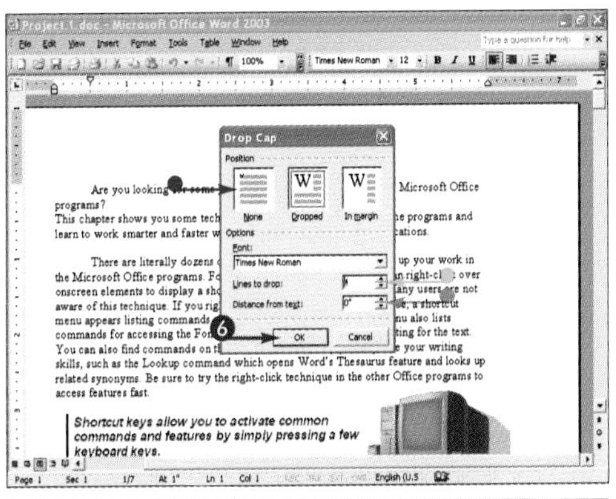

- To set additional space between the drop cap and the paragraph text, click the up or down arrows, or type the number of a measurement you want.
- To change the font, click here and select a font style.
- To return a drop cap to normal character text click the None position option.

6. Click OK.

- Word applies the drop cap.

***Note:** Because Word places drop caps in text boxes, you can move, resize, and apply formatting to the text box, such as a background color or a border.*

Did You Know?

For eye-catching drop caps, use a decorative font, such as Algerian or Old English MT. Although it is not a good idea to add drop caps to every paragraph in a document, when used sparingly, they can create a good visual break for people viewing your document.

Customize Comment Text

By default, comment text in your Word documents appears as 10-point Times New Roman type. If you intend to create and read a lot of comments in a document, you may want to change the font and size to make the text more legible.

Word formats comment text in accordance with a preset style. A style is a set of formatting characteristics you can apply to text.

To customize comment text, you must open the Styles and Formatting task pane and then modify the Comment Text style. Depending on what styles are in view, you may need to add the Comment Text style to the task pane.

1. Click the Styles and Formatting button.

   The Styles and Formatting task pane appears.

2. Click here and select Custom.

   The Format Settings dialog box appears.

3. Click the Comment Text option.
4. Click OK.

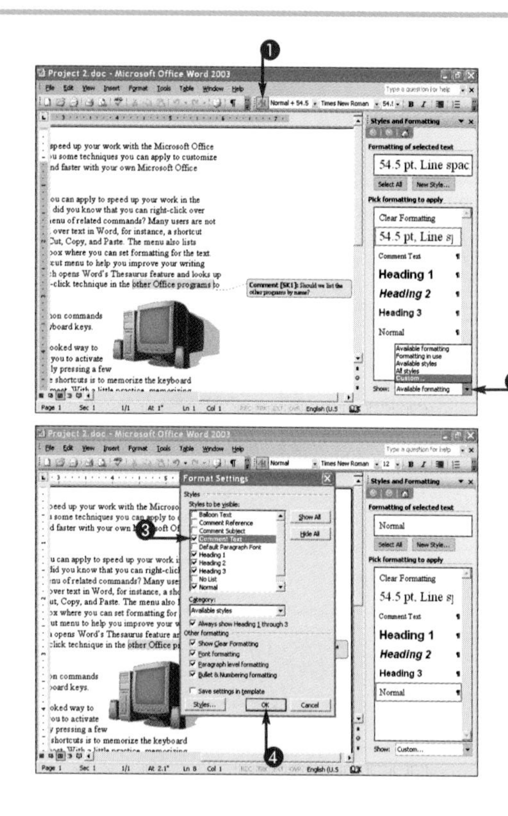

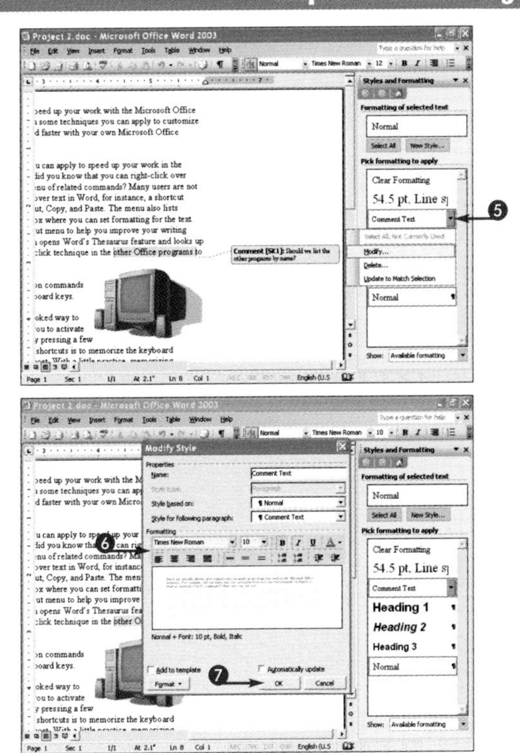

5. Click here and select Modify.

The Modify Style dialog box appears.

6. Make the changes you want to the font and font size, or other formatting options.
7. Click OK.

Word applies the new comment style to existing comment text boxes as well as comments you add later.

Customize It!

The Modify Style dialog box includes a wide variety of formatting options you can apply to your comment text. You can set alignment, line spacing, paragraph spacing, and indents. You can also change the font color and style, such as bold or italics. You can click Format to reveal additional categories of attributes you can apply to styles.

Add Captions to Your Graphics

If your document includes graphic items, you can add captions to describe the items for the reader.

Using the Caption feature in Word, you can automatically number the captions within your document. If you move a graphic object, Word automatically renumbers captions for you. You can label captions as figures, equations, or tables, or you can create your own labels, such as photograph or item. You can also place your captions above or below the item.

After creating a caption and a label, you can edit the caption text at any time. The caption text box works like any other text box in Word.

1. Select the graphic object to which you want to add a caption.
2. Click Insert.
3. Click Reference.
4. Click Caption.

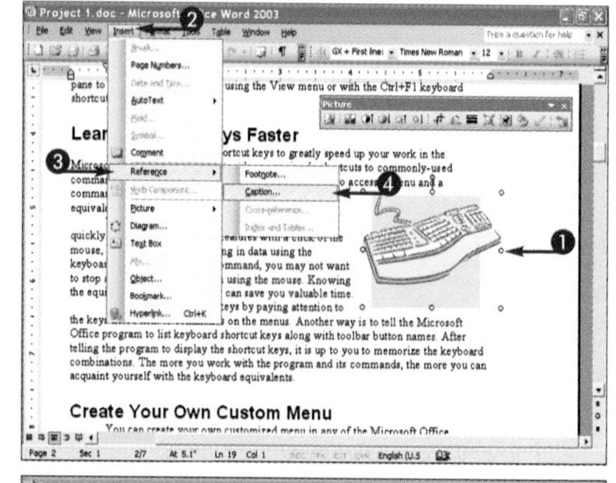

The Caption dialog box appears.

5. Click here and select a label.

- To add a new label, click New Label and type in the new label text.

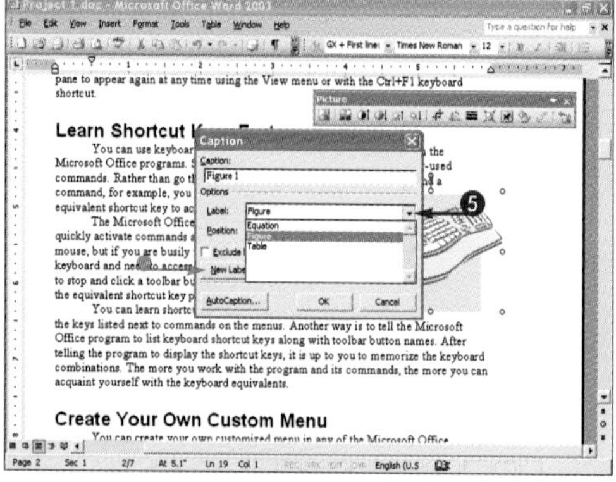

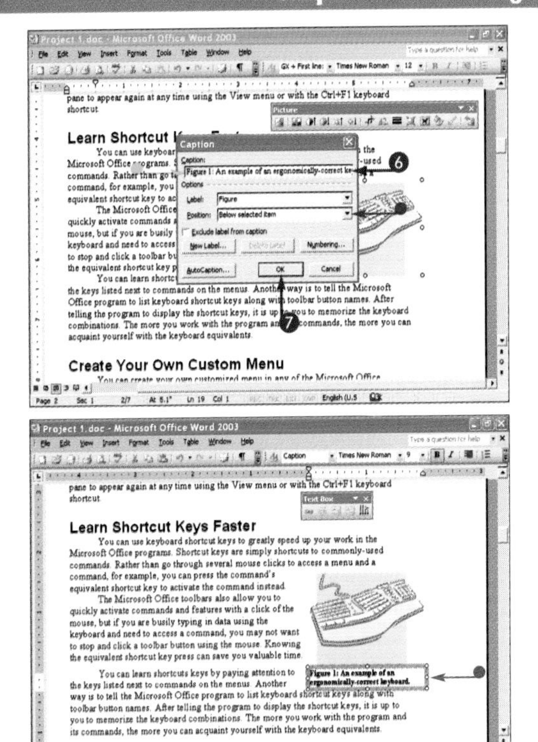

- The numbered label appears in the Caption field.

6. Type any additional caption text you want to include.

- You can click here to select the caption position.

7. Click OK.

- Word applies the caption to the graphic object.

Note: *Captions appear in text boxes, which means you can move, resize, and apply formatting to the text box, such as a background color or a border.*

To remove a caption text box, select the text box, then press the Delete key.

To edit the text, you can make changes directly in the caption text box.

Did You Know?

If you need to add callouts to an illustration you import into Word, you can do this using AutoShape callouts. AutoShapes appear on the Drawing toolbar, and the Callouts category of pre-drawn shapes includes 20 types of callouts. After selecting a callout shape, click where you want it go to, resize and move the shape, and reposition the line pointing to the callout.

Type Out a Table

Most users create a table in Word using the Insert Table button, which allows them to drag over the number of columns and rows they want to insert. But did you know that you can use the keyboard to type out a table? This technique is useful if you are a fast typist and do not want to use the mouse to create a table. By typing out a string of plus and minus signs, you can start a table on any line in your document. If your table requires more rows, you can add them as you enter table cell data.

1. Click where you want to insert a table.
2. Type a plus sign (+).
3. Type a minus sign (-) for the number of character spaces you want to have in the first column.
4. Type a plus sign to start the next column.
5. Repeat steps **3** and **4** for each column you want to add.

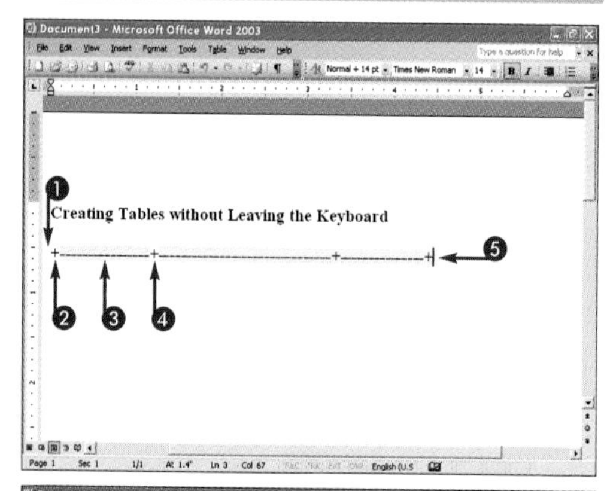

6. Press Enter after typing the final plus sign to end the last column.

- Word creates the table.

To add more rows to the table, press the Tab key after entering cell data in the last table cell.

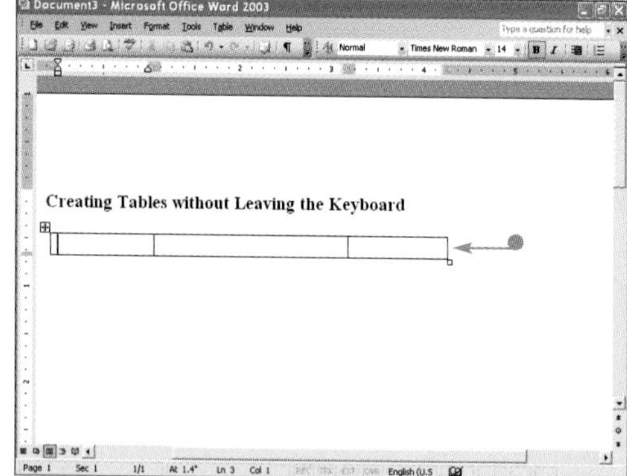

Keep Table Column Headings in Sight

Column headings describe what data is in each column. If you create a long table in Word that spans more than one page, you may lose sight of your column headings as you enter data, and you may have to scroll back and forth to the top of the table to see what information each column should contain. Fortunately, Word has a technique you can use to keep column headings visible. The Repeat Row Headings command, which is only visible in Print Layout view, instructs Word to repeat the column titles for each page on which the table appears.

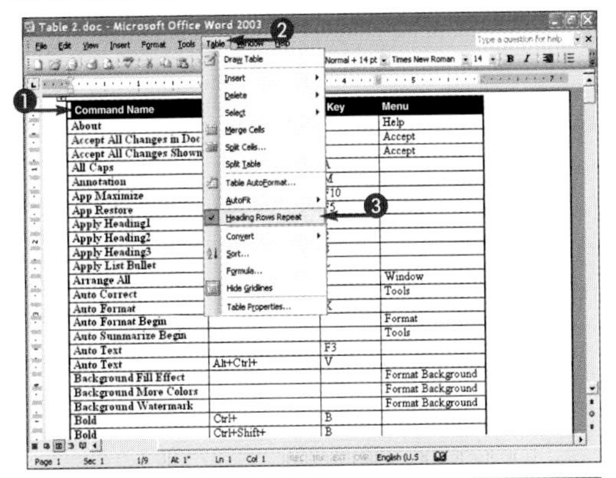

1. Click the first row containing the column headings you want to view.
2. Click Table.
3. Click Heading Rows Repeat.

- Word repeats the column headings at the top of any subsequent pages on which the table appears.

In this example, page 2 now shows column headings.

Place a Table within a Table

Did you know that you can place tables within tables? For example, you may create a table that displays a listing of classes and professors, and a table within each class listing that displays times and room numbers. Placing a table within a table helps you further organize your document's data.

You can use the Insert Table command on the Table menu to add a table within the current cell of an existing table, or you can use the Insert Table button on the Standard toolbar. Either method adjusts the current table cell height and width to accommodate the new table within the existing table.

1. Click inside the cell in which you want to add a table.
2. Click the Insert Table button.
3. Drag across the number of columns and rows for the new table.

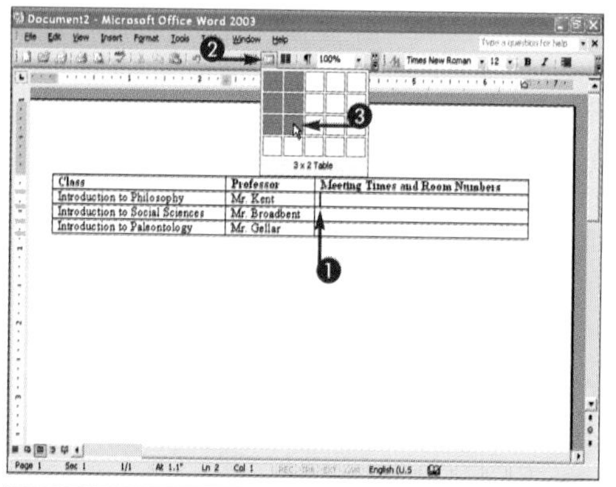

- Word inserts the new table within the existing table.

You can populate the sub-table as needed.

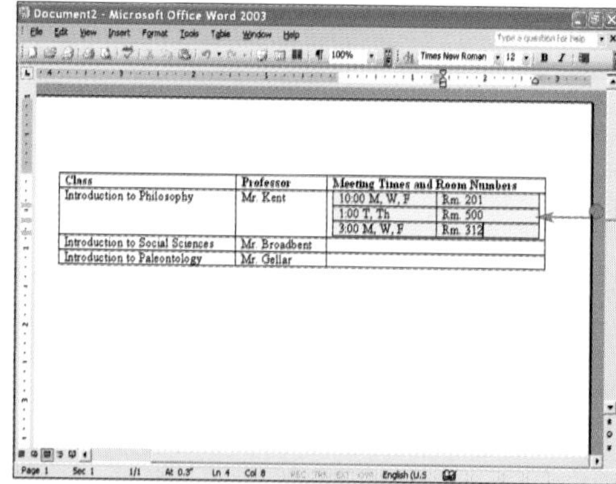

Align Shapes with Grid Lines

If you add shapes, clip art, and other graphic objects to your document, you may find it difficult to line them up. Microsoft Word features a drawing grid that helps you position graphic objects on a page. You access the grid through the Drawing toolbar. By default, the grid does not appear when you draw customized shapes and AutoShapes with the Drawing toolbar. However, you can turn the grid on as needed, and turn it off again after you align your shapes.

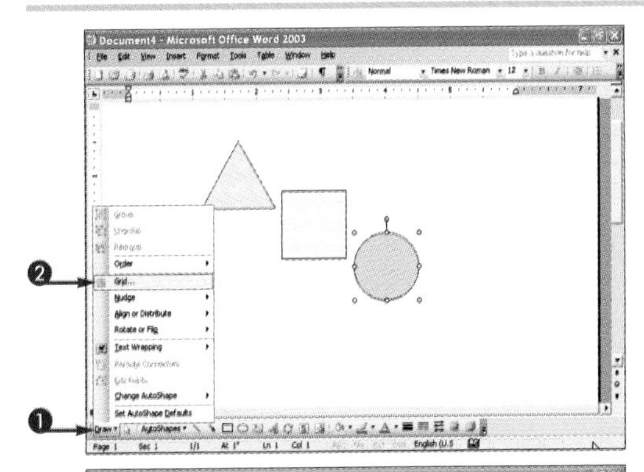

1. Click Draw on the Drawing toolbar.
2. Click Grid.

Note: *To display the Drawing toolbar, click View, then Toolbars, then Drawing.*

The Drawing Grid dialog box appears.

3. Click the Display gridlines on screen option.

- You can adjust horizontal and vertical gridline spacing.

4. Click OK.

- Word displays the grid.
- You can align shapes and objects by clicking and dragging them along the gridlines.

Add Gradient Fills to Text Boxes

Text boxes in Word usually contain captions for photographs and other graphic objects. You can use them in other ways to draw attention to important text. You can use text boxes to set text apart from the rest of your document and add fill colors behind the text to make the text stand out even more.

By default, text boxes include a plain white background, or fill color. You can set another fill color as well as patterns, textures, and gradient fill effects.

When selecting any type of fill, whether a solid color or a gradient effect, you should always choose colors or patterns that do not detract from the legibility of your text.

1. Add a new text box, or select an existing text box.
2. Double-click the text box edge.

***Note:** Be sure to double-click over the edge. If you double-click over the text, Word inserts the cursor for you to edit the text.*

The Format Text Box dialog box appears.

3. Click the here and select Fill Effects.

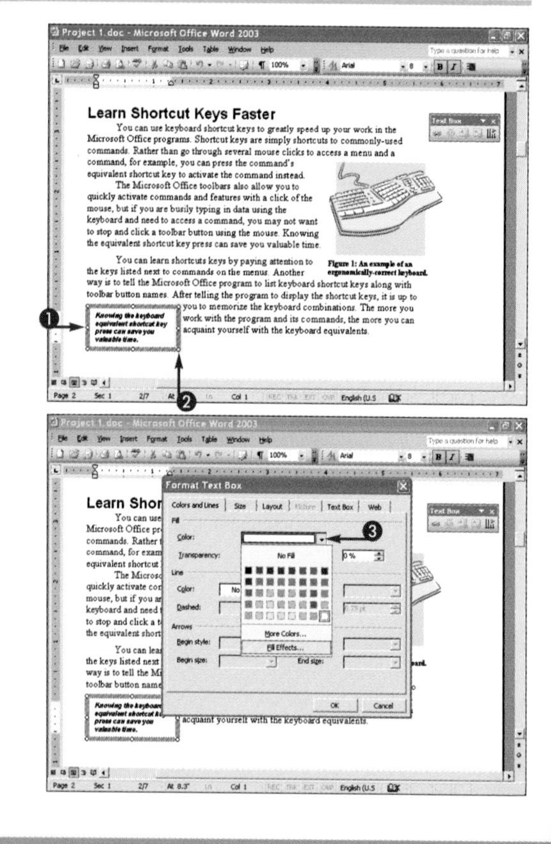

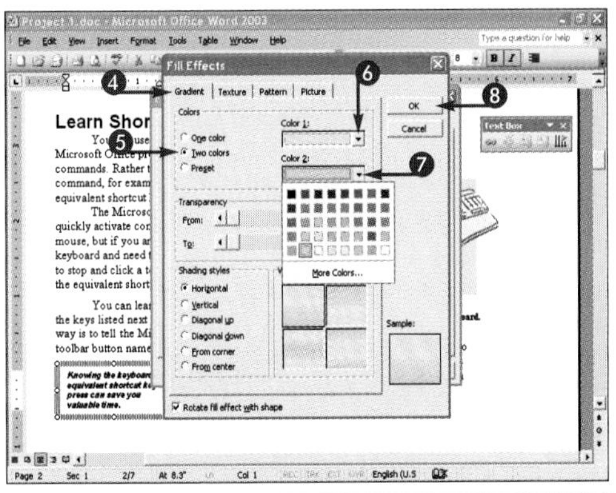

The Fill Effects dialog box appears.

4. Click the Gradient tab.
5. Click the Two colors option.
6. Click here select your first color.
7. Click here and select your second color.
8. Click OK twice to exit the dialog boxes.

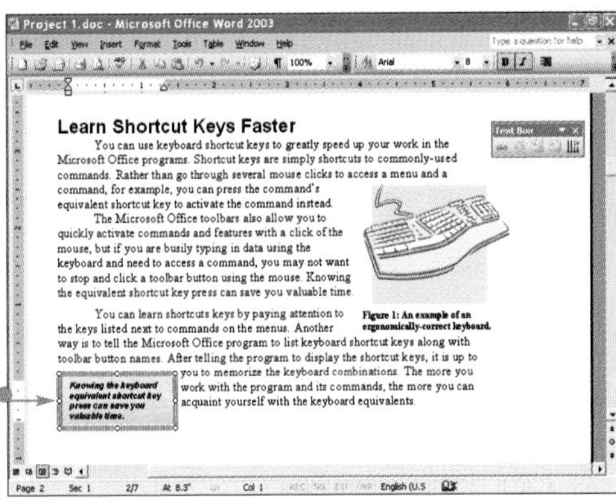

- Word applies the gradient effect to the text box background.

To move a text box, drag the mouse pointer over the border until it becomes a four-sided arrow pointer, then click and drag the box.

TIP

Apply It!

In addition to gradient fill effects, you can add a pattern, texture, or picture to the background of a text box. From the Format Text Box dialog box, click the Fill Colors (▾) and select Fill Effects. The Fill Effects dialog box appears. Each tab offers a different type of background fill.

Create a Watermark

Watermarks are useful for documents you print and share with others. You can use a logo, text, or picture as a watermark behind your document text.

You can use graphic objects or text as a watermark. When choosing a picture as a watermark, you can apply a washout effect to make the image appear even lighter in the background. Depending on the size of the original picture file, you can use the Scale option to resize the image.

For best results, you should use a picture that does not detract from the document text.

INSERT A PICTURE WATERMARK

1. Click Format.
2. Click Background.
3. Click Printed Watermark.

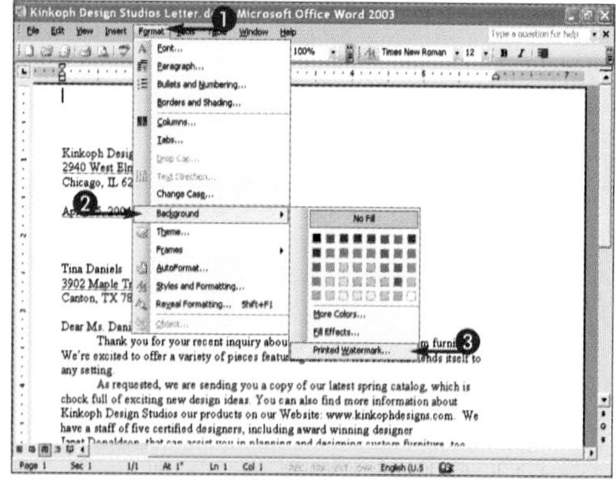

The Printed Watermark dialog box appears.

4. Click the Picture watermark option.
5. Click Select Picture.

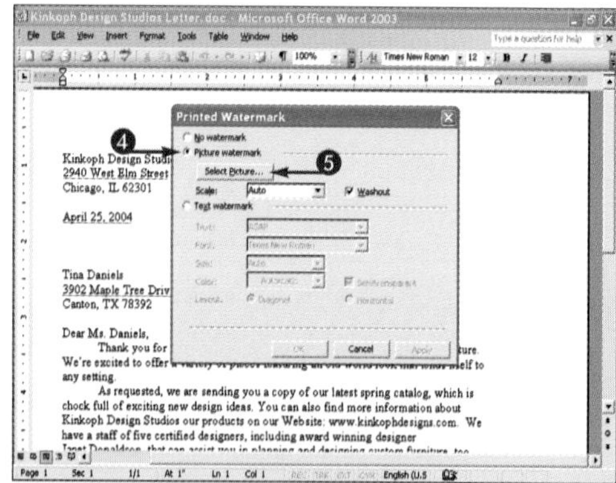

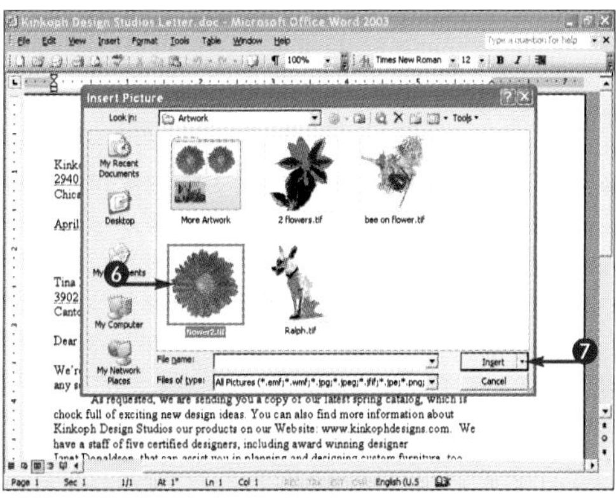

The Insert Picture dialog box appears.

6. Select the picture file you want to use.
7. Click Insert.

- You can click the Washout option to make your picture more transparent.
- To resize the image, click here and select a size.

8. Click OK.

Customize It!

If your watermark picture still overpowers your document even after you apply the Washout option, you can use a graphics program, such as Adobe Illustrator or Photoshop to increase the transparency of the image.

Create a Watermark *(continued)*

When using text as a watermark, you can select from several presets, such as CONFIDENTIAL or COPY. Word offers 10 different preset text choices and 10 text choices in Spanish. You can also enter your own watermark text by typing directly into the Text field.

You can also control the font, size, color, and layout position of the text watermark.

You can also make the text watermark less transparent by deselecting the Semitransparent option.

Watermarks appear on every page in your document. To view a watermark, you can switch to Print Layout view mode or view the file in Print Preview mode.

- Word applies the watermark to every page in your document.

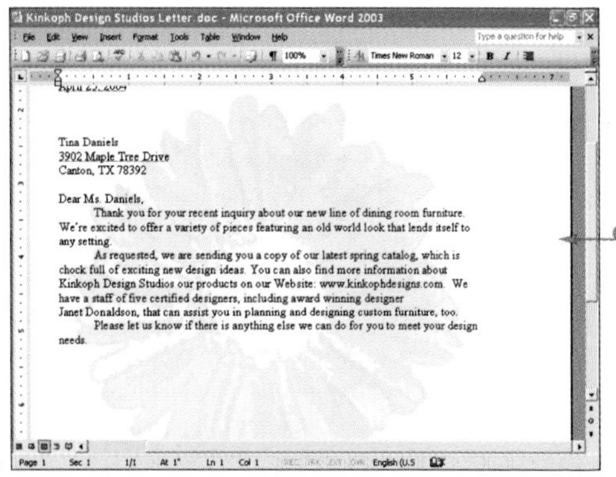

INSERT A TEXT WATERMARK

1. Click Format.
2. Click Background.
3. Click Printed Watermark.

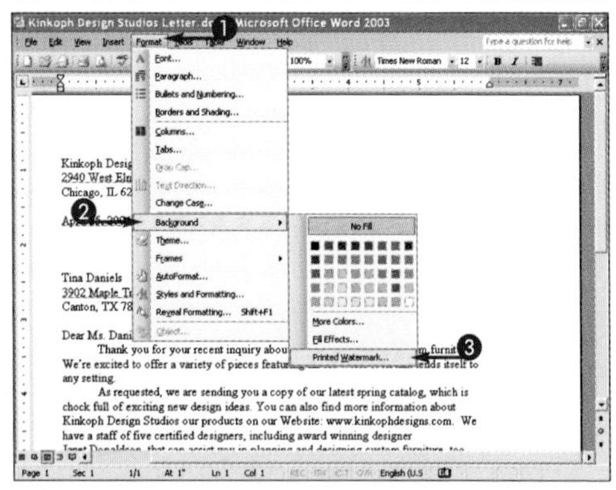

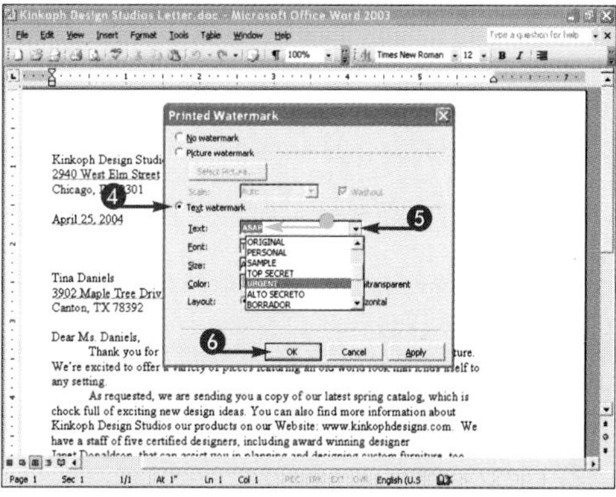

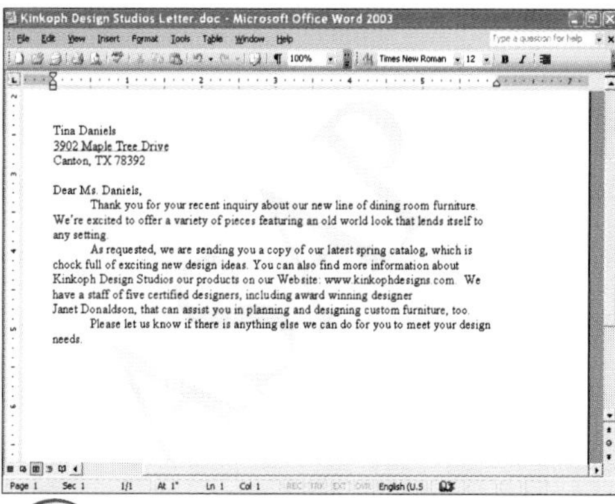

The Printed Watermark dialog box appears.

4. Click the Text watermark option.
5. Click here and select the watermark text you want to apply.
   - You can also type new watermark text directly into the Text field.

   Change any other text options you want to assign, such as font, size, color, or layout position.
6. Click OK.

   Word applies the text watermark to every page in the document.

Did You Know?

You can use a graphic object, such as an AutoShape you draw with the Drawing toolbar tools, as a watermark. To do so, you must copy and paste the object into the document header. The document header appears at the top of every page. You cannot use the Printed Watermark dialog box to insert shapes and other drawn objects onto the document background.

Chapter 3

Increase the Power of Your Spreadsheet with Excel

Microsoft Excel is much more than just a simple spreadsheet program. You can also use Excel to create database lists, balance a checkbook, build dynamic charts, analyze data, and so much more. Along with the basics of using the program, such as learning how to name cells, build formulas, and work with functions, you can take advantage of many other features.

This chapter offers a variety of tips and techniques you can use to make Excel work more productively for you. For example, you can learn how to tell Excel to open a particular workbook automatically every time you open the program window or how to keep your eye on a particular worksheet cell no matter where you scroll in the sheet. These techniques are handy if you revisit the same worksheet over and over again. You can also learn tips for customizing how Excel displays gridlines, formulas, row and column labels. You can use the text-to-speech tool to tell Excel to read back cells as you check data on a printout or ledger. You can update and retrieve stock quotes on a worksheet, or locate data from multiple sheets using the VLookup function. Other handy and timesaving techniques include freezing headings to keep your labels in view at all times, adding a calculator to the toolbar, or turning Excel data into a bitmap picture that you can then insert as an illustration into another file.

Regardless of how you use Excel, this chapter is sure to offer you some nifty tricks to make building worksheets more enjoyable.

Quick Tips

Automatically Open Your Favorite Workbook

By default, Excel opens a new, blank spreadsheet every time you launch the program. If you work on the same spreadsheet every time you use Excel, you can tell the program to automatically open a particular workbook for you.

To set up a workbook to open automatically, you must store the workbook file in the XLSTART folder. If you select the default folder setting for storing Excel on your computer when you installed Excel, you can find the XLSTART folder within the Program Files folder.

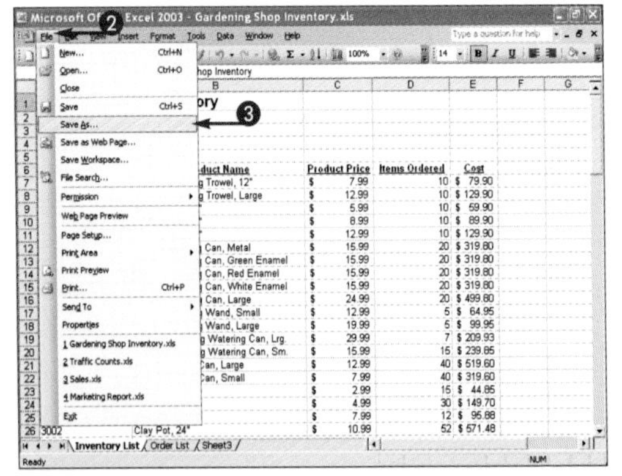

1. Open the workbook you want to save as your default file.
2. Click File.
3. Click Save As.

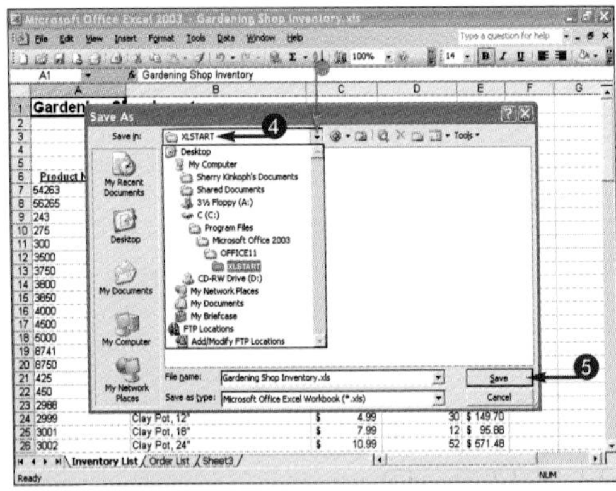

The Save As dialog box appears.

4. Navigate to the XLSTART folder.
   - You can click the Save here to switch folders and drives.
5. Click Save.

The next time you open Excel, the workbook you specify opens automatically.

Access More Files by Increasing the Recent Files List

You can use the recent files list to quickly access the spreadsheets with which you worked most recently in Excel. By default, Excel keeps track of the four most recent workbook files, and displays the list, called the recent files list, at the bottom of the File menu. You can display the File menu and select the workbook you want to open.

If necessary, you can increase the number of files that appear in the recent files list. This gives you quick access to additional files.

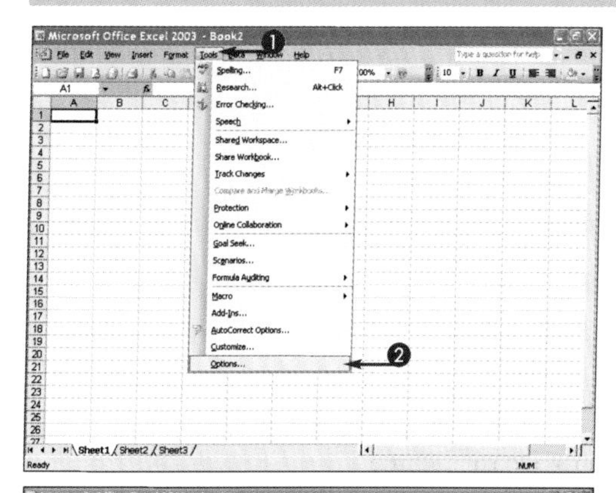

❶ Click Tools.

❷ Click Options.

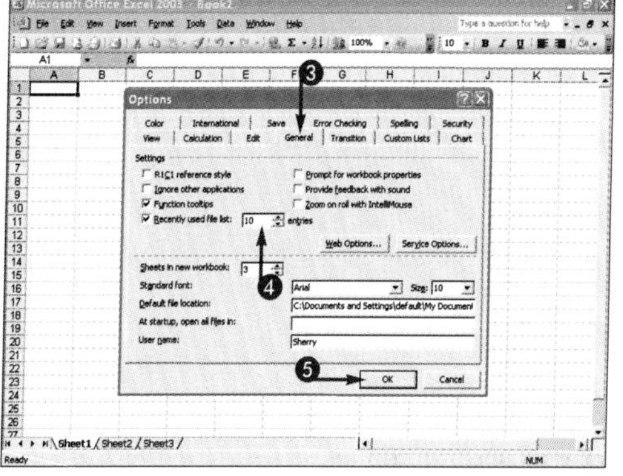

The Options dialog box appears.

❸ Click the General tab.

❹ Type a new number in the Recently used file list field.

You can also click the up or down arrows to increase or decrease the number.

❺ Click OK.

Excel now displays a list of the number of recent files you specify.

Set a New Default Font and Size

You can control the font and size that Excel automatically applies to every worksheet you open. By default, Excel applies the Arial font for all of the worksheet data you enter into cells, and sets the font size to 10 points.

You can change the font and size of your worksheet data as you create and use your worksheets, as well as apply any other formatting. However, you may find it easier to establish a default font and size before you begin adding data.

You can use the Options dialog box to set a new default font and size. Once you set the new font and size, every new worksheet you open utilizes the default settings.

1. Click Tools.
2. Click Options.

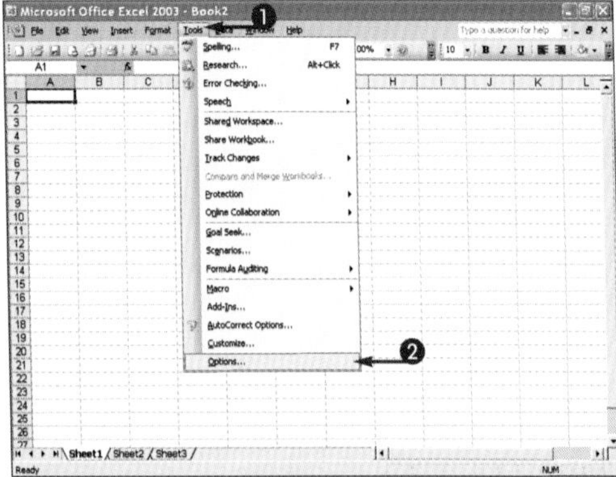

The Options dialog box appears.

3. Click the General tab.
4. Click here and select the font you want to assign.

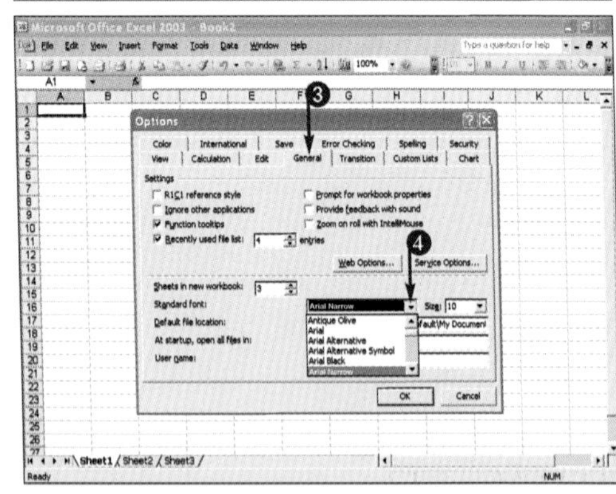

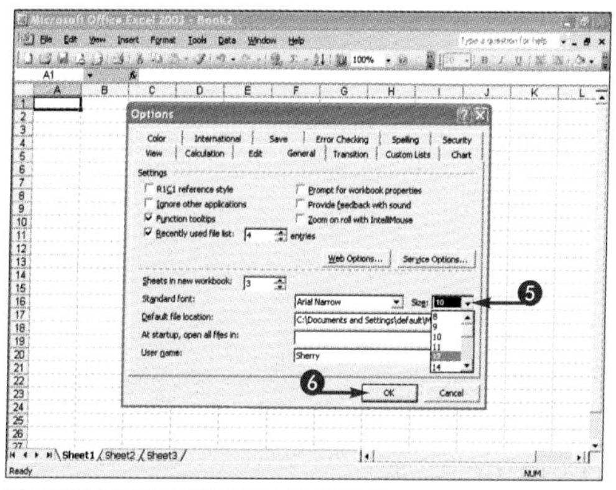

5. Click here and select a size you want to assign.
6. Click OK.

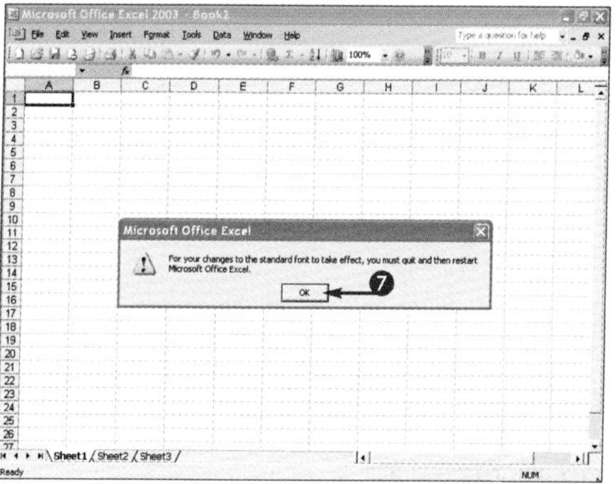

A prompt window appears, warning you that you need to restart Excel in order to use the new font and size settings.

7. Click OK.

You can continue working on the current worksheet, or restart Excel.

The next time you start Excel, all new worksheets you create utilize the new default font and size.

Apply It!

To quickly clear all the formatting you assign to your cells, press Ctrl+A to select all the cells, click Edit, then Clear, and then Formats.

Change Gridline Color

Essential to the structure of worksheets in any spreadsheet program, gridlines allow you to distinguish cells, columns, and rows. By default, gridlines appear in a light-gray color. You can change this color to make the lines more visible onscreen, especially if the default color is difficult to see on a worksheet.

You use the Options dialog box to establish gridline color, as well as to turn gridlines on or off. Because gridlines help you to see how your cell data corresponds to column and row headings, consider leaving the gridlines feature turned on.

1. Click Tools.
2. Click Options.

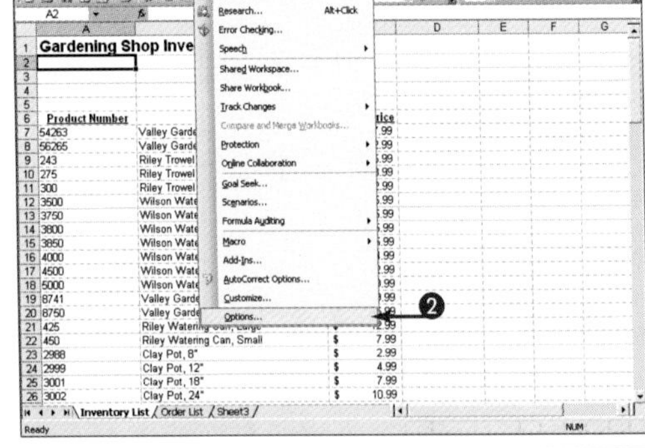

- The Options dialog box appears.

3. Click the View tab.
4. Click here and select a new color.
5. Click OK.

- Excel applies the new color.

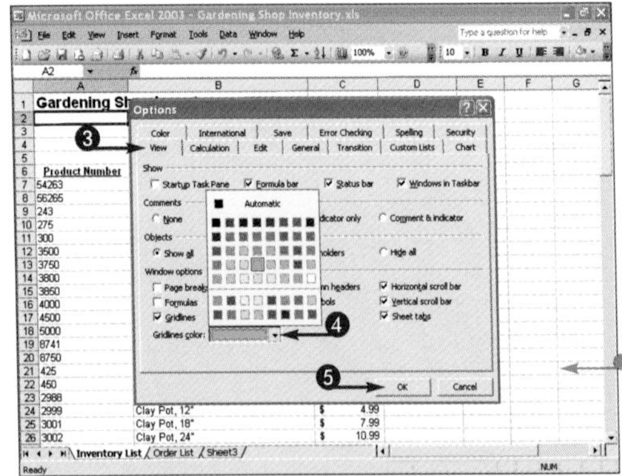

Increase Readability by Printing Gridlines

You can choose to print the worksheet gridlines along with the cell data when you print out an Excel workbook file. By default, gridlines do not print out with the data. However, by including the gridlines with the printout, you can more easily see how the row and column cells relate to each other.

Once you activate the gridline option, the gridlines print for that particular workbook. If you open another workbook and want to include the gridlines in the printout, you must activate the option again.

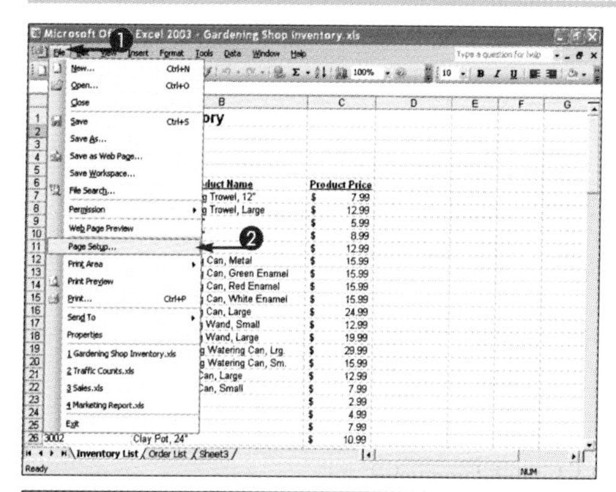

1. Click File.
2. Click Page Setup.

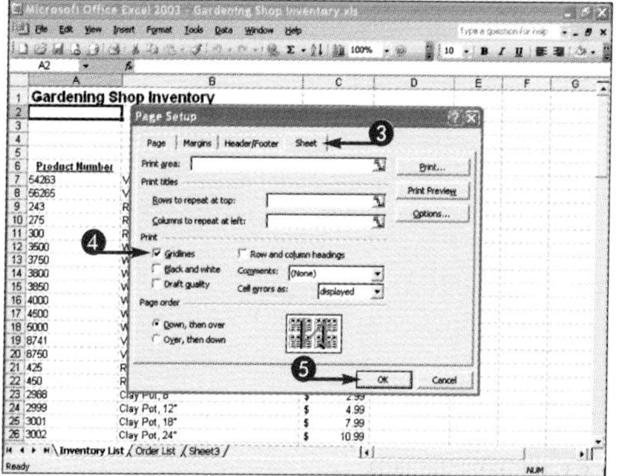

The Page Setup dialog box appears.

3. Click the Sheet tab.
4. Click the Gridlines option.
5. Click OK.

When you print the file, the worksheet gridlines appear along with the data.

Center Align Printed Data

By default, Excel aligns all printed data to the left and top margins of the page, unless you specify otherwise. However, some of your worksheets may look better if you center the data on the page. You can use the Page Setup dialog box to determine how you want the printed data to align on the page. You can select the Horizontally option to center the data between the left and right margins, or the Vertically option to center the data between the top and bottom margins. You can also apply both centering alignments at the same time.

1. Click File.
2. Click Page Setup.

   The Page Setup dialog box appears.

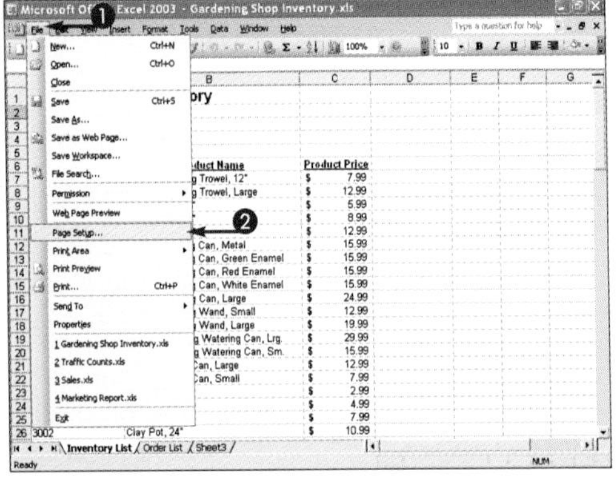

3. Click the Margins tab.
4. Click an alignment option.
   - You can also adjust the margin settings to control the page margins.
5. Click OK.

   Excel centers the worksheet data on the printed page.

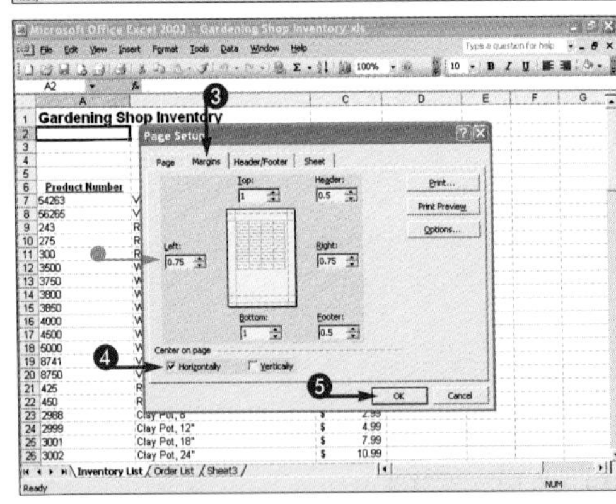

Print Formulas Instead of Formula Results

Ordinarily, when you print out a worksheet, you print the results of your formulas, and not the formulas themselves. However, you may occasionally want to print the formulas instead of the results.

You can use the Options dialog box to turn on the formula display option. When you activate this option, formula results do not appear in the cells containing formulas. Excel also highlights the cells associated with the formula, and color-codes them on the worksheet. When you print the worksheet, the formula prints as well. To view the results again, you must turn off the formula display setting in the Options dialog box.

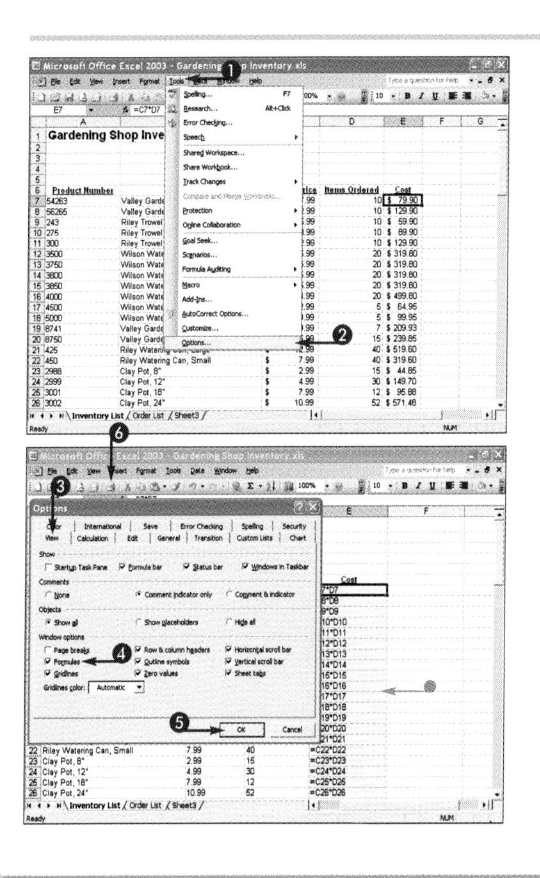

1. Click Tools.
2. Click Options.

   The Options dialog box appears.

3. Click the View tab.
4. Click the Formulas option.
5. Click OK.

   - Excel displays all the formulas in your worksheet instead of formula results.

6. Click the Print button.

   Excel prints the formulas along with the other worksheet data.

Organize Worksheets by Color-Coding Tabs

You can color-code your worksheet tabs to make it easier to distinguish the contents and identity of each tab. If you use multiple workbooks containing the same types of worksheets, you can apply the same tab color to the same types of worksheets to keep the worksheet data organized and easy to identify. To assign colors to your tabs, you can use the Format Tab Color dialog box, which offers a full palette of colors from which you can choose, as well as a No Color option for turning off the tab color.

1. Right-click over the tab.
2. Click Tab Color.

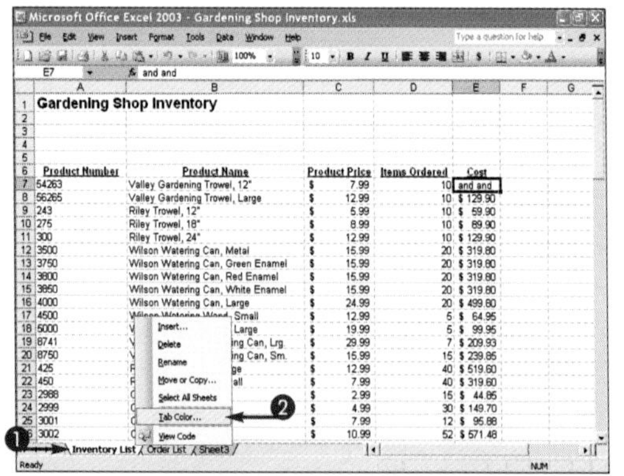

The Format Tab Color dialog box appears.

3. Click a color.
4. Click OK.

   Excel applies the color to the tab.

   To view the color of the current tab, click another tab in the workbook.

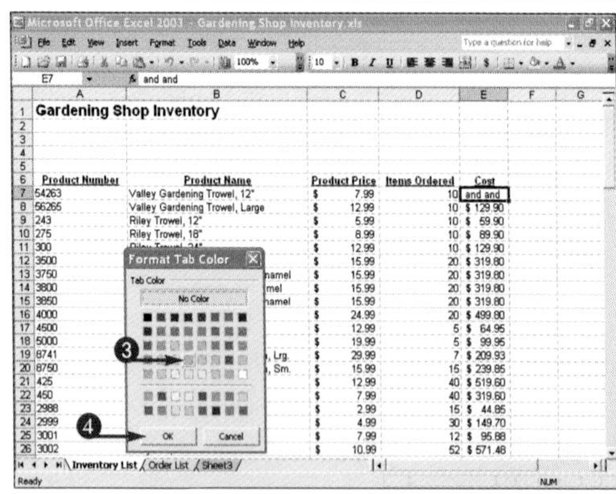

Change Default Column Labels

You can change worksheet column headings from letters to numbers to correlate with row headings. This reference style, the R1C1 style, refers to cell addresses by row and column numbers. By default, Excel uses the A1 style.

You can switch to R1C1 style to make your Excel worksheets and interface compatible with those of anyone else using R1C1 style. A1 style is relative by default, so to make cells in a formula absolute, you must add a dollar sign to the front of the cell address, as in E8. R1C1 style is absolute by default, so to make cells relative, you must add brackets to the cell numbers, as in R[5]C[8].

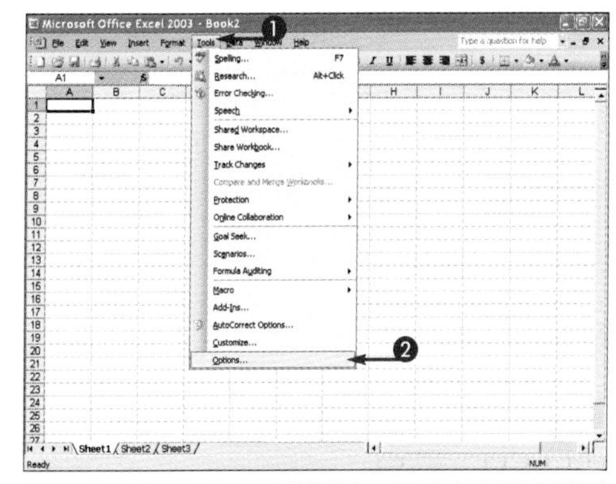

1. Click Tools.
2. Click Options.

   The Options dialog box appears.

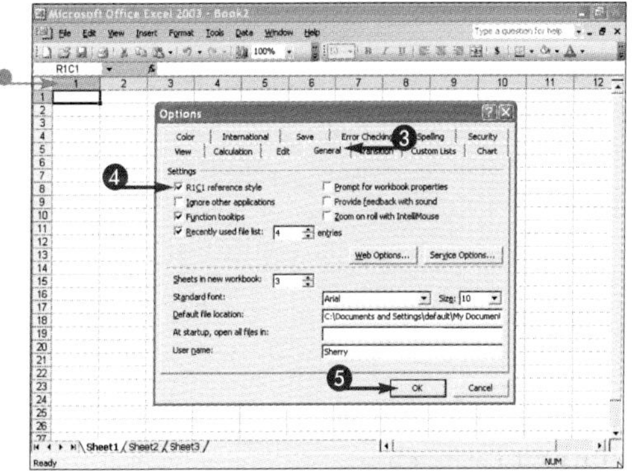

3. Click the General tab.
4. Click the R1C1 reference style option.
5. Click OK.

- Excel changes the column headings from letters to numbers.

Keep Cells in View with a Watch Window

The longer your worksheet becomes, the more difficult it is to keep important cells in view as you scroll around the worksheet. You can use the Watch Window to monitor selected cell values in your worksheet. You can even use the Watch Window to view cells in other worksheets or sheets in a linked workbook.

The Watch Window is a mini-window that floats on top of the worksheet. No matter where you scroll on the worksheet, the Watch Window always stays onscreen where you can see it. The Watch Window acts much like the Excel toolbars; you can dock it on any side of the screen.

ADD A WATCH WINDOW

1. Right-click over the cell you want to watch.
2. Click Add Watch.

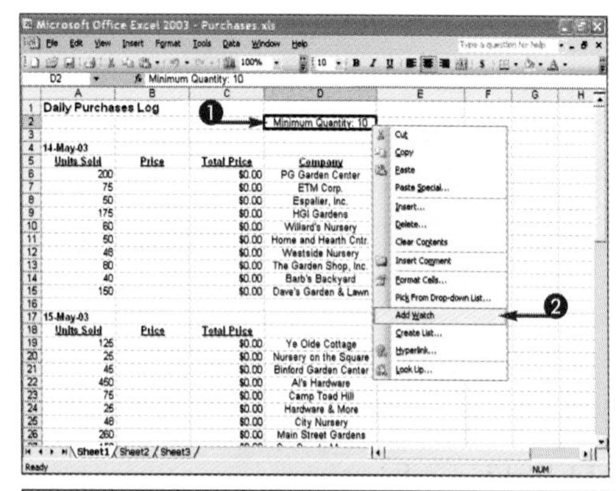

- The Watch Window appears.
- If you scroll through the worksheet, the Watch Window stays onscreen.

If you make changes to the data referenced in the watch cell, the changes appear immediately in the Watch Window.

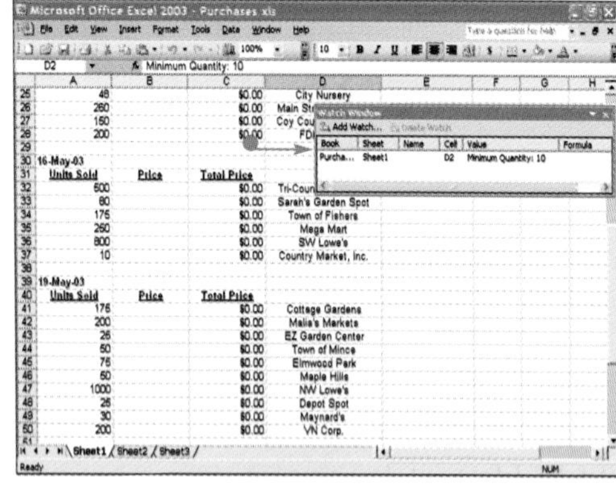

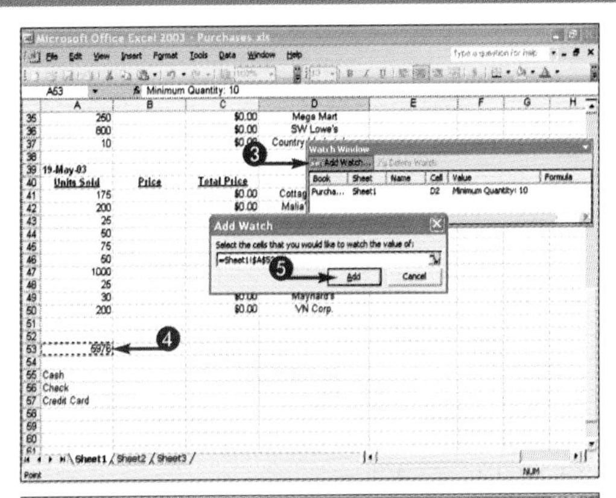

ADD A SECOND WATCH WINDOW

3. Click Add Watch.

   The Add Watch dialog box appears.

4. Select the cell or cells you want to watch.
5. Click Add.

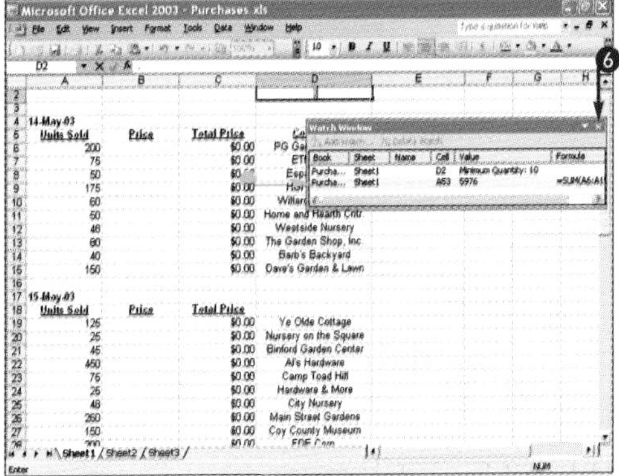

- Excel adds the cell or cells to the Watch Window.

6. When finished with the Watch Window, click the Close button.

   Excel closes the Watch Window dialog box.

Did You Know?

If you frequently use the Watch Window to monitor cells, you can use names that identify cell contents. For example, if you watch a cell range of sales totals, you can name the range Sales_Totals. Range names are more useful than default addresses, such as C12. To name any cell or range of cells, click inside the cell name box on the Formula bar, and type a name. Press Enter, and Excel saves the name. Cell and range names must start with a letter or an underscore, and cannot include spaces.

Protect Cells from Unauthorized Changes

You can protect your worksheet to prevent unauthorized changes to the cells. The changes also include formatting, formulas, and layout.

To protect certain cells, you must first unlock the cells that you do not want to protect. You can use the Format Cells dialog box to unlock cells.

You can now use the Excel Protect Sheet feature to establish which worksheet elements other users can change within the worksheet. You can also use the feature to assign a password to the worksheet.

1. Select the cells that you do not want to protect.
2. Right-click over the selected cells.
3. Click Format Cells.

   The Format Cells dialog box appears.
4. Click the Locked option.
5. Click OK.

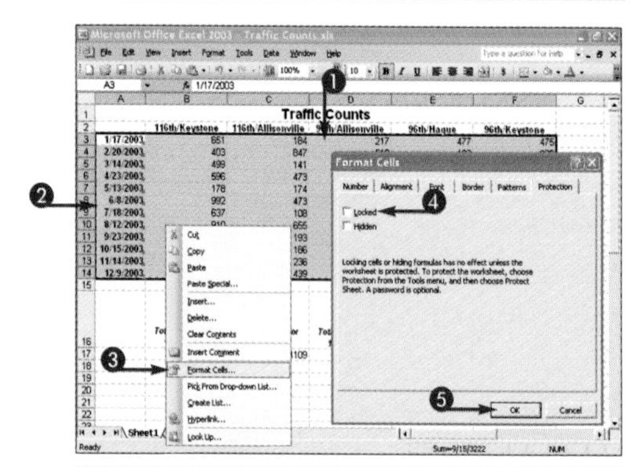

6. Click Tools.
7. Click Protection.
8. Click Protect Sheet.

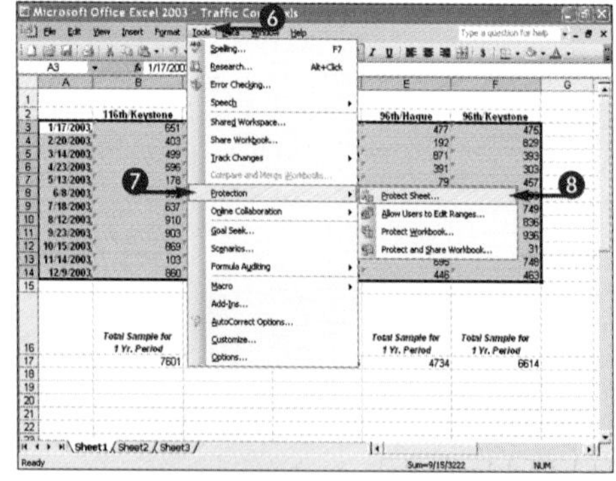

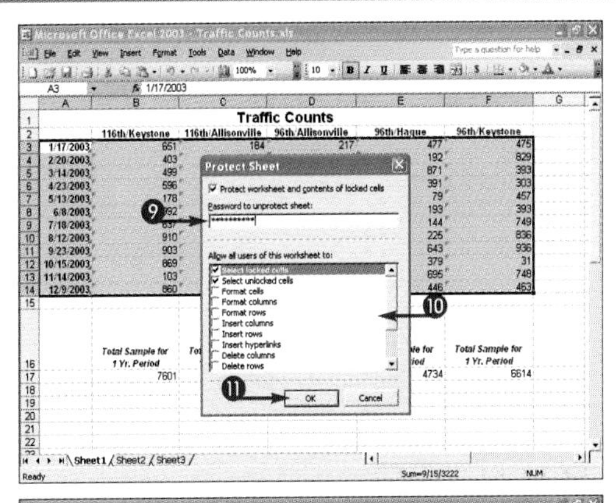

The Protect Sheet dialog box appears.

9. Type a password for the worksheet.
10. Select the items that you want other users to be able to change in the worksheet.
11. Click OK.

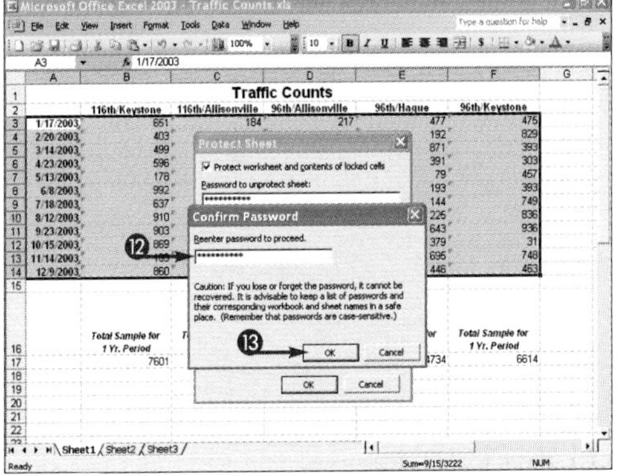

12. Type the password again.
13. Click OK.

Excel now protects the worksheet.

Did You Know?

To change protection settings for cells, you can activate the Unprotect Sheet command. However, you must know the password. To unprotect a worksheet, click Tools, then Protection, and then Unprotect Sheet. Type the password, and click OK.

Freeze Headings for Easier Scrolling

As you work with longer worksheets, it is important to keep your column or row labels in view. The longer or wider your worksheet becomes, the more time you spend scrolling back to the top of the worksheet to see which heading is which. Excel has a freeze feature you can use to lock your row or column headings in place. You can freeze them into position so that they are always in view. If you print out the worksheet, the frozen headings do not print. Row and column headings appear as they normally do, in their respective positions on the worksheet.

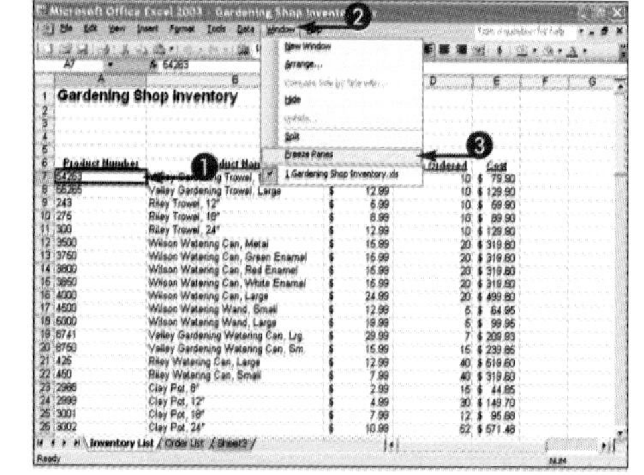

1. Click the cell below the row you want to lock or to the right of the column you want to lock.
2. Click Window.
3. Click Freeze Panes.

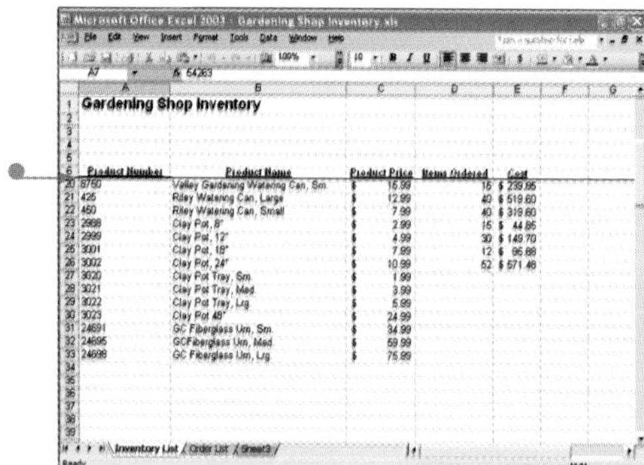

- Excel adds a solid line to set off the frozen headings.

  When you scroll through the worksheet, the row or column headings remain onscreen.

Note: *To unfreeze the frozen headings, click Window, then Unfreeze Panes.*

Wrap Text in Worksheet Cells

If you type a line of numbers or text that exceeds the width of a worksheet cell, the text automatically spans multiple columns. To have the text appear in a single cell, you can instruct Excel to wrap the text to the next line. Excel automatically enlarges the depth of the cell to accommodate new text lines. You use the Format Cells dialog box to activate the Wrap text option to achieve this effect.

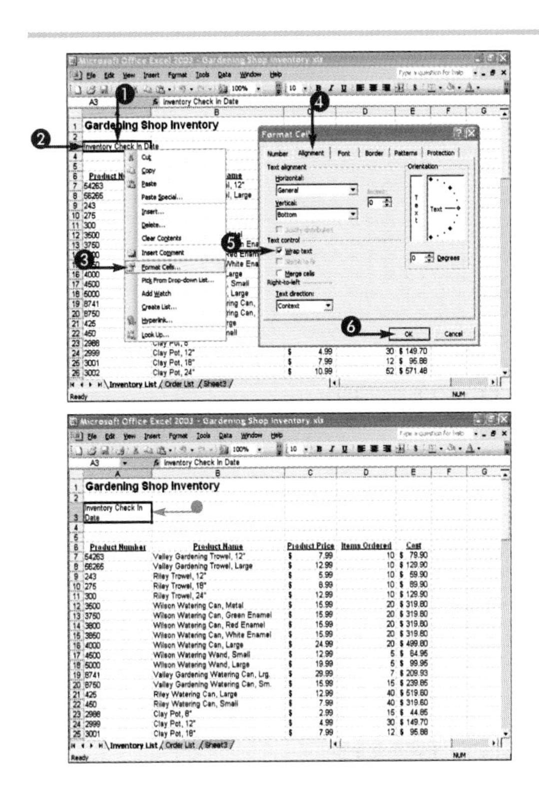

1. Select the cell that you want to wrap.
2. Right-click the selected cell.
3. Click Format Cells to display the Format Cells dialog box appears.
4. Click the Alignment tab.
5. Click the Wrap text option.
6. Click OK.

- Excel wraps the text to the next line in the cell.

Excel also increases the height of the cell row to accommodate the new text line.

Add Visual Interest with Slanted Text

You can add visual interest to your text by slanting the text upwards or downwards in the cell. You can also use this technique to make a long column heading take up less horizontal space on the worksheet.

You can make cell text angle upwards or downwards by degrees of rotation. By default, the orientation angle is set to 0 degrees. If you set the text orientation to a positive number, such as 25, Excel angles the text in an upward direction. If you set the text orientation to a negative number, such as –40, Excel angles the text in a downward direction.

1. Click the cell or cells containing the text you want to angle.
2. Click Format.
3. Click Cells.

   You can also press Ctrl+1 to open the Format Cells dialog box.

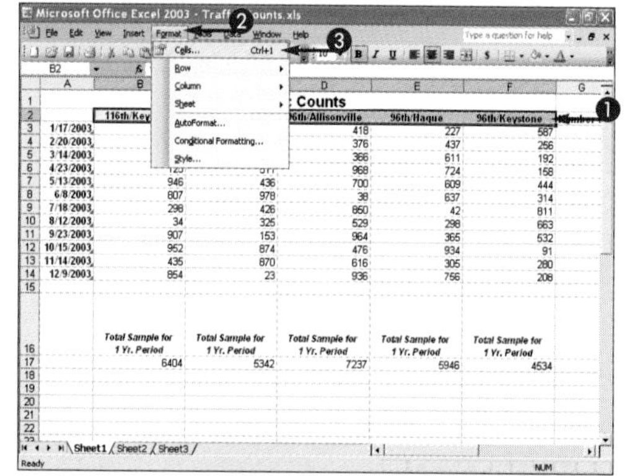

The Format Cells dialog box appears.

4. Click the Alignment tab.
5. Click an orientation marker.

- You can also type a degree of rotation or use the spin arrows to set a degree.

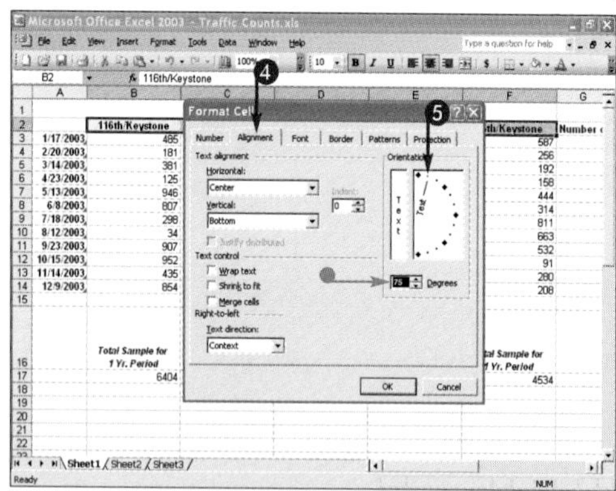

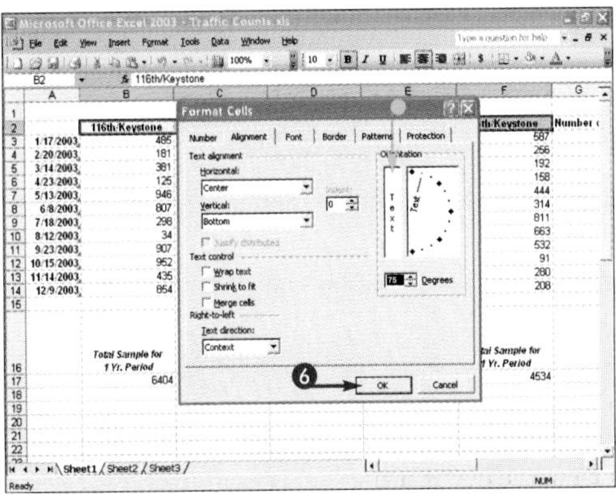

- You can click the vertical text area to display your text vertically instead of horizontally in the cell.

6. Click OK.

- Excel angles the cell text.

The row height automatically increases to contain the slanted text.

You can resize the column width to free up space and make your cells more presentable.

Did You Know?

If you display the Chart toolbar, you can click the Angle Clockwise ( ) or Angle Counterclockwise ( ) buttons to slant cell text.

Magnify Cells with the Fit Selection Setting

You can use the Fit Selection zoom setting to magnify your view of any group of cells that you select in your worksheet. If you use the other zoom settings, such as 200%, Excel magnifies your view without any regard for the cells you select.

You can use the Zoom button on the Standard toolbar to access the Fit Selection setting, or you can access this setting through the Zoom dialog box. However, you achieve faster results if you use the Zoom button instead of the Zoom dialog box.

1. Select the cells you want to magnify onscreen.
2. Click here and click Selection.

Microsoft Office Excel 2003 - Gardening Shop Inventory.xls

Gardening Shop Inventory

Product Number	Product Name	Product Price	Items Ordered	Cost
54263	Valley Gardening Trowel, 12"	$	10	$ 79.90
56265	Valley Gardening Trowel, Large	[illegible]	10	$ 129.90
243	Riley Trowel, 12"	$ 5.99	10	$ 59.90
275	Riley Trowel, 18"	$ 8.99	10	$ 89.90
300	Riley Trowel, 24"	$ 12.99	10	$ 129.90
3500	Wilson Watering Can, Metal	$ 15.99	20	$ 319.80
3750	Wilson Watering Can, Green Enamel	$ 15.99	20	$ 319.80
3800	Wilson Watering Can, Red Enamel	$ 15.99	20	$ 319.80
3850	Wilson Watering Can, White Enamel	$ 15.99	20	$ 319.80
4000	Wilson Watering Can, Large	$ 24.99	20	$ 499.80
4500	Wilson Watering Wand, Small	$ 12.99	5	$ 64.95
5000	Wilson Watering Wand, Large	$ 19.99	5	$ 99.95
8741	Valley Gardening Watering Can, Lrg.	$ 29.99	7	$ 209.93
8750	Valley Gardening Watering Can, Sm.	$ 15.99	15	$ 239.85
425	Riley Watering Can, Large	$ 12.99	40	$ 519.60
450	Riley Watering Can, Small	$ 7.99	40	$ 319.60
2988	Clay Pot, 8"	$ 2.99	15	$ 44.85
2999	Clay Pot, 12"	$ 4.99	30	$ 149.70
3001	Clay Pot, 18"	$ 7.99	12	$ 95.88
3002	Clay Pot, 24"	$ 10.99	52	$ 571.48

Excel magnifies the cells you select.

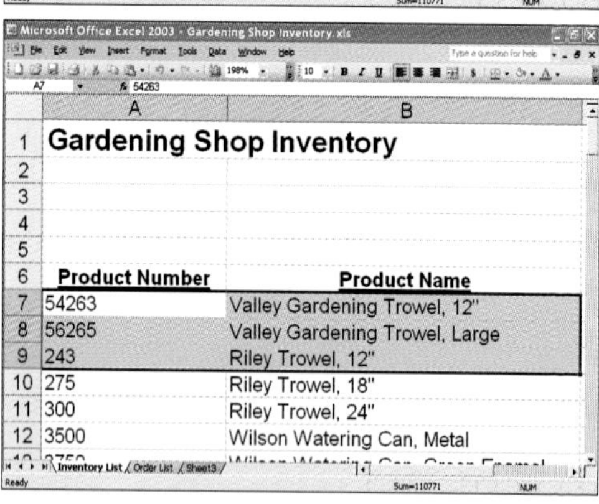

Add Pizzazz with a Background Picture

You can add a background picture behind your worksheet cell data. When you add a picture to a worksheet, the image only appears on the active worksheet. The remaining worksheets in the workbook appear with the default white background.

Be sure to select a picture that does not compete with the appearance of your worksheet data.

Depending on the size of the original image, Excel may tile the picture across the background. If you do not want the image to tile, you can resize it in a graphics program.

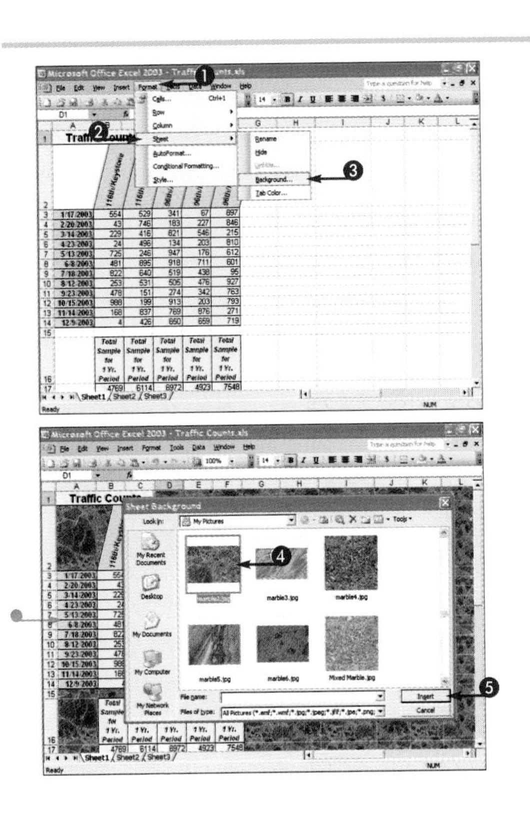

1. Click Format.
2. Click Sheet.
3. Click Background.

   The Sheet Background dialog box appears.

4. Select the picture file you want to use as a background.
5. Click Insert.

- Excel adds the image behind the worksheet cells.

***Note:** To remove a background you no longer want, display the worksheet and click Format, then Sheet, and then Delete Background.*

Add a Calculator to the Excel Toolbar

You can add a digital version of a handheld calculator to an Excel toolbar so that you can perform your own mathematical calculations. By activating the Calculator button, you can open the Calculator window and use the number pad buttons, or the numeric keypad on your keyboard, to enter calculations.

To add the Calculator button to an Excel toolbar, you must open the Customize dialog box. When you activate the dialog box, all toolbars and menus switch to edit mode. This allows you to make changes to the commands and buttons and to customize their appearance.

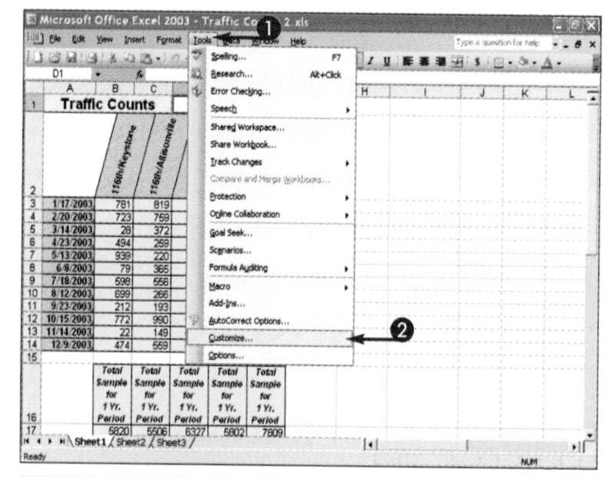

1. Click Tools.
2. Click Customize.

***Note:** To add the Calculator button to another toolbar besides the default toolbars, first open the toolbar to which you want to add the feature.*

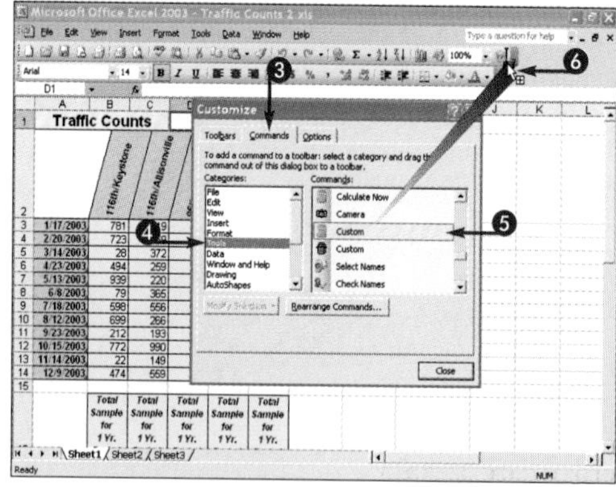

The Customize dialog box appears.

3. Click the Commands tab.
4. Click the Tools category.
5. Click the Custom command.
6. Drag the Custom icon to the toolbar where you want the Calculator button to appear.

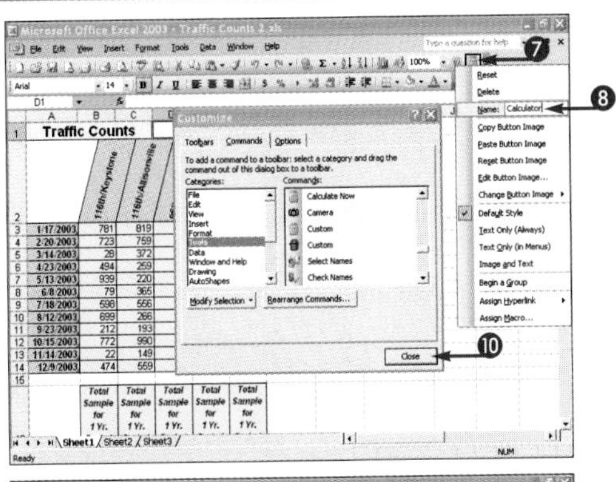

Excel adds the Calculator button to the toolbar.

7. Right-click over the button.
8. Type Calculator into the Name field to replace the Custom name.
9. Press Enter.

   Excel renames the button.

10. Click Close.

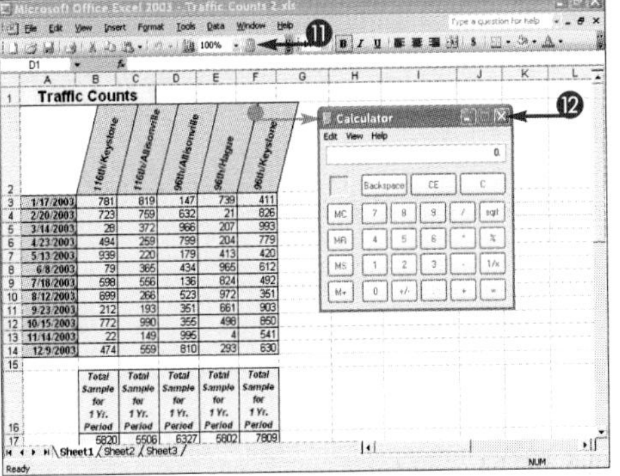

11. Click the Calculator button.

- Excel opens the Calculator window where you can perform calculations.

12. Click the Close button to close the Calculator window after performing your calculations.

Did You Know?

If you want to activate the numeric keypad on your keyboard to enter numbers that you are calculating in the Calculator window, be sure to press the Num Lock key first if you do not already have it displayed as active on the status bar. When active, the letters NUM appear bold on the status bar.

Center Text Across Columns without Merging Cells

You can make your worksheets more visually appealing by centering title text, such as a range heading, across several columns.

Using the Center Across Selection option in the Format Cells dialog box, you can achieve the same appearance as if you merged the cells. This technique leaves intersecting row and columns safe for cutting and copying later.

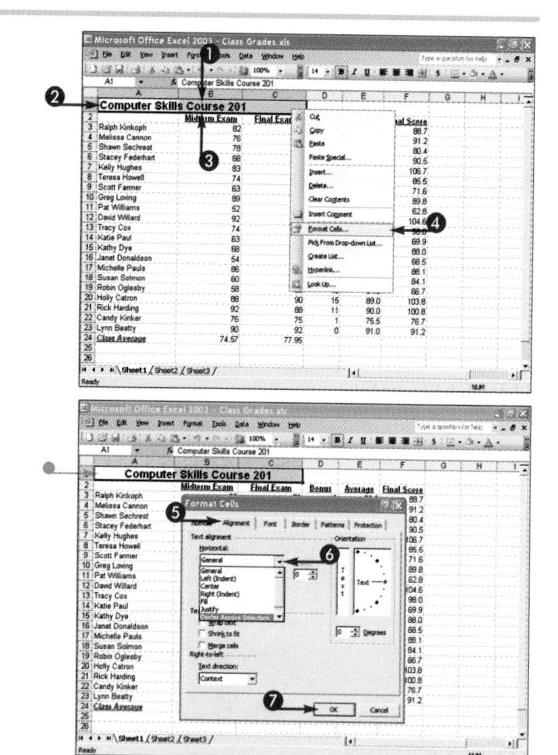

1. Type your title text in the leftmost cell of the range of columns.
2. Select the cell and extend the selection to include the remaining cells over which you want to center the title.
3. Right-click over the selected cells.
4. Click Format Cells.

   You can also press Ctrl+1 to open the Format Cells dialog box.

   The Format Cells dialog box appears.
5. Click the Alignment tab.
6. Click here and select Center Across Selection.
7. Click OK.

- Excel centers the text across the columns you selected.

Add Comments to Formulas

You can add comments to your formulas to explain the formula construction or purpose. For example, you can add instructions about how to use the formula elsewhere in the worksheet.

Ordinarily, when you want to add a comment to your Excel worksheet, you use comment text boxes. Comments can include anything from a note about a task to an explanation about the data that the cell contains. To add a comment to a formula, you use the N() function instead of comment text boxes. The N() function enables you to add notes about the formula within the formula itself.

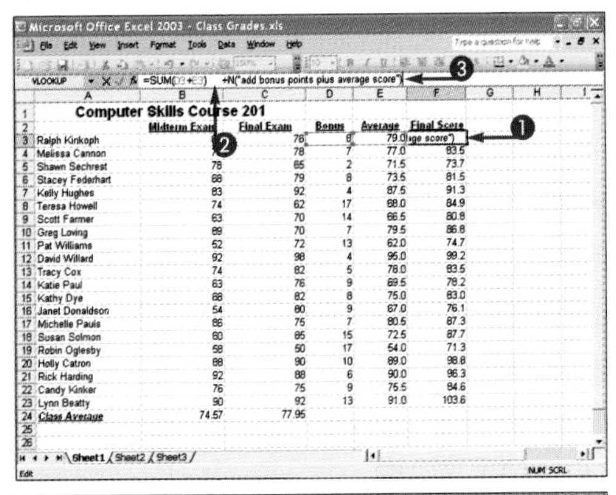

	Midterm Exam	Final Exam	Bonus	Average	Final Score
Ralph Kinkoph		76	6	79.0	ge score")
Melissa Cannon		78	7	77.0	83.5
Shawn Sechrest	78	65	2	71.5	73.7
Stacey Federhart	68	79	8	73.5	81.5
Kelly Hughes	83	92	4	87.5	91.3
Teresa Howell	74	62	17	68.0	84.9
Scott Farmer	63	70	14	66.5	80.8
Greg Loving	89	70	7	79.5	86.8
Pat Williams	52	72	13	62.0	74.7
David Willard	92	98	4	95.0	99.2
Tracy Cox	74	82	5	78.0	83.5
Katie Paul	63	76	9	69.5	78.2
Kathy Dye	68	82	8	75.0	83.0
Janet Donaldson	54	80	9	67.0	76.1
Michelle Pauls	86	75	7	80.5	87.3
Susan Solmon	60	85	15	72.5	87.7
Robin Oglesby	58	50	17	54.0	71.3
Holly Catron	88	90	10	89.0	98.8
Rick Harding	92	88	6	90.0	96.3
Candy Kinker	76	75	9	75.5	84.6
Lynn Beatty	90	92	13	91.0	103.6
Class Average	74.57	77.95			

1. Click the cell that contains the formula to which you want to add a comment.
2. Click inside the Formula field.
3. Type **+N("?")**, replacing ? with the comment text you want to add.
4. Press Enter.

Microsoft Office Excel 2003 - Class Grades.xls

F3 =SUM(D3+E3)+N("add bonus points plus average score")

Computer Skills Course 201

	Midterm Exam	Final Exam	Bonus	Average	Final Score
Ralph Kinkoph	82	76	4	79.0	82.6
Melissa Cannon	76	78	16	77.0	93.5
Shawn Sechrest	78	65	16	71.5	87.8
Stacey Federhart	68	79	10	73.5	83.7
Kelly Hughes	83	92	11	87.5	98.6
Teresa Howell	74	62	8	68.0	75.6
Scott Farmer	63	70	19	66.5	85.1
Greg Loving	89	70	9	79.5	88.2
Pat Williams	52	72	5	62.0	66.6
David Willard	92	98	2	95.0	96.9
Tracy Cox	74	82	0	78.0	78.3
Katie Paul	63	76	11	69.5	80.5
Kathy Dye	68	82	3	75.0	78.3
Janet Donaldson	54	80	17	67.0	84.5
Michelle Pauls	86	75	17	80.5	97.3
Susan Solmon	80	85	15	72.5	87.2
Robin Oglesby	58	50	19	54.0	72.8
Holly Catron	88	90	8	89.0	96.8
Rick Harding	92	88	19	90.0	109.4
Candy Kinker	76	75	6	75.5	81.8
Lynn Beatty	90	92	7	91.0	98.5
Class Average	74.57	77.95			

- Excel adds the comment to the formula, but the cell displays only the formula results.

Turn Excel Data into a Pasteable Picture

You can turn a group of Excel worksheet cells that contain data into a picture that you can paste into another sheet or workbook, or even into another program.

When you turn a group of cells into a picture, Excel includes the worksheet gridlines in the image by default, unless you turn off the gridlines option.

You can use the Copy Picture command to copy cells, and then the Copy Picture dialog box to select the format and appearance you want for the picture. For the best picture quality, you can select the As shown on screen and Picture options.

❶ Select the cells that contain the data that you want to turn into a picture.

❷ Press and hold the Shift key.

❸ Click Edit.

❹ Click Copy Picture.

***Note:** The Copy Picture command only appears on the menu when you press the Shift key.*

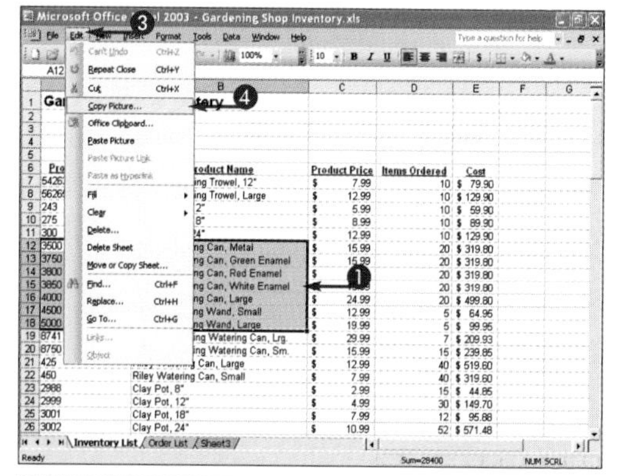

The Copy Picture dialog box appears.

❺ Click the As shown on screen option.

❻ Click the Picture option.

❼ Click OK.

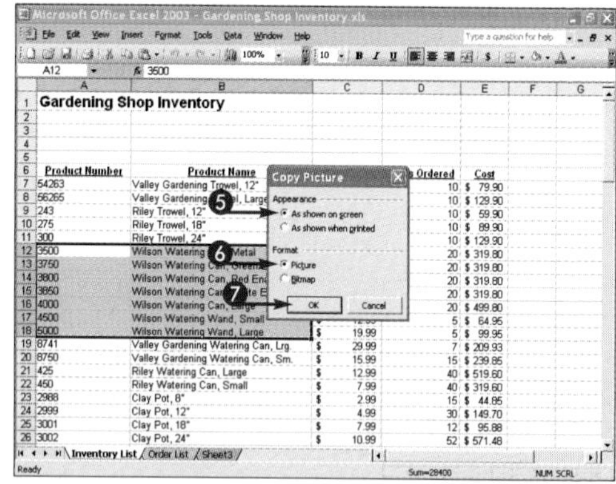

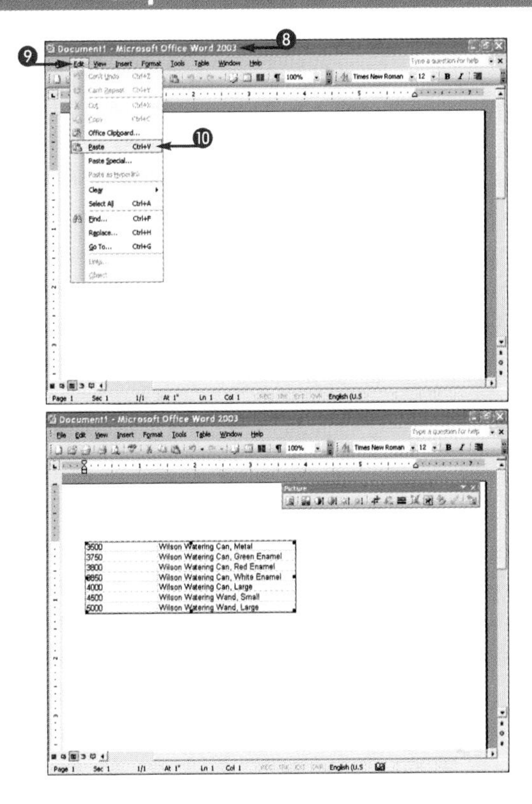

8. Open the worksheet or program file in which you want to paste the Excel picture.

   This example pastes an Excel picture into a Microsoft Word file.

9. Click Edit.
10. Click Paste.

    You can also press Ctrl+V to paste the item.

- The Excel picture appears in the document.

You can select the picture and click and drag the selection handles to move and resize the object.

Did You Know?

You can change the fill or line color for Excel data that you turn into a picture. To do so, double-click the picture to open the Format Picture dialog box, and change the fill color or line color.

Generate Random Numbers in Your Cells

You can use the RAND() function to generate random numbers in your worksheet cells.

After assigning the function to one cell, you can use the fill handle to populate other cells in the worksheet with more random numbers. The numbers you generate with the RAND() function take on the default numbering style for the cells. By default, Excel applies the General number format, which means that decimal numbers may appear. To limit your random numbers to whole numbers, you can open the Format Cells dialog box and set the number format to Number style and the decimal places to zero.

1. Click the cell to which you want to add the Random function.
2. Click inside the Formula field.
3. Type **=RAND()*?**, replacing ? with the maximum random number you want Excel to generate.
4. Press Enter.

- Excel generates a random number for each cell you select.
- You can drag the fill handle across as many cells as you want to fill with random numbers.

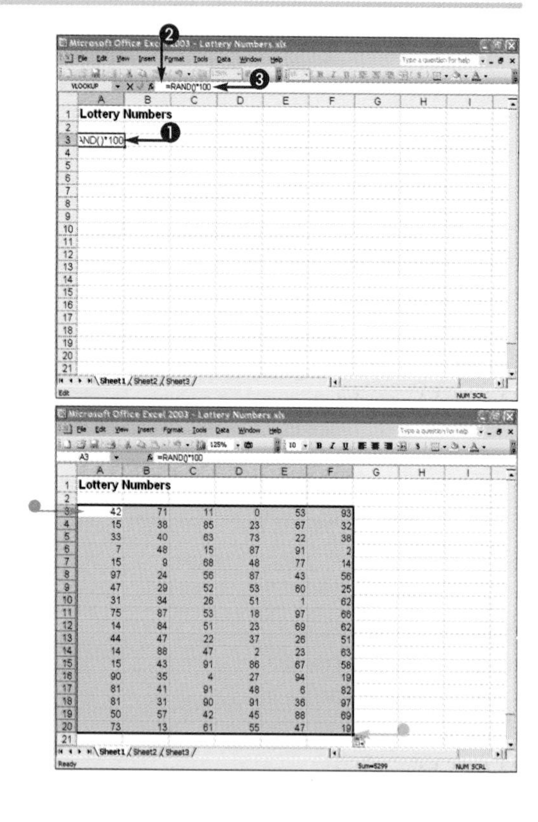

Prevent Excel from Converting Fractions

If you try to enter a fraction into a worksheet cell, Excel automatically converts the fraction into a date. For example, if you type ½, Excel converts the number into the date January 2. To keep your fractions from converting, you must type a zero and press the spacebar before typing your fractions. Without the zero, Excel thinks you want to enter a date.

If you enter mixed numbers, such as 1½, Excel does not change the fraction to a date. It is only when you enter a fraction by itself that Excel converts it to a date by default.

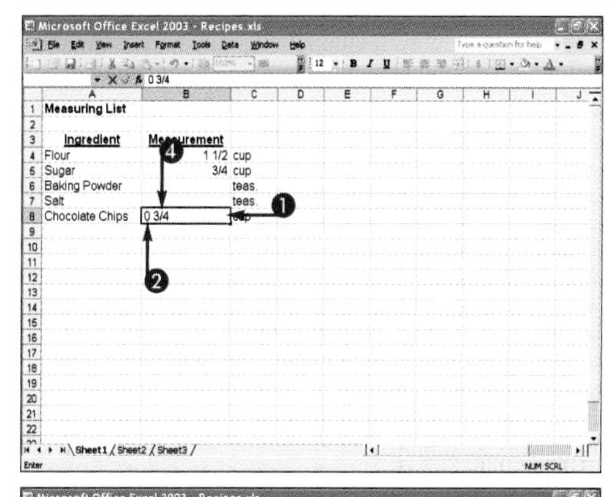

1. Click the cell to which you want to add a fraction.
2. Type **0**.
3. Press the spacebar.
4. Type a fraction.

5. Press Enter.

- Excel does not change the fraction to a date.

Retrieve a Stock Quote

You can use the Excel smart tags to download the latest quotes on your favorite stocks. You can download this stock quote data into your current worksheet or into a new sheet in your workbook. To use this feature, you must have Internet access, and you must activate the Excel smart tags.

When you enter a stock symbol and select the option from the smart tag of the cell, Excel connects to the MSN MoneyCentral Web site to gather the latest information about the stock symbol you specify. Excel then inserts the information that it downloads into your worksheet. The information includes active links to the Web site for viewing charts, news, and looking up other stock symbols.

1. Establish an Internet connection.
2. Type the stock symbol into the cell using all capital letters.
3. Press Enter.

- Excel adds a small red triangle to the bottom-right corner of the cell.

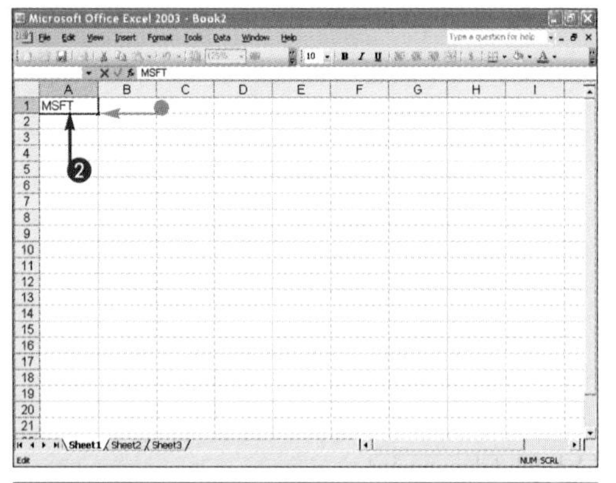

4. Move the mouse pointer over the red triangle in the cell.

   A smart tag appears.
5. Click the smart tag icon.
6. Click Insert refreshable stock price.

   The Insert Stock Price dialog box appears.

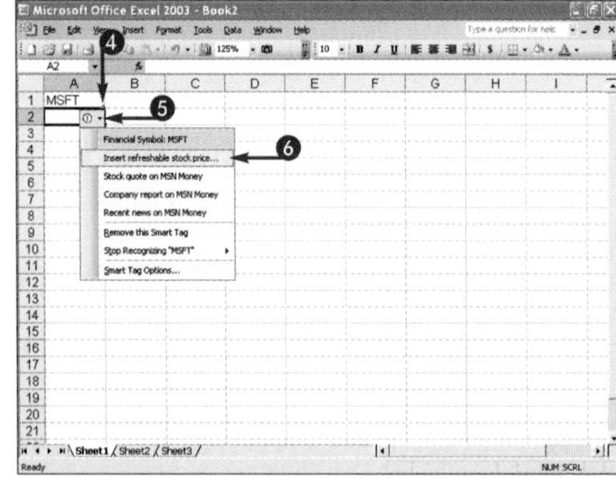

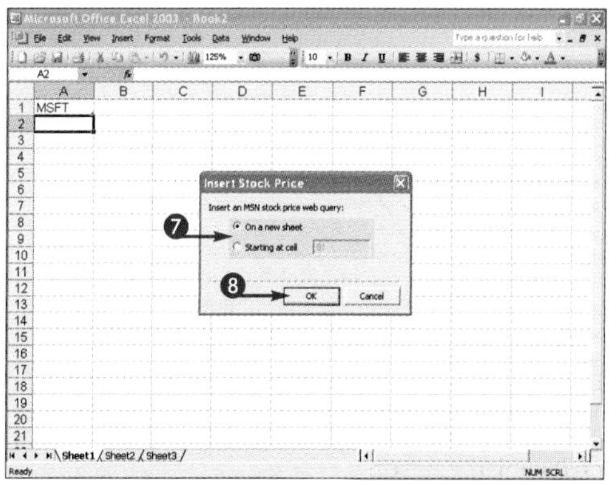

7. Select how you want to display the stock quote.

   Select On a new sheet to display the stock quote on another worksheet which Excel automatically adds to the current workbook.

   Select Starting at cell to display the quote starting at the current cell, or you can specify a cell.

8. Click OK.

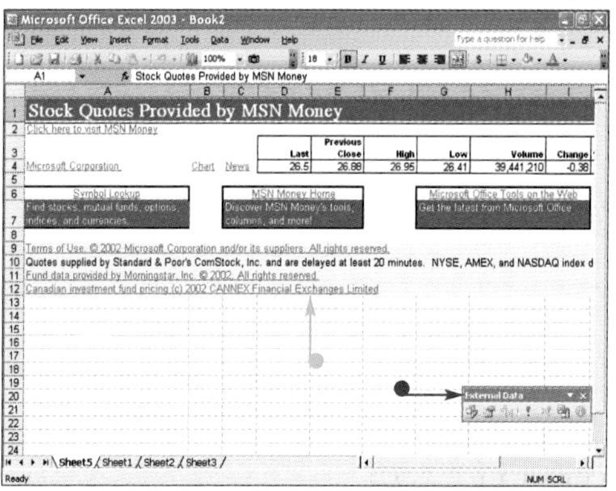

Excel gathers the stock quote information from the MSN MoneyCentral Web site and displays it on a new or current worksheet.

- You can click a link to open your Web browser and view more information.
- Excel also displays the External Data toolbar.

Apply It!

To activate smart tags to use the stock quote feature, click Tools, then AutoCorrect Options. In the AutoCorrect dialog box, click the Smart Tags tab, and select the Label data with smart tags option (☐ changes to ☑). Click OK. You can now type a stock symbol in all caps to trigger a smart tag and look up a stock quote.

Count the Number of Days between Two Dates

You can instruct Excel to calculate the number of days between any two dates. You must first enter the second date, and then subtract it from the first date. For example, to count the number of days between now and Christmas, enter the holiday date first, and subtract the current date from the holiday date. You must use the numeric equivalent, which consists of the number for the month, followed by the number for the day, and finally the number for the year. You must separate each number with a forward slash and include quote marks around the entered dates.

1. Click in the cell in which you want to insert the formula.
2. Type **="?"**, replacing ? with the second date.
3. Type **-**.
4. Type **"?"**, replacing ? with the first date.

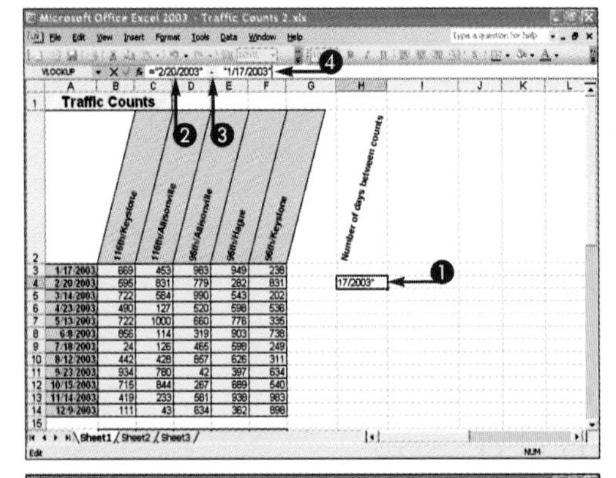

5. Press Enter.
- Excel calculates the number of days between the two dates.

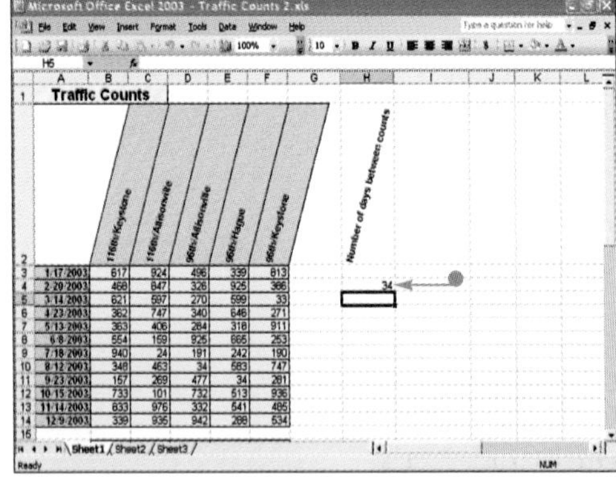

Join Text from Separate Cells

You can use the Concatenate function to join text from separate cells into a text string.

When you use the Concatenate function, it is important to include spaces between the text strings. In the formula, you can indicate spaces by entering actual spaces within quotes. If the combined names require other punctuation, such as a comma, use a comma within quotes between the cell references. After establishing the formula for the first name in the list, copy the formula down the rows of the worksheet to join together the remaining names in the list.

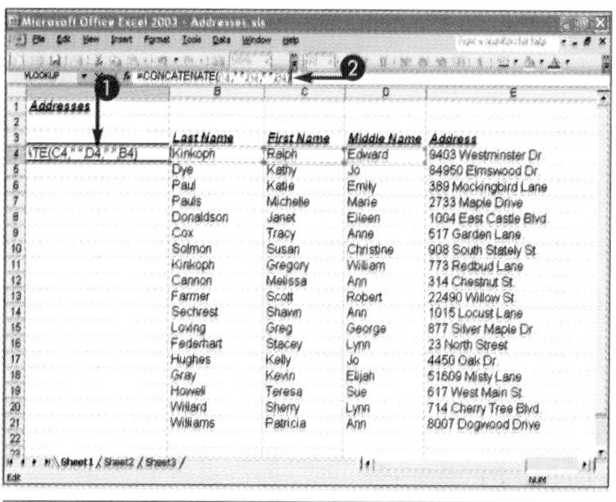

1. Click inside the cell in which you want to display the text that you join together.
2. Type **=CONCATENATE(?," ",?," ",?)**, replacing the ? symbols with the cell addresses that contain the component names.

Note: *Be sure to write the cell references in the order in which you want them to join together.*

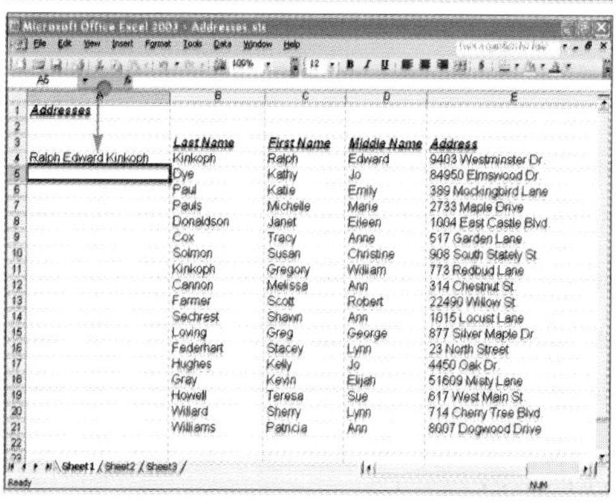

3. Press Enter.

- Excel combines the component cell text into one cell.

Copy Page Setup Settings from One Worksheet to Another

You can use the Page Setup dialog box to specify page and print settings for a worksheet in your workbook.

Fortunately, you can copy the Page Setup settings from one worksheet to another and save some time. To do this, you must first group your worksheets. Using the Ctrl key, you can select the worksheets for which you want to use the same Page Setup settings and activate the settings with a single click in the Page Setup dialog box.

1. Click File.
2. Click Page Setup.

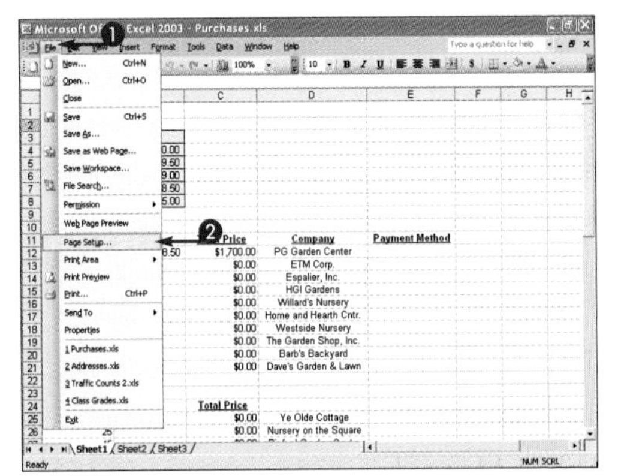

The Page Setup dialog box appears.

3. Specify the Page Setup settings that you want to assign to a worksheet in your workbook.

Note: *See the Excel help files to learn more about setting up your pages with the Page Setup dialog box.*

4. Click OK.

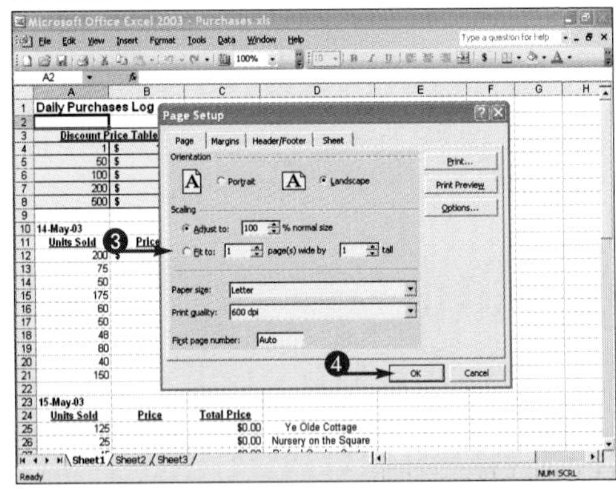

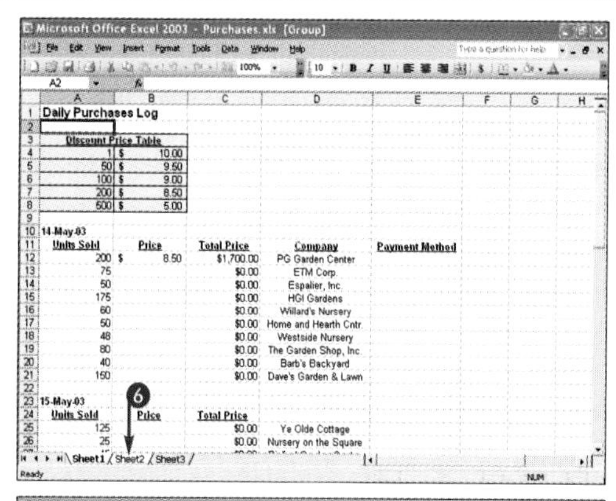

5. Press and hold the Ctrl key.
6. Click the sheet tab of the worksheet to which you want to copy the Page Setup settings.

   Excel highlights both worksheet tabs to indicate that group mode is active.

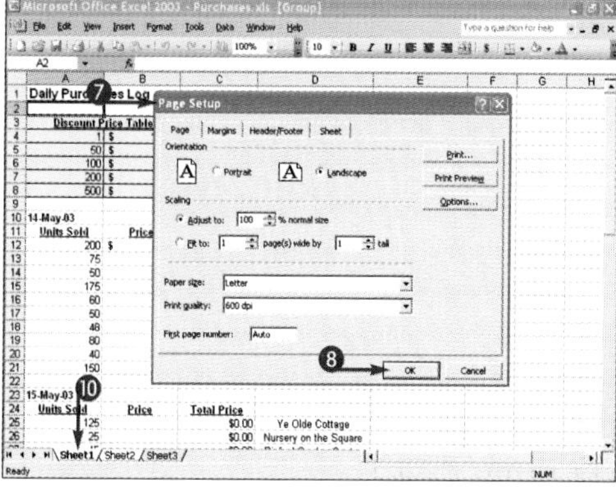

7. Repeat steps **1** to **3** for the second worksheet.
8. Click OK.

   Excel applies the same Page Setup settings to the second worksheet.
9. Press and hold the Shift key.
10. Click the current worksheet.

    Excel turns off group mode.

Did You Know?

You can also use the Page Setup dialog box to create header and footer text that appears at the top and bottom of for your worksheet printouts. Open the Page Setup dialog box and click the Header/Footer tab. Click Custom Header or Custom Footer, and select from the available built-in fields buttons. Click OK to add your selections to the Page Setup dialog box. Click OK to exit Page Setup.

Find Data on Multiple Sheets with the VLookup Function

You can use the `VLookup` function to look up values vertically in a table.

To perform this technique, you must create a table that holds the values you want to look up. You must also make sure the value labels appear in the left-most column of the worksheet. To build the formula, you must reference the lookup_value, the table containing the lookup data, which is called the table_array, and a column index number, col_index_num. In the example below, the lookup value is a quantity of units sold, and the lookup table is a table of discount pricing located above the purchases list. Because the lookup table is two columns wide, the column index number is 2.

1. Click the cell in which you want the lookup results to appear.
2. Click the Paste Function button in the Formula bar.

   The Insert Function dialog box appears.
3. Select the Lookup & Reference category.
4. Double-click VLOOKUP in the function list.

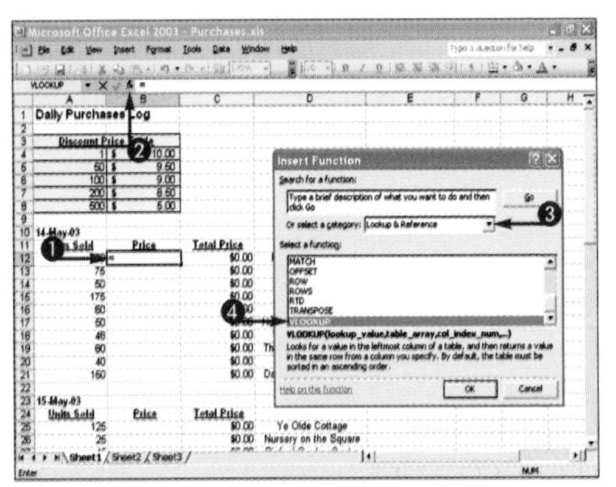

The Function Arguments dialog box appears.

5. Click the Lookup_value field and click the cell containing the value you want to look up.

   In this example, the value is 200 units.
6. Click the Table_array field and select the lookup table you want to search.

Note: *To select a cell or cell range from another sheet, click the sheet tab and select the range.*

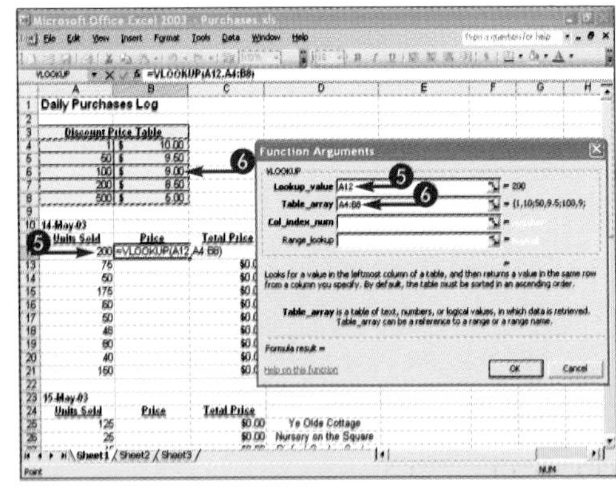

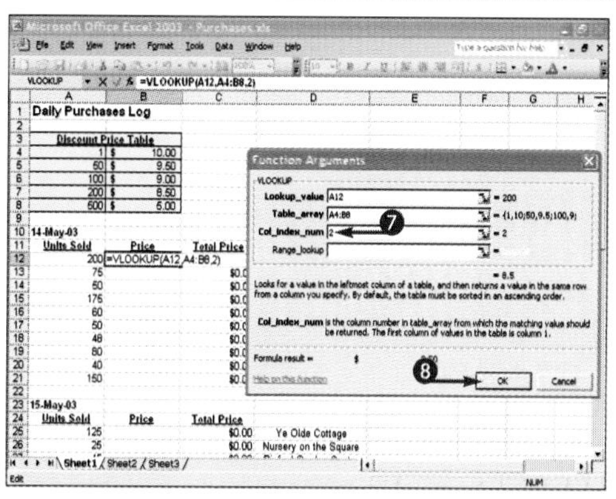

7. Click the Col_index_num field and type the column number where Excel can find the corresponding value.

   In this example, the Discount Price Table consists of two column widths, so the number 2 appears in the field.

8. Click OK.

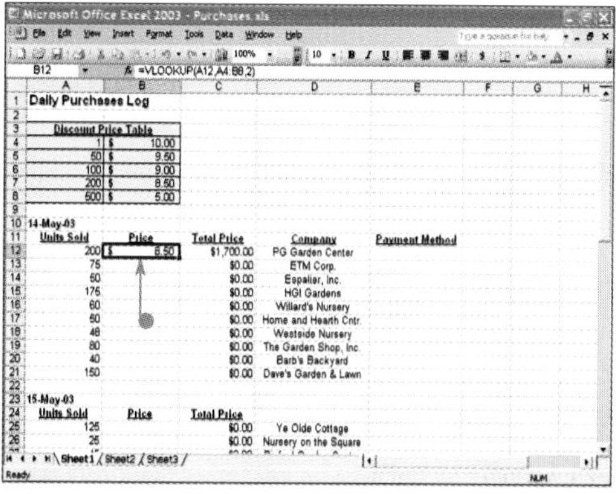

- Excel calculates the results.

Did You Know?

You can also use the `HLookup` function, which stands for horizontal lookup, to look up data horizontally across a table.

Chapter 4

Enhance Your PowerPoint Presentations

PowerPoint is an excellent tool for communicating all types of ideas and visuals to an audience. You can create a variety of different kinds of slide show presentations, including presentations you can display on the Web. Whether you are explaining a marketing strategy to your coworkers, or just presenting a book report to your class, PowerPoint offers you all the tools necessary to present a dynamic, eye-catching slide show.

One reason for the popularity of PowerPoint is that it is such an easy program to use. It comes with a variety of slide designs and layout templates, so all you have to do is add your own text and images. However, if you want your slide shows to stand out, you need to tap into some of the more advanced features of the program, such as the animation effects, transition controls, and drawing tools.

The tasks in this chapter introduce you to ways to speed up your workflow as well as enhance the appearance of your presentations. For example, you can reduce your presentation file size by compressing graphics, or you can turn slides into bitmap images that you can use to illustrate other files.

Because PowerPoint is so visual, it is easy to be distracted by all the visual items you can add to your presentation and to lose the focus of your original message. When applying various techniques, make sure you do not overwhelm your audience and distract from your presentation message.

Quick Tips

Turn a Word Outline into a PowerPoint Presentation

You can turn an existing Word outline into a slide show in PowerPoint.

PowerPoint converts your Word document into a simple presentation. It does not assign slide designs or layouts. It is up to you to add formatting, slide designs, and to illustrate the slides with any graphic items, such as clip art, shapes, or photos.

When importing Word outlines into PowerPoint, you must first install the outline converter. If this is the first time you attempt to import an outline, Word prompts you to install the converter.

1. Click File.
2. Click Open.

   The keyboard shortcut for opening the Open dialog box is Ctrl+O.

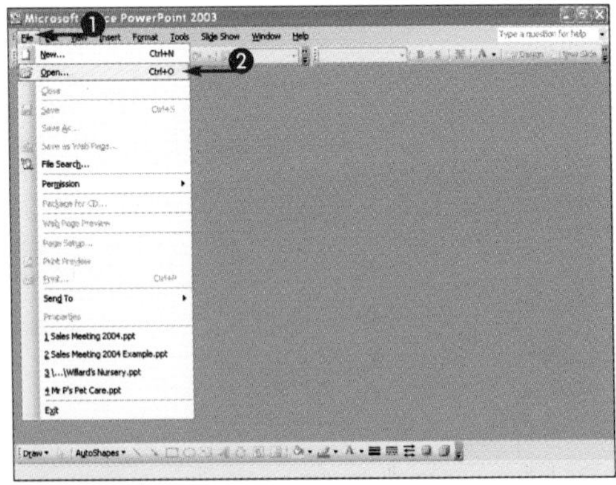

The Open dialog box appears.

3. Click here and then All Outlines.

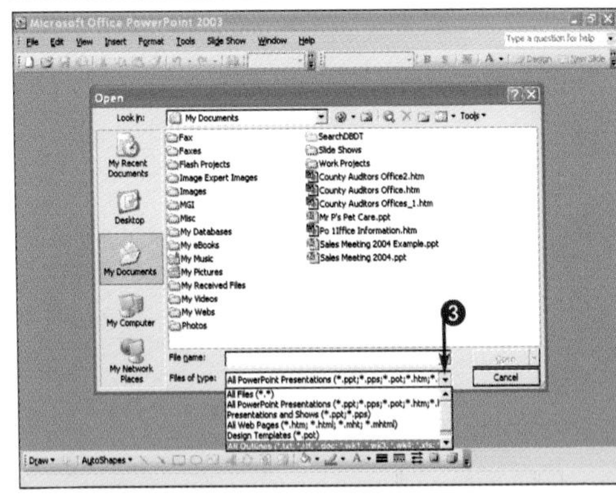

4. Locate and select the Word document you want to convert into a slide show.
5. Click Open.

- PowerPoint converts the content of the file into a presentation and lists each slide in the Slides pane.

Did You Know?

You can also use the Word Send To option to send an outline document to PowerPoint. In Word, click File, click Send To, and then click Microsoft PowerPoint. PowerPoint opens and converts the outline document into a slide show presentation.

Convert a Slide into a Bitmap Image

You can use the Copy and Paste commands to turn a single slide into a bitmap image, which you can then use as a graphic object in other programs, including the Office applications.

However, if you paste the bitmap into another program, you cannot save it as another graphic file type.

To use this technique, you take the slide you want to convert into Notes Page view, where the PowerPoint slide appears as a bitmap image by default. You can apply the Copy command, and then paste the image into another program, or you can copy it into another slide or presentation and save it as a graphic file.

1. Click View.
2. Click Notes Page.

   PowerPoint switches to Notes Page view mode.

Note: *If you use the Notes Page view a lot and want to quickly access it, add a button for the view to your toolbar.*

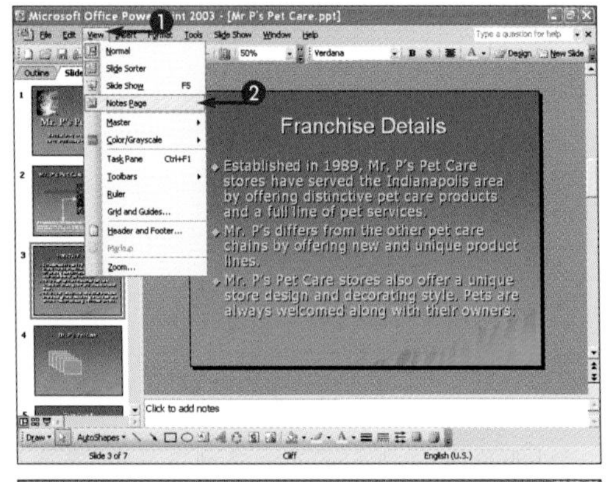

3. Right-click over the slide image.
4. Click Copy.

   PowerPoint places the image in the Windows Clipboard.

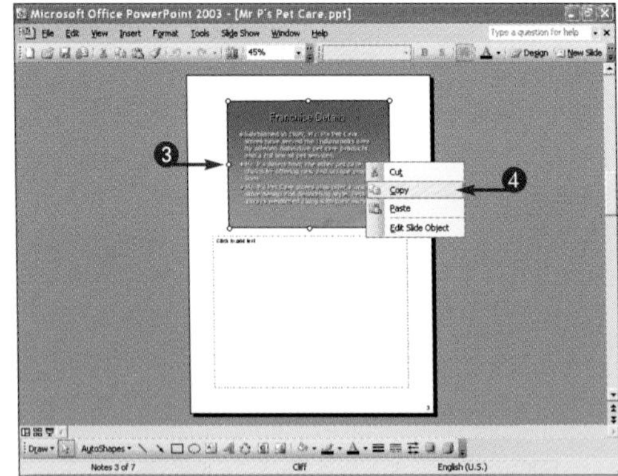

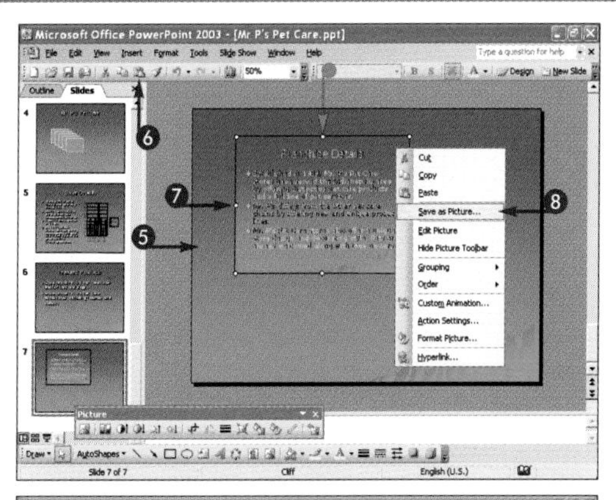

5. Open a new presentation or slide.
6. Click the Paste button.

   You can also press Ctrl+V.

- PowerPoint inserts the slide bitmap image.

7. Right-click over the image.
8. Click Save as Picture.

   The Save As Picture dialog box appears.

9. Type a name for the image file.
10. Click here and select a graphic file format.
11. Click Save.

    PowerPoint saves the slide as a graphic file for reuse in other programs.

    You can close the new presentation without saving the newly pasted slide image.

Did You Know?

You can use the Copy and Paste commands to paste a slide image from Notes Page view into Word or Excel. After right-clicking to copy the file as shown below, open Word or Excel and press Ctrl+V to paste the slide image into a document or worksheet. You can now move and resize the slide image as a bitmap object.

Repeatedly Draw the Same Shape

Ordinarily, when you select a tool on the Drawing toolbar, the tool is active for one-time use only. For example, when you click the Arrow tool button, you can draw a single arrow onscreen, after which the tool becomes inactive again. If you want to draw another arrow, you must reselect the Arrow tool button. However, you can use a shortcut technique to keep the same drawing tool active until you decide you no longer want to draw the shape or line.

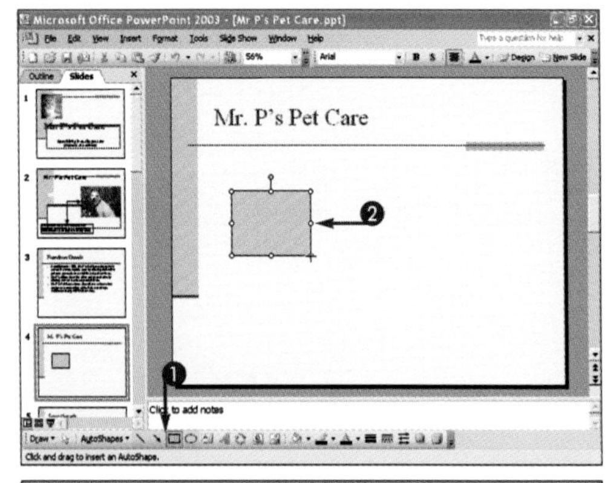

1. Double-click the drawing tool you want to keep active.

   The tool appears active on the toolbar.

2. Draw the object or shape on the slide.

   In this example. The Rectangle tool is selected.

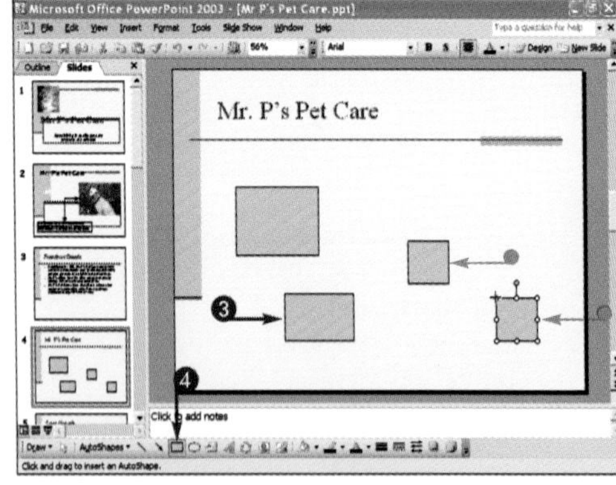

3. Draw the object or shape again elsewhere on the slide.

   - You can continue drawing the same object repeatedly on the slide.

4. Click the drawing tool button you activated in step **1** again to deactivate the tool.

Note: *You can also deactivate the tool by selecting another drawing tool.*

Create Evenly Spaced Duplicate Shapes

You can automatically duplicate shapes and space them evenly on a slide. Using this shortcut technique, you can duplicate an existing shape, position it where you want it to go, and then continue to repeatedly duplicate the same shape.

You can use this technique to duplicate shapes you draw with the Rectangle, Oval, Arrow, and Line tools, as well as shapes you create using the PowerPoint AutoShapes tools. The technique also works on text boxes and WordArt objects.

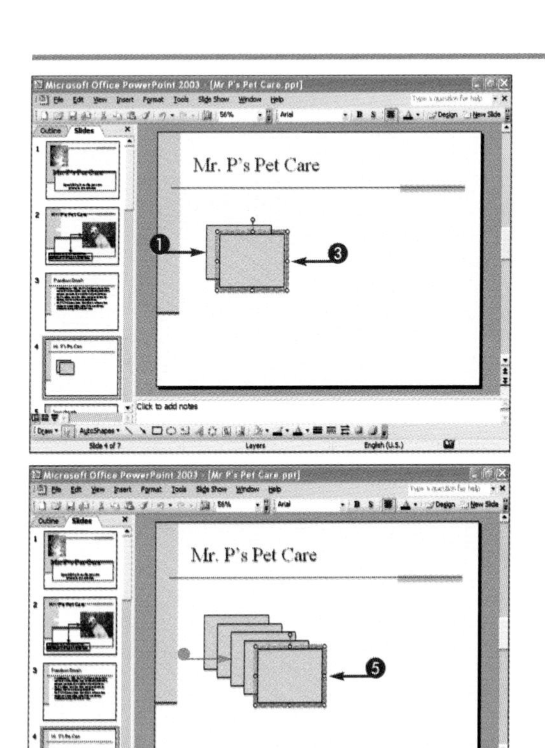

1. Click the shape or object you want to duplicate.
2. Press Ctrl+D.

   PowerPoint duplicates the shape.
3. Drag the duplicate shape to move it and establish the spacing you want for the duplicate objects.
4. Press Ctrl+D.
   - PowerPoint duplicates the shape and the spacing you set in step **3**.
5. Repeat step **4**.

   PowerPoint duplicates the shape and the spacing you want.

Add Connector Lines to Objects

You can use the AutoShapes connector lines to connect slide objects. *Connector lines* are simply lines that PowerPoint automatically draws for you between two objects. You can use connector lines to create your own version of a flowchart or diagram. Connector lines allow you to establish links between various objects on a slide, much like flowchart elements show links to each other.

Connector lines come in several different styles. Once you add a connector line between two slide objects, you can move either or both objects, and the connector line resizes to maintain the connection between them. You can add formatting to connector lines.

1. Display the slide containing the two objects you want to connect.

Note: *You can connect AutoShapes, text boxes, WordArt, clip art, pictures, OLE objects, and more.*

2. Click AutoShapes.
3. Click Connectors.
4. Click the connector style you want to apply.

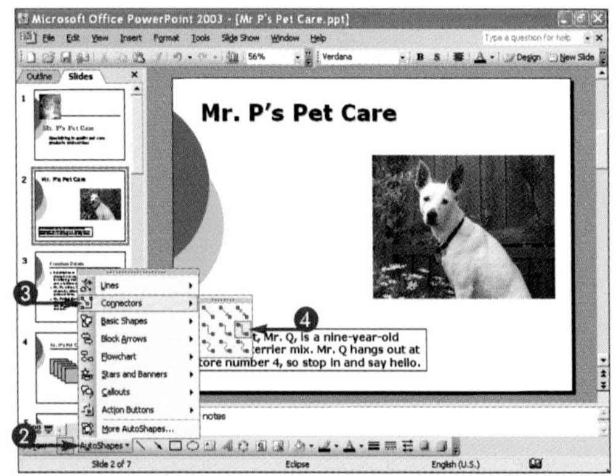

↖ changes to ⊹.

5. Move ⊹ over the first item.

- Blue connector handles surround the object.

6. Click the handle you want to use as the anchor point.

   PowerPoint establishes the handle you click as the first anchor point.

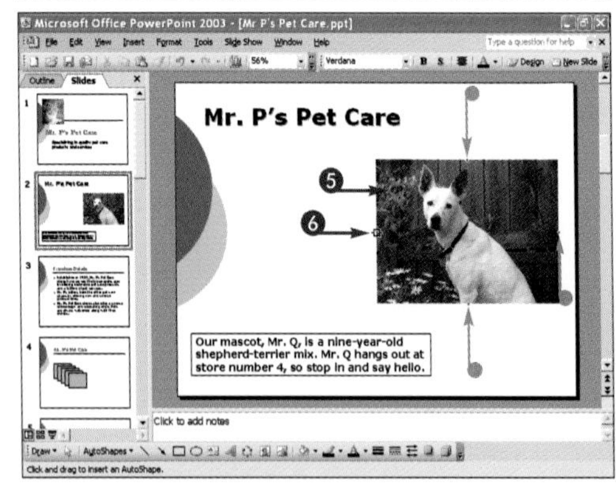

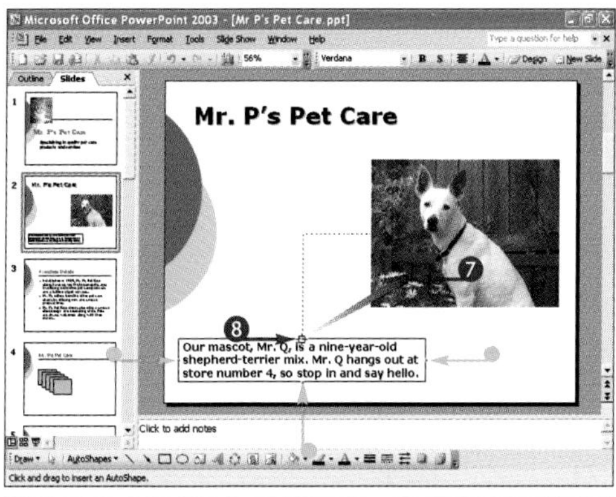

7. Drag ⊹ over the object to which you want to connect.

   A dashed line trails your connector line as you drag to the other object on the slide.

- Blue connector handles surround the object.

8. Click the handle you want to use as the second anchor point.

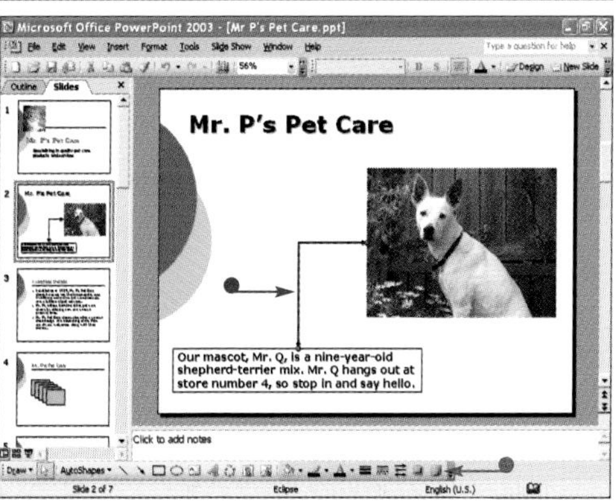

- PowerPoint draws a connector line between the two objects.
- You can apply formatting to the connector line using the drawing tools.

Did You Know?

If you prefer the look of AutoShape's block arrows, which have a chunkier style and can curve, you can use them to simulate connectors. However, you establish the connections between two objects by drawing the shapes yourself. No blue connector handles appear to assist you, and if you move a slide object, the Block Arrow shape does not resize to maintain the connection between the items.

Save File Size by Compressing Pictures

You can compress pictures in your PowerPoint document to reduce the file size of the presentation. The more pictures you add to illustrate your slides, the larger your presentation file size becomes.

The Compress Pictures dialog box displays options for reducing image resolution, discarding the cropped areas of an image, and compressing the image file size.

Depending on the image type, you can compress a particular image on a slide, or you can choose to compress all the images in the presentation.

1. Double-click the picture you want to compress.

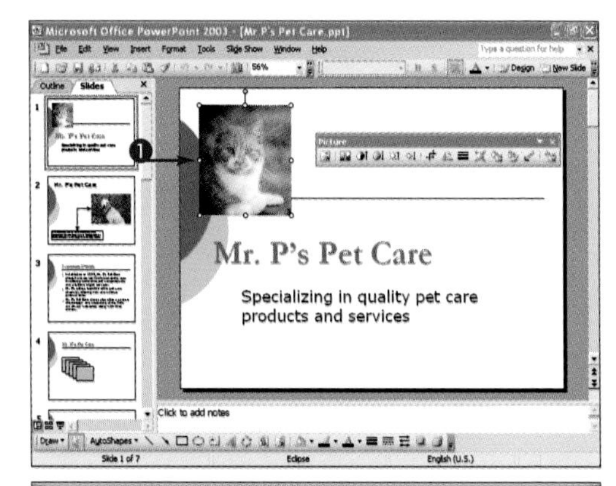

The Format Picture dialog box appears.

2. Click the Picture tab.
3. Click Compress.

The Compress Pictures dialog box appears.

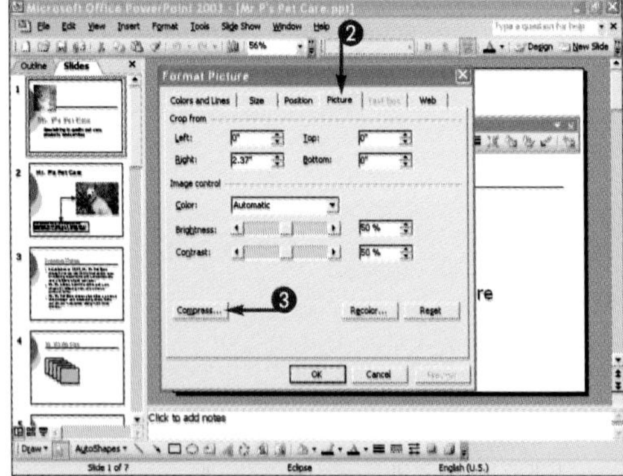

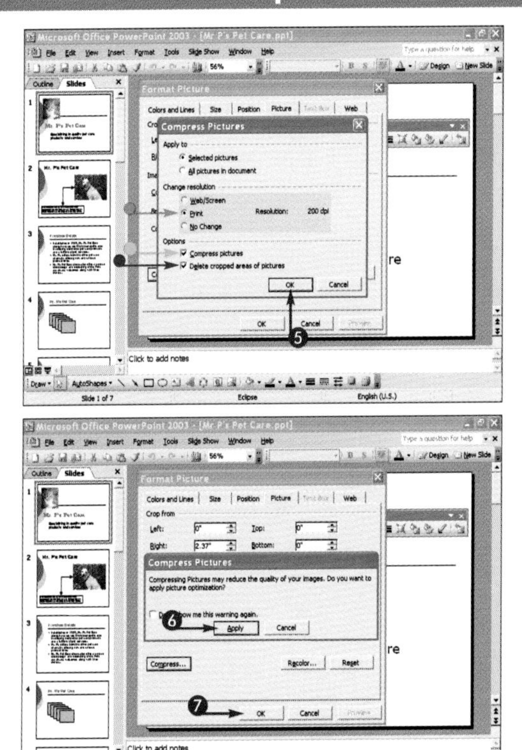

4 Select compression options.

Note: *You must compress all the clip art in the presentation, not just a single clip art image.*

- To reduce image resolution, click a resolution option.
- Select this option to compress the image.
- To remove any excess cropping, click here.

5 Click OK.

A prompt window appears, warning you about possible quality reduction.

6 Click Apply.

PowerPoint compresses the image.

7 Click OK to close the Format Picture dialog box.

Did You Know?

You can also access the Compress Pictures dialog box through the Picture toolbar. After you select an image, simply click the Compress Pictures button ( ) on the toolbar, the fifth button from the right. To open the Picture toolbar, click View, click Toolbars, and then click Picture.

Create Better-Looking Shadowed Text

The Shadow Style command, found on the Drawing toolbar, allows you greater control over how you position the shadow under your text. With the Shadow Settings toolbar, you can control the color of your shadow effect, nudge the shadow to just the right spot, and turn the effect on or off. You can use the directional buttons on the Shadow Settings toolbar to determine the direction of the shadow effect behind the text, as well as the spacing of the shadow from the text.

1. Select the text or text box to which you want to apply an object shadow.
   - If the text already has a shadow, remove the shadow by clicking the Shadow button on the Formatting toolbar.
2. Click the Shadow Style button on the Drawing toolbar.
3. Click Shadow Settings.

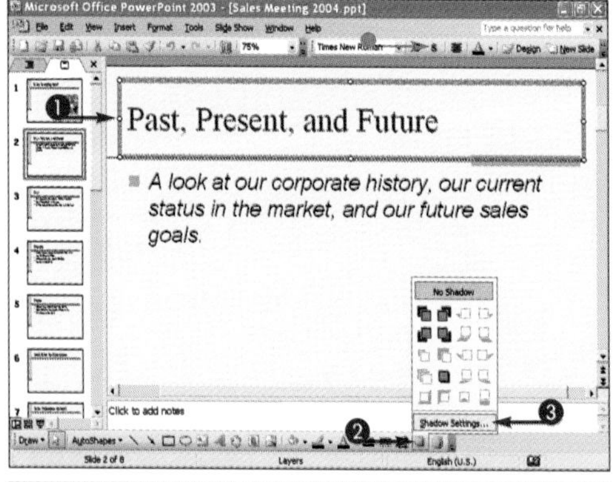

The Shadow Settings toolbar appears.

4. Click a shadow direction.
   - PowerPoint applies a shadow effect.

   Repeat step **4** to nudge the shadow in any direction to create the effect you want.

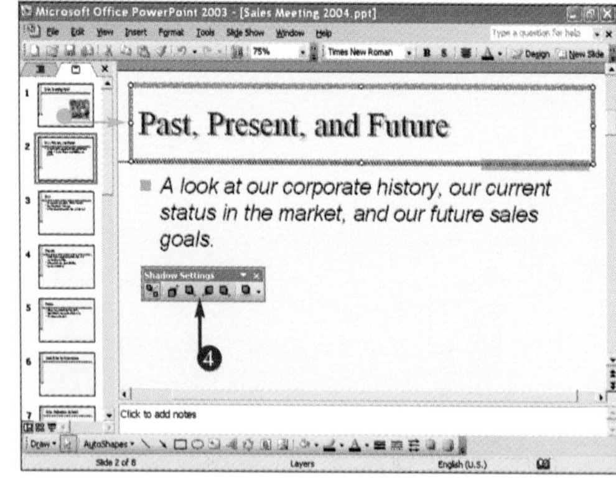

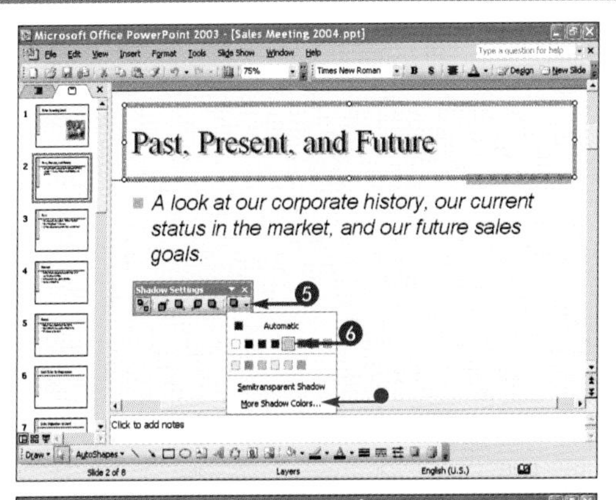

5. Click the Shadow Color button.
6. Select a color for the shadow.
   - To select from more colors than those that appear, click the More Shadow Colors option and select another color.

- PowerPoint applies the shadow color.
- To turn off the shadow effect, click the Shadow On/Off button.

7. Click the Close button to close the toolbar.

Did You Know?

Shades of the color gray make the best types of shadow effects in PowerPoint. To maintain text legibility, choose a shadow color that appears lighter than the text color. If you choose too dark a color, you cannot really see a shadow effect, but your text letters appear thicker instead.

Turn a Photo into a Slide Background

You can turn a photo into a slide background to use throughout your presentation.

The key to using a photo as a background is to make sure that the photo details or appearance do not distract the audience from viewing the message text on your slide. PowerPoint imports photos as is. The Background feature does not offer a setting for making your photo more transparent after you import it. If the photo is too dark or has too much detail, you may need to change the text box objects on each slide. For example, you can choose a more legible font or color for the slide text, or assign a fill color to the text objects to make your text stand out from the photo background.

1. Right-click over an empty area on the slide background.
2. Click Background.

   The Background dialog box appears.
3. Click here and click Fill Effects.

The Fill Effects dialog box appears.

4. Click the Picture tab.
5. Click Select Picture.

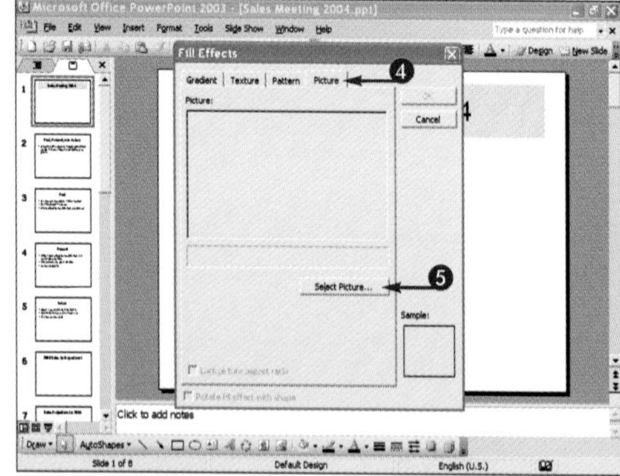

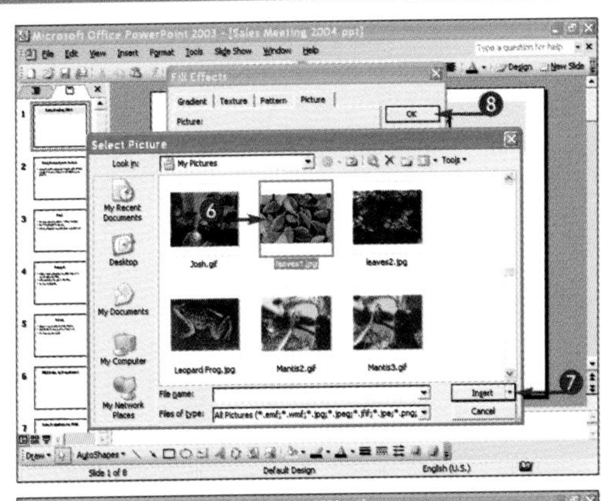

The Select Picture dialog box appears.

6. Locate and select the picture you want to use as a background.
7. Click Insert.

   PowerPoint inserts the figure into the Picture tab list.

8. Click OK to exit the Fill Effects dialog box.

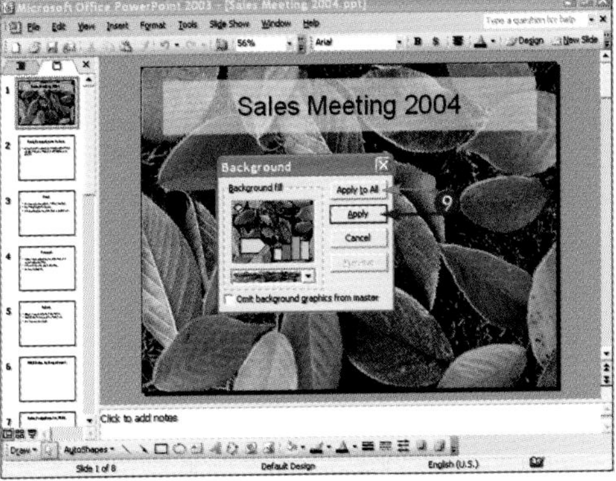

9. Click Apply.

- You can click Apply to All to use the photo as the background for all the slides in your presentation.

PowerPoint applies the photo to the slide background.

Apply It!

You can add a fill to any text box to make your text stand out from the slide background. By default, all text objects you add are set to No Fill status. To change this, double-click the text object to open the Format AutoShape dialog box. Click the Colors and Lines tab, click the Fill Color ▾, and select a new fill color. Click OK to apply the color to the text box.

Tile a Picture in the Slide Background

You can repeat the same image across the background of a slide using an effect called *tiling*.

PowerPoint does not resize your image for tiling, so if your image is large to begin with, the tiling effect uses the same full-size image across the background.

The key to successful tiling is to select a small, uncomplicated image. However, if the tiled image still interferes with the legibility of your slide text, you can always change the fill color of the text box to make your message text stand out.

1. Right-click over the slide background.
2. Click Background.

   The Background dialog box appears.
3. Click here and then click Fill Effects.

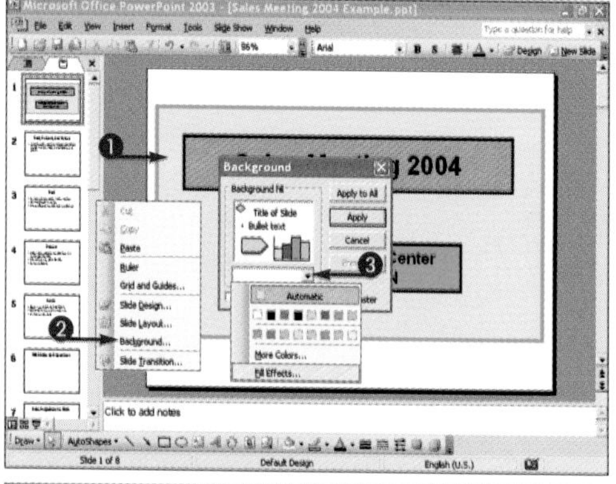

The Fill Effects dialog box appears.

4. Click the Texture tab.
5. Click Other Texture.

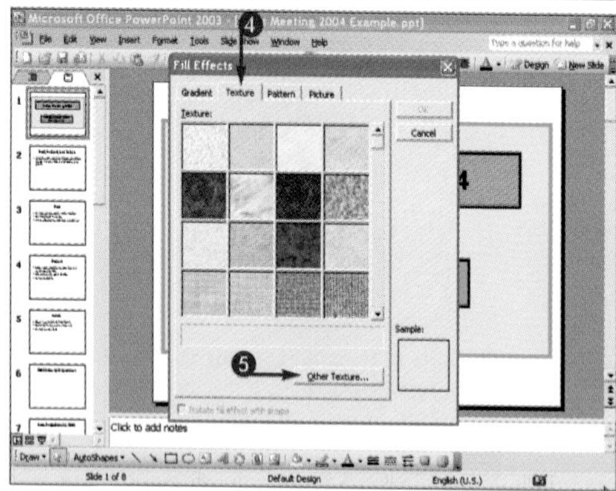

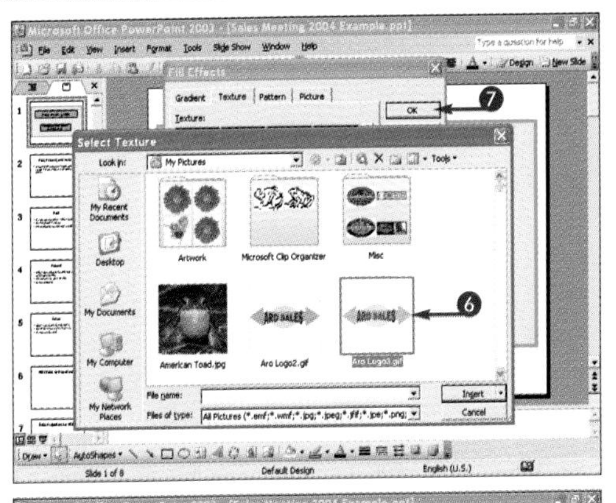

The Select Texture dialog box appears.

6. Double-click the image you want to use as a tiled background.

   PowerPoint adds the image to the Texture list of the Fill Effects dialog box.

7. Click OK to close the Fill Effects dialog box.

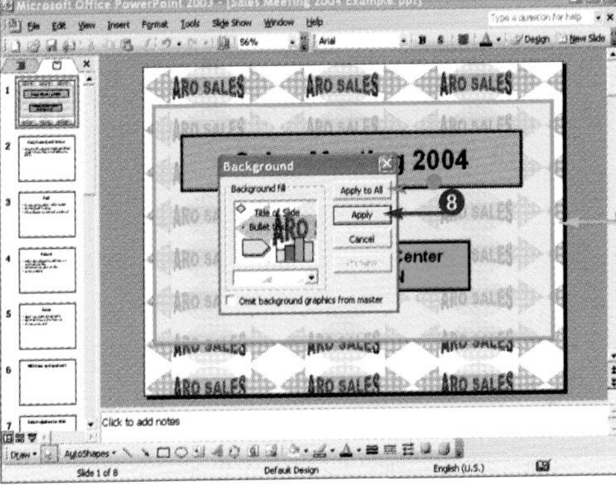

8. Click Apply.

- You can click Apply to All to use the image as the tiled background for all the slides in your presentation.
- PowerPoint tiles the image across the slide background.

Did You Know?

You can also use the Texture tab in the Fill Effects dialog box to insert other textures as slide backgrounds. You can check the Microsoft Web site Clip Gallery for more textures you can download and apply. Click Help, then Office on Microsoft.com and log onto the Microsoft Web site.

Enhance Presentations with Flash Movies

You can insert Flash animations, which use the SWF file format, into a PowerPoint presentation and play them during a slide show.

To add a Flash movie, you create an ActiveX object in your slide using the Control Toolbox. ActiveX object is a set of technologies that generate interactive features. Like other objects you add to your slides, you can control the size of the ActiveX object, in this case, the window in which your Flash movie file plays. After drawing the ActiveX object, you use the object's Properties dialog box to designate the full path or URL to the SWF file. PowerPoint creates a link to the SWF file.

1. Display the slide to which you want to add a Flash movie.
2. Click View.
3. Click Toolbars.
4. Click Control Toolbox.

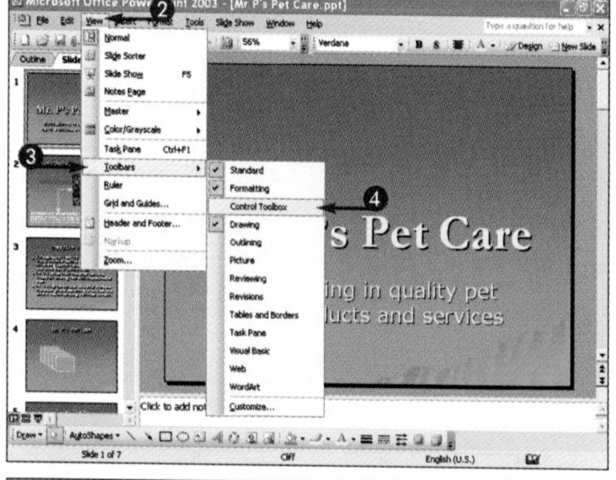

The Control Toolbox toolbar appears.

- You can resize the Control Toolbox by dragging the toolbox border.

5. Click the More Controls button.
6. Click Shockwave Flash Object (↖ changes to +).

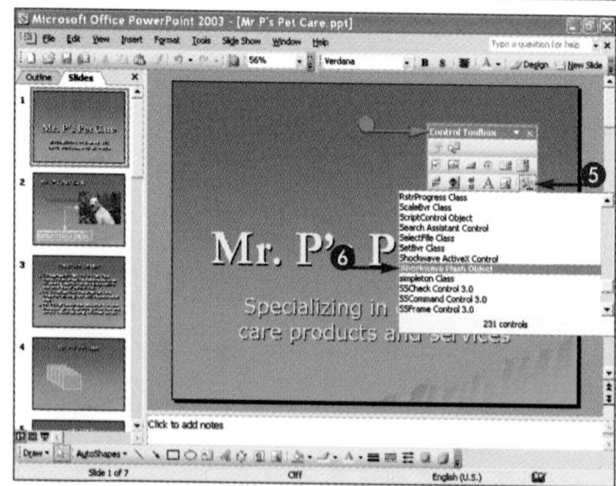

7. Draw a box to contain the Flash movie.

   PowerPoint creates a Flash object window to play the Flash file.

8. Right-click over the box.
9. Click Properties.

   The Properties window appears.

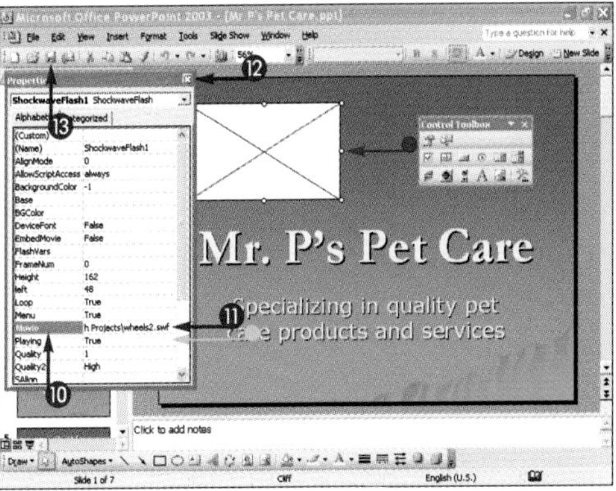

10. Click the `Movie` property.
11. Type the path or URL to the Flash file.
    - Make sure you set the `Playing` property to `True`.
12. Click the Close button.
13. Click the Save button.
    - The next time you run the slide show, the Flash animation plays.

Warning!

PowerPoint does not automatically include the Flash movie if you use the Pack and Go feature to save your presentation to a disk or CD-ROM. You must copy the Flash file separately, and save a copy of it on the computer on which you play the presentation. You must also reestablish the link in the Properties dialog box for PowerPoint to find the file.

Create Scrolling Credits

You can create the illusion of scrolling credits at the beginning or end of your slide show.

You can control the speed of the effect and whether the animation plays automatically or with a mouse click.

To create this effect, you must place a text box outside the actual slide parameters. By placing the text box above the top of the slide, you can ensure that the text appears to scroll completely off the top of the slide.

1. Display the slide to which you want to add scrolling credits.
2. Click the Text Box tool.
3. Draw a text box above the top of the slide.

- You can use the Zoom feature to zoom out, to allow yourself more room to draw the text box above the slide.

4. Type your credits text.

- You can apply formatting to the text.

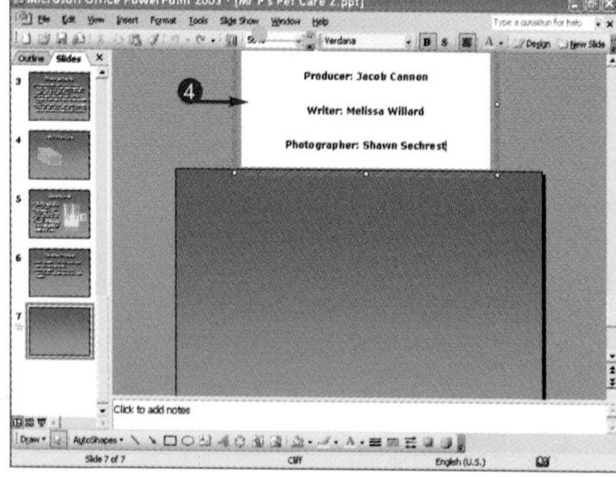

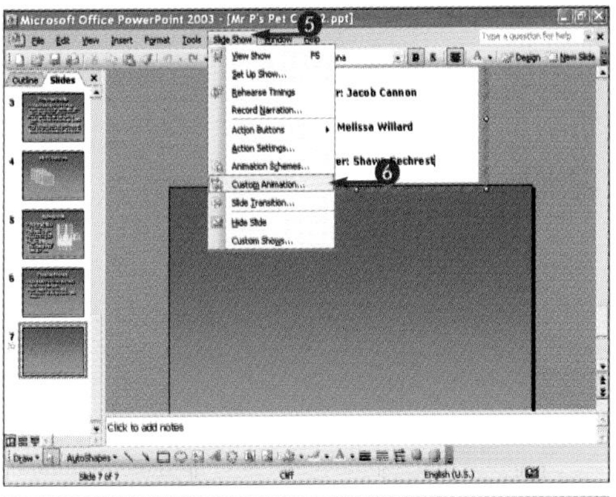

5. Click Slide Show.
6. Click Custom Animation.

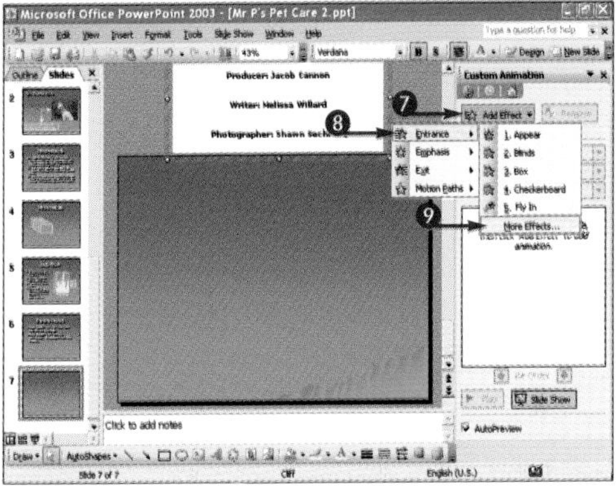

The Custom Animation pane appears.

7. Click Add Effect.
8. Click Entrance.
9. Click More Effects.

Did You Know?

To create a text box that accommodates the text you type, simply click where you want the text box to appear and start typing. As you type, the text box width increases. If you press Enter, the text box depth increases. To define the size of the text box, draw the text box by clicking and dragging. Any text you type stays within the borders you define.

continued

Create Scrolling Credits *(continued)*

Just because you place a text box outside of the slide's parameters does not mean that the text box is not part of the slide. Although the text box is not actually visible on the slide itself, the scrolling text you create within the text box is clearly visible on the slide during the animation effect.

Although the text box does not sit directly on the slide, the text you type into it is still a part of the slide show.

By default, the Crawl In effect makes the text crawl from bottom-to-top. However, you can choose any direction, including from the top, bottom, left, or right.

The Add Entrance Effects dialog box appears.

10. Click Crawl In.

    PowerPoint previews the effect.

11. Click OK.

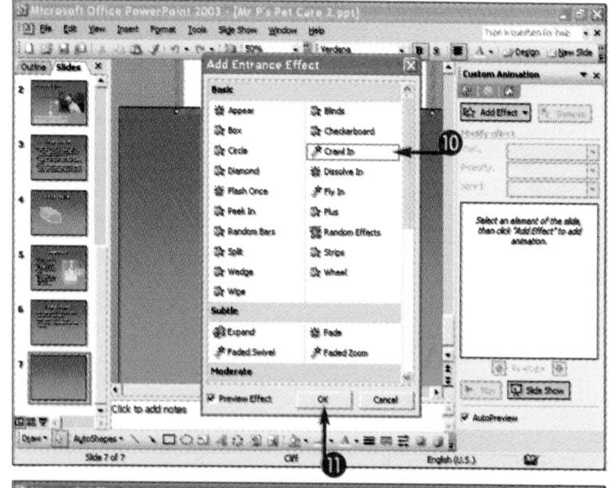

12. Click here and select a Start option.

    To make the animation occur after any previously assigned animation effects, click the After Previous option.

    To allow the user to control the start of the scrolling effect, select the On Click option.

    To start the scrolling effect at the same time as another animation effect, select the Start with Previous option.

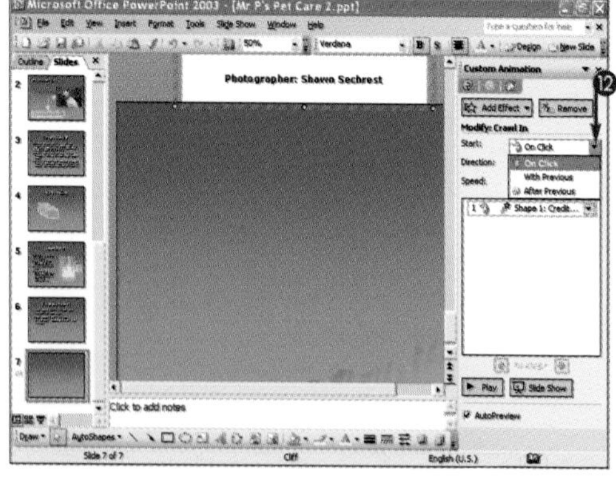

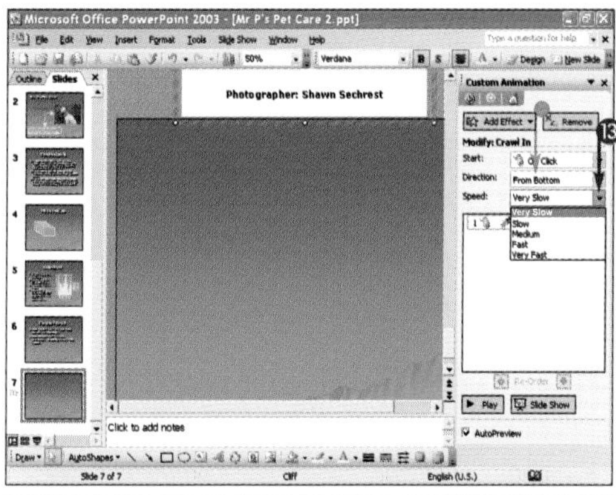

- PowerPoint selects the From Bottom direction by default.

13. Click here and select a speed.

    To make your credits scroll slowly, select Very Slow.

14. Click Play.

- To see the effect onscreen, you must select the AutoPreview option.
- PowerPoint plays the animation effect.

Did You Know?

To slow down the scrolling effect, add blank lines between the credits in the credits text box. Keep in mind that this enlarges the overall size of the text box and that you may need to move it again to keep it outside the slide parameters.

Launch a Mini Slide Show Window

You can launch a mini slide show to quickly see how your edits affect the show.

When you use the mini slide show window, you can switch back and forth between the mini slide show window and the main PowerPoint program window. With this shortcut technique, you can view a miniature version of your slide show, yet still access the PowerPoint window and all the editing commands and features whenever you want. You can leave the mini slide show window open and view your edits as soon as you make them. The mini slide show window stays open until you close it.

1. Press and hold the Ctrl key.
2. Click Slide Show view mode.

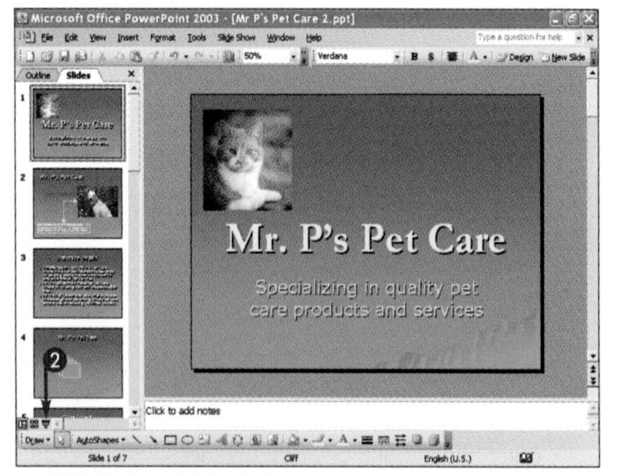

A mini slide show window appears.

An icon for the mini slide show window appears on the taskbar.

- You can use the same controls for advancing slides as you do in full-screen view mode.

If the mini slide window is active, you can press Esc to close the window.

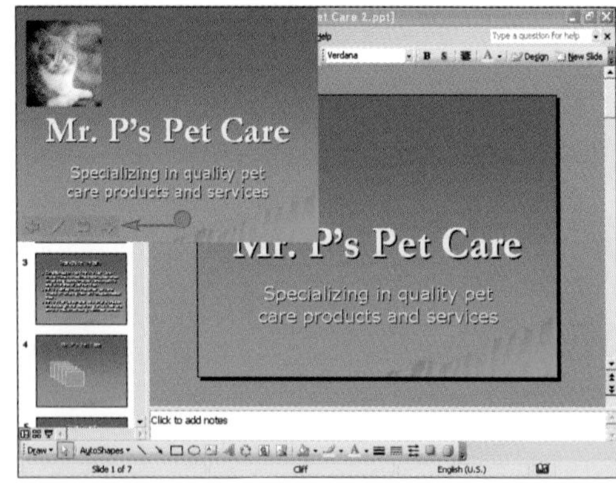

Make Your Slide Show Start Automatically

Ordinarily, PowerPoint stores any presentations with a .ppt file extension, which requires you to open the PowerPoint program window. However, you can save your PowerPoint presentation in the PowerPoint Show, or PPS, file format, to make it start automatically when you double-click the filename. By saving the presentation file as a PPS file type, you avoid opening the PowerPoint program window to launch the show.

1. Click File.
2. Click Save As.

The Save As dialog box appears.

3. Click here and select PowerPoint Show (*.pps).
4. Click Save.

PowerPoint saves the file.

You can double-click the file in the folder in which you store it to launch the show.

Using Word to Customize Handouts

You can export your PowerPoint presentation to Microsoft Word and customize any handout text you want to include with each slide.

Using the Send To command, you can send your entire presentation or just the outline to Word. You can also determine how you want the layout of the presentation to appear in Word. When you export the presentation, Word creates a table that includes a column for slide numbers and a column for miniature pictures of each slide.

When selecting a layout, you can decide whether to export any speaker notes, or just blank lines for your audience to add their own notes.

1. Click File.
2. Click Send To.
3. Click Microsoft Word.

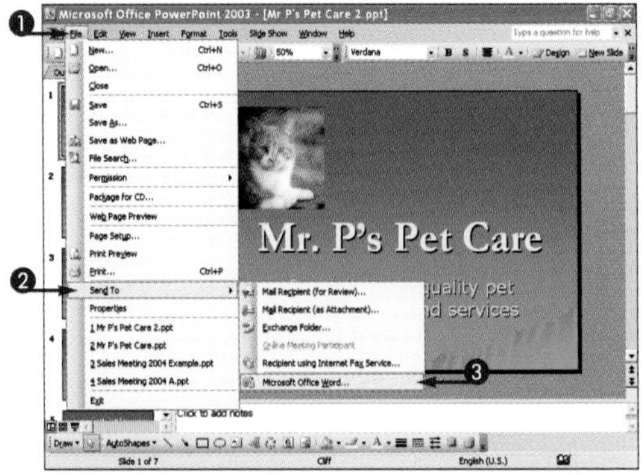

The Send To Microsoft Word dialog box appears.

4. Click a layout.

- Select this option to place notes next to slides.
- Select this option to place blank lines next to slides.
- Select this option to place notes below slides.
- Select this option to place blank lines below slides.

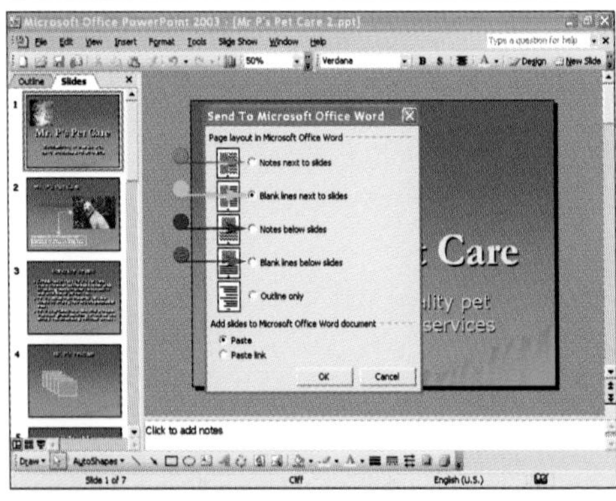

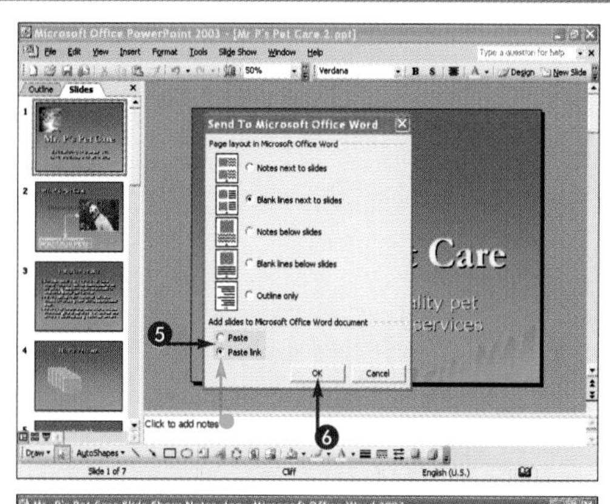

5. Click a paste option.
   - To link the slides in Word to PowerPoint, select this option.
6. Click OK.

PowerPoint exports the presentation and opens the Word program window.

You can now add or edit the handout text.

Did You Know?

If you select the Paste Link option (○ changes to ◉) in the Send To Microsoft Word dialog box, the slide miniatures in Word link to the actual slides in PowerPoint. Double-click a slide image in Word to immediately return to PowerPoint and view the same slide. Any edits you make in PowerPoint appear in the slide miniatures in Word.

Chapter 5

Customize & Optimize Your Outlook Features

One of the handiest organizing tools available, Outlook lets you easily work with and manage e-mail messages. You can also use it to keep track of appointments and other scheduled events, manage information about all the people with whom you interact, record and manage tasks you need to accomplish, create notes, and more. You may use all of the features of Outlook, or focus on a few key features, such as e-mail and the calendar. Regardless of how you use the program, you can always make your work easier with a few shortcuts and timesaving techniques.

Out of all of the Microsoft Office programs, Outlook has undergone the most visible changes from previous versions. It has a new interface and improved features, such as those for handling junk e-mail. As with all of the Office programs, you can find your own favorite shortcuts by right-clicking on various features. When you right-click, a shortcut menu of related commands appears, and you can quickly make a selection.

In this chapter, you will find several ways to customize the program as well as a few features that are not well known. For example, did you know you can look up an online Web map for any address in your Contact's folder? Or that you can turn that same contact's address into an envelope or label? Outlook also works intuitively with Word. For example, if you type a person's name in Word, a smart tag appears with options for adding the name to the Outlook contact list.

Quick Tips

Send Message Replies to Another Recipient

You can set up Outlook to send message replies to another person.

When you apply this feature to an outgoing e-mail, Outlook ensures that the replies you would normally receive in your Inbox are redirected to another e-mail address. Using the Message Options dialog box, you can specify an e-mail address from your Address Book, or you can manually enter another address in the field.

After specifying a different e-mail address, you can close the Message Options dialog box and send your e-mail. This feature only applies to the outgoing message you compose. To apply this feature to another e-mail, you can repeat the steps below.

1. Compose a new e-mail message.
2. Click Options.

   The Message Options dialog box opens.

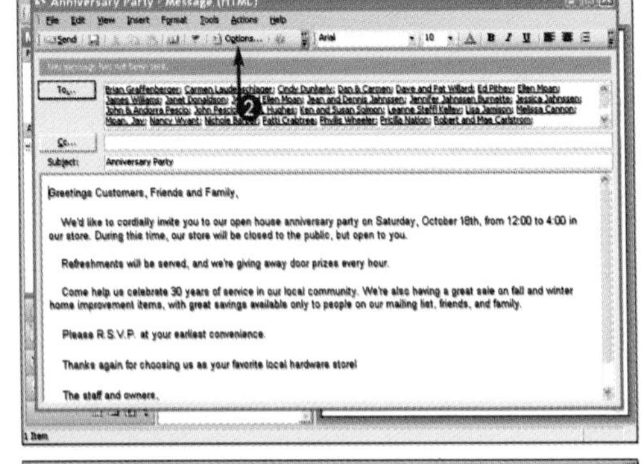

3. Click the Have replies sent to options.

   - Outlook automatically inserts your name.

4. To send replies to someone in your Address Book, click Select Names.

   You can also type the e-mail address to which you want the replies sent directly in the field.

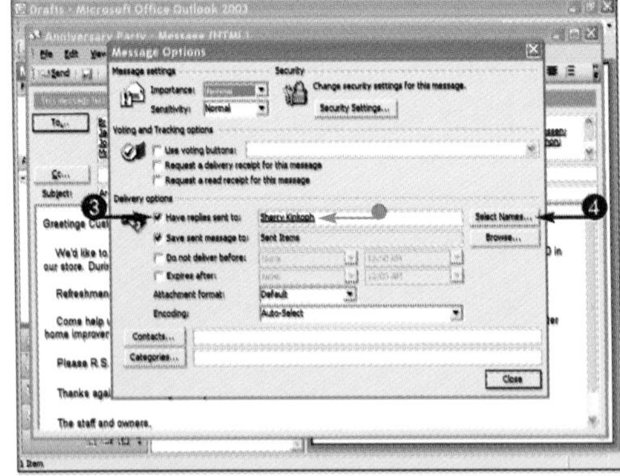

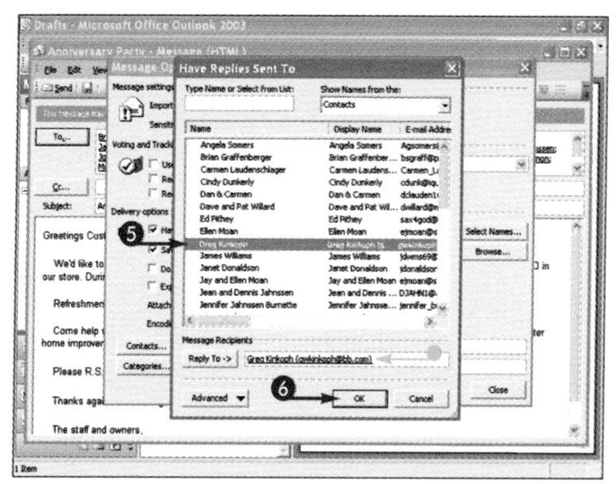

The Have Replies Sent To dialog box opens.

5. Double-click the name of the person to whom you want the replies sent.

- Outlook adds the name to the Reply To field.

6. Click OK.

Note: *You cannot have message replies sent to a distribution list.*

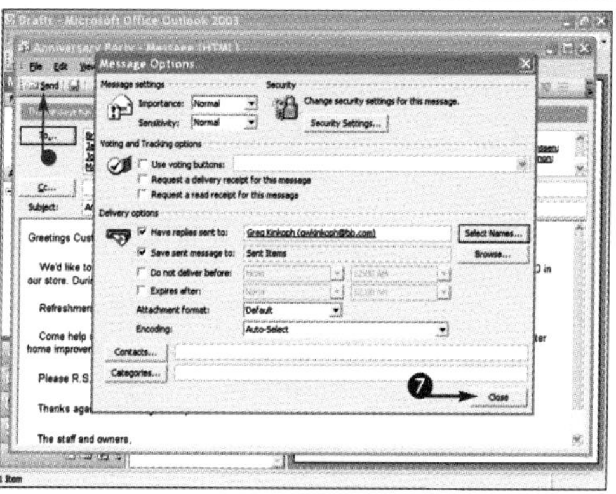

7. Click Close.

- You can now send the message.

Outlook sends message replies the selected recipient.

Did You Know?

You can look up related messages in your Outlook mailbox. This technique is also useful for finding messages that are part of the same conversation. Start by opening one of the message replies. Click Tools, Find All, and then Related Messages. The Advanced Find dialog box opens and lists all the related messages.

Customize a Personal Distribution List

You can use a personal distribution list to send e-mail messages to a select group of people from your Outlook Address Book. A distribution list can really help you speed up the task of e-mailing several people with the same message. You can also add and remove names from a personal distribution list.

Outlook marks distribution lists with a special icon that shows several faces. Outlook stores all distribution lists you create in the default Contacts folder. This allows you to quickly and easily assign categories to the lists, as needed.

1. Click File.
2. Click New.
3. Click Distribution List.

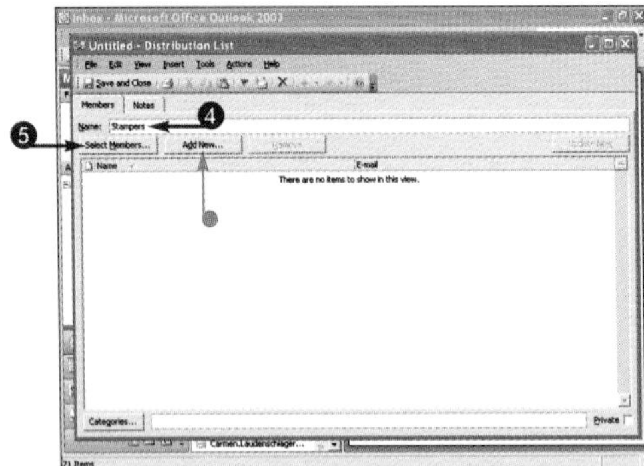

The Distributions List window appears.

4. Type a name for the list.
5. Click Select Members.

- To add new names and e-mail addresses to the list, you can click Add New.

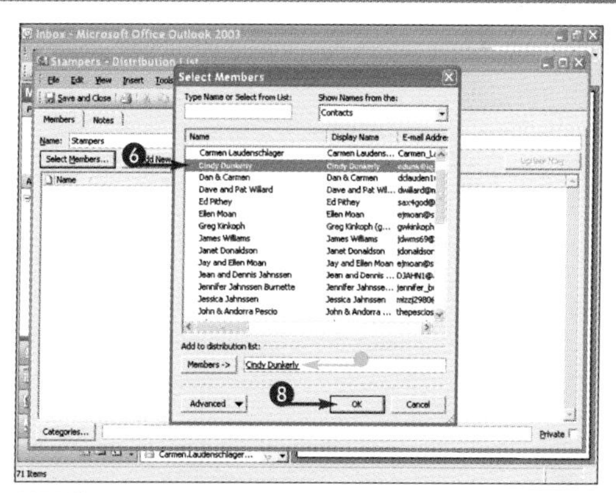

The Select Members dialog box opens.

6. Double-click the name you want to add.
- Outlook adds the contact to the distribution list.
7. Repeat step **6** to continue adding names to the list.
8. Click OK.

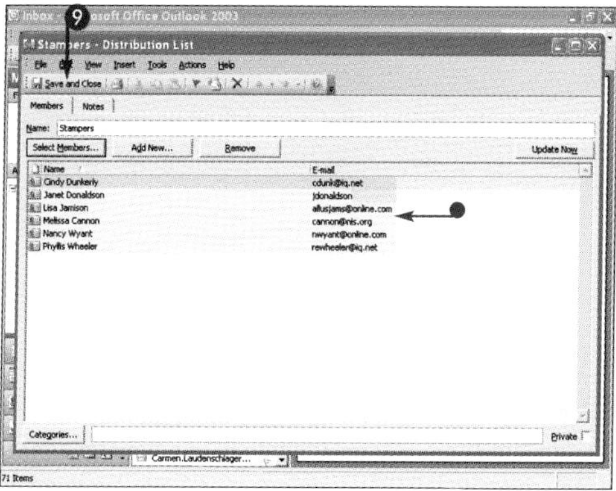

- The distribution list shows the selected names.
9. Click Save and Close.

Office adds the list to your Address Book of e-mail addresses.

Apply It!

To utilize a distribution list in an e-mail message, click To in the message window, then double-click the distribution list and click OK. When you compose and send the message, Outlook sends it to everyone on the list.

Create a Custom Signature

You can add a signature to the bottom of your e-mail messages to include additional information about yourself or your company. You can also use signatures to share a favorite quote. Signatures are simply personalized information or a picture that you add to the end of your message.

You can use signatures to convey a message, such as how to respond to your e-mail. For example, if you send out an electronic newsletter in your e-mail that includes the latest product news of your company, you can add a signature at the bottom of the message that tells people how to unsubscribe to the list.

1. Click Tools.
2. Click Options.

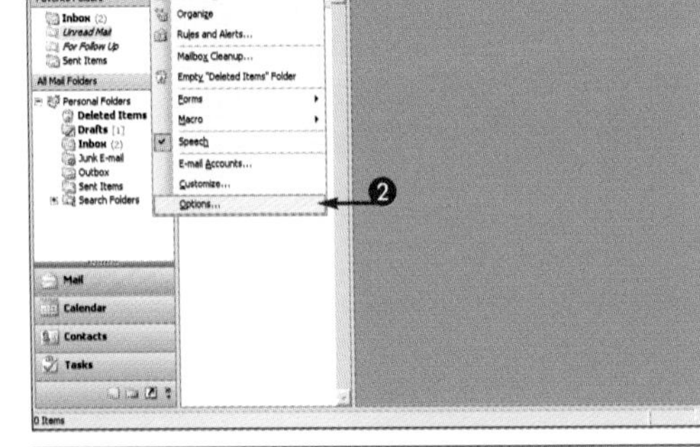

The Options dialog box appears.

3. Click the Mail Format tab.
4. Click Signatures.

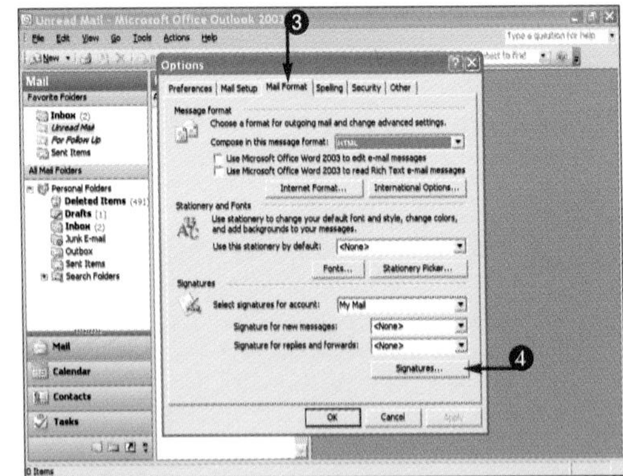

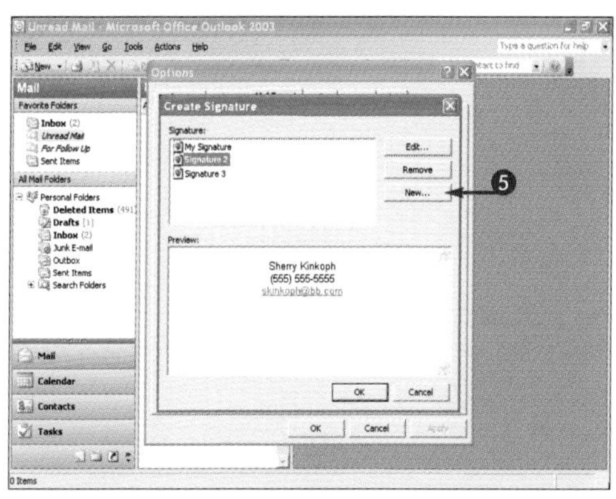

The Create Signature dialog box appears.

5. Click New.

The Create New Signature dialog box appears.

6. Type a name for the signature.

- To base the new signature on an existing signature, select this option and specify a signature.
- To use a file as a signature, select this option and select the file.

7. Click Next.

Did You Know?

You can use Microsoft Word to create signatures that include pictures. Click Tools, then click Options. Click the General tab. Click E-mail Options, then click the E-mail Signature tab. Click inside the Create your e-mail signature box and type your signature text. Click the Insert Picture button ( ) to select a picture. Outlook automatically adds the signature to the list of available signatures.

continued

Create a Custom Signature *(continued)*

When you create a new signature, you can indicate what formatting you want to use. You can also control the alignment of text in a signature or add bullets in front of the signature text.

You can save several signatures to use with different types of messages, as well as apply different signatures to message replies and forwards.

You can also attach a *v-Card*, a virtual business card, to your signature. You can turn an Outlook contact into a v-Card that you can share with other users. Attaching a v-Card does not add the v-Card text to your actual signature, but automatically attaches the information as a file attachment to the message.

8. Type the text you want to use as your signature text.

- To change the formatting, select the text, click Font and select another font, size, or text color.
- To change the alignment, select the text, click Paragraph and select another alignment.

9. Click Finish.

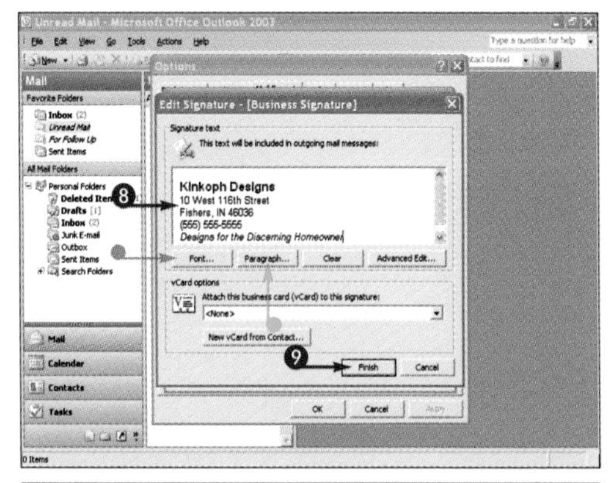

- Office adds the signature to the list of available signatures.

10. Click the signature to preview it.

11. Click OK.

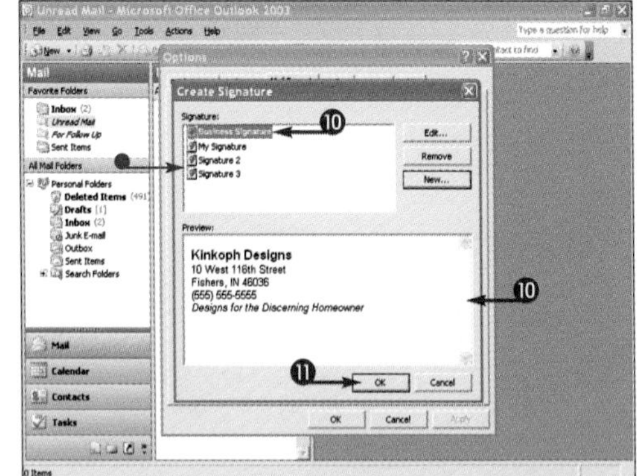

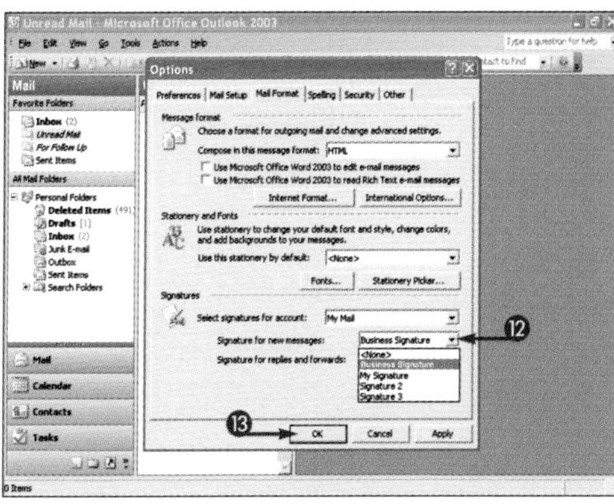

⓬ Click here and select the signature you want to use for new e-mail messages.

⓭ Click OK.

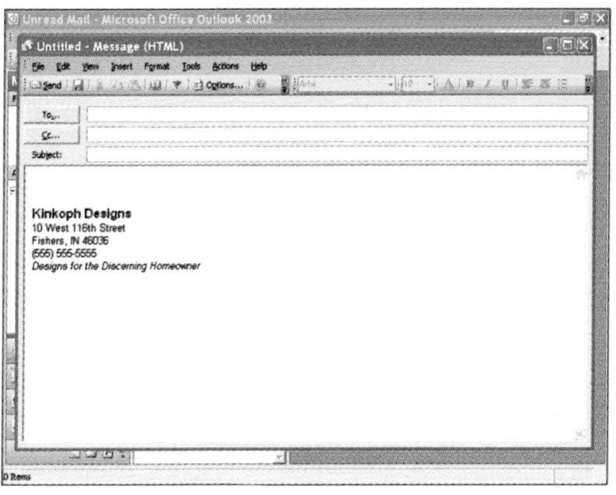

Outlook applies the selected signature to any new messages you create.

Customize It!

You can copy and paste text and pictures into the Edit Signature dialog box. Simply select the item you want to copy and press Ctrl+C. Click in the Edit Signature dialog box where you want to insert the item and press Ctrl+V.

Clean a Mailbox of Space-Stealing Files

The more e-mail you receive through Outlook, the larger your Outlook mailbox becomes. If you use Outlook on a network, you may need to clean out your mailbox from time to time if it exceeds the size limits that your network allows. It is a good idea to clean out your mailbox regularly even if you do not use Outlook in a corporate network environment. As messages pile up in your mailbox, they consume space on your computer as well.

If you worry about removing important messages, you can create a customized search to locate only the messages consuming the most space, such as those with file attachments.

1. Click Tools.
2. Click Find.
3. Click Advanced Find.

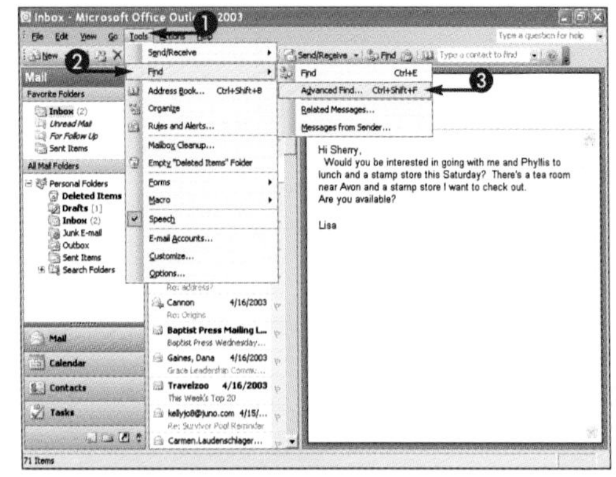

- The Advanced Find dialog box appears.

4. Make sure you select Messages in the Look For box.
5. Click the More Choices tab.
6. Click here and select greater than.

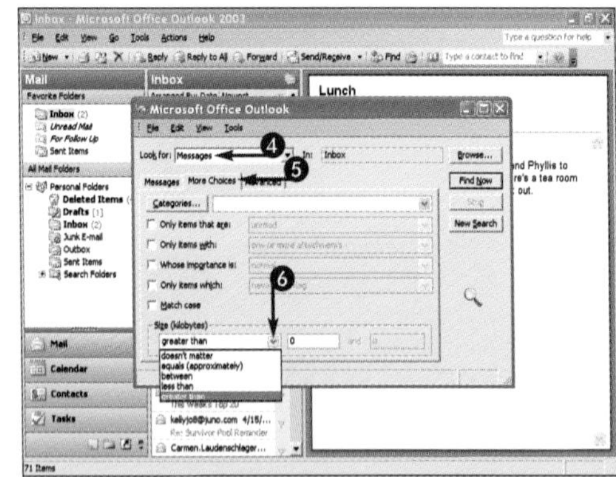

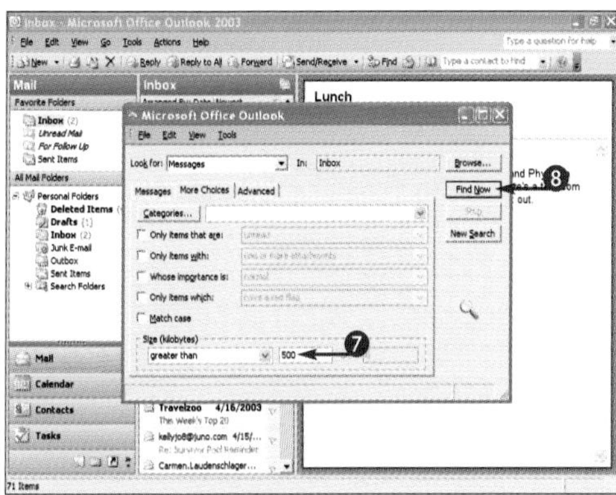

7. Type a file size number.

   A number such as 500 tells Outlook to look for files that are 500 kilobytes or larger.

8. Click Find Now.

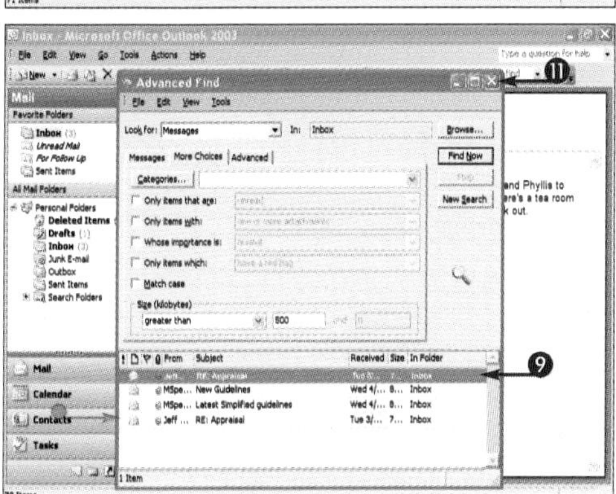

- Outlook lists all the files with a size greater than or equal to what you specify.

9. Select the file you want to remove.

10. Press the Delete key.

    Outlook deletes the file.

Note: *Deleting the message and file attachment permanently deletes the file.*

11. Click the Close button.

Apply It!

To save a search you want to use again, click File, and then click Save Search to open the Save Search dialog box. Type a distinct name for the search and click OK. To reuse the search, open the Advanced Find dialog box and click File, click Open Search and select the search.

Print a Master Copy of an Address Book

Storing all of your contact names and addresses, including e-mail addresses, electronically can cause concern, especially if you worry about losing your data during a system crash.

The Outlook Address Book window does not offer a print option. However, you can print your contacts from Contact view. The Outlook Contacts feature allows you to record information about people you contact, such as family members, business contacts, and colleagues. In addition, it includes your e-mail address book.

The Print dialog box offers several different print styles.

1. Switch to Contacts view.
2. Click File.
3. Click Print.

The Print dialog box appears.

4. Scroll through the Print Style list and click a style you want to use.
5. Click OK.

Outlook prints your contacts, including e-mail addresses.

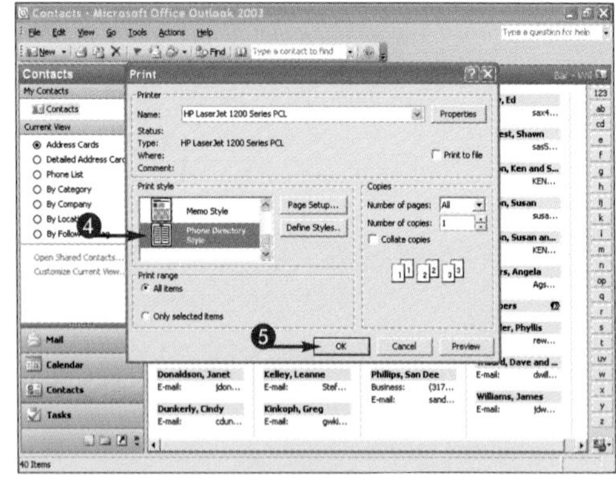

Print a Contact Address on an Envelope or Label

You can use the Outlook Contacts list to create envelopes and labels. With help from the Word Envelopes and Labels feature, you can quickly print out any name and address from your Outlook Address Book. You can leave Outlook open while you switch over to the Word window to access the Envelopes and Labels feature. The steps below focus on creating an envelope out of a contact using the Envelopes and Labels dialog box, however, you can also click the Labels tab and create a label just as easily.

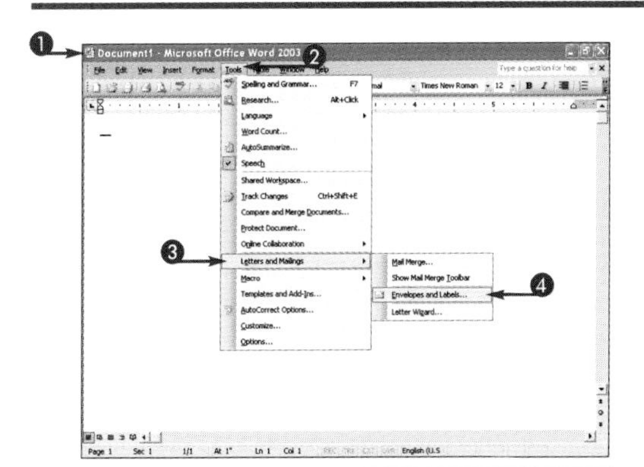

1. With Outlook still open, switch to the Word window.
2. Click Tools.
3. Click Letters and Mailings.
4. Click Envelopes and Labels.

   The Envelopes and Labels dialog box opens.

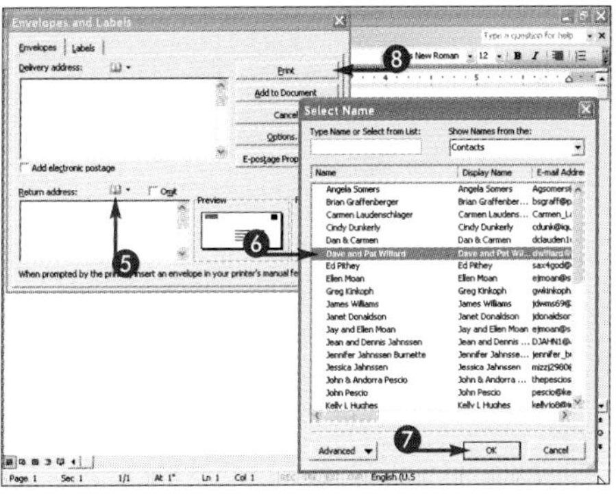

5. Click the Insert Address icon.

   The Select Name dialog box opens.
6. Click the contact you want to use.
7. Click OK.
8. Click Print.

   Outlook prints your contact addresses.

Display a Map to an Outlook Contact

You can use your Internet connection to quickly find a map to the address of any contact in the Outlook Contacts folder.

This feature only works if you have an Internet connection. When you activate this feature, your default Web browser window opens and connects you to the MSN Web site for looking up maps and addresses.

Using the Microsoft MapPoint Technology, you can look up an address anywhere in the United States.

❶ Double-click a contact in the Contacts list.

The contact information appears.

- If the contact has more than one address, you can click here and select an address to look up.

❷ Click Actions.

❸ Click Display Map of Address.

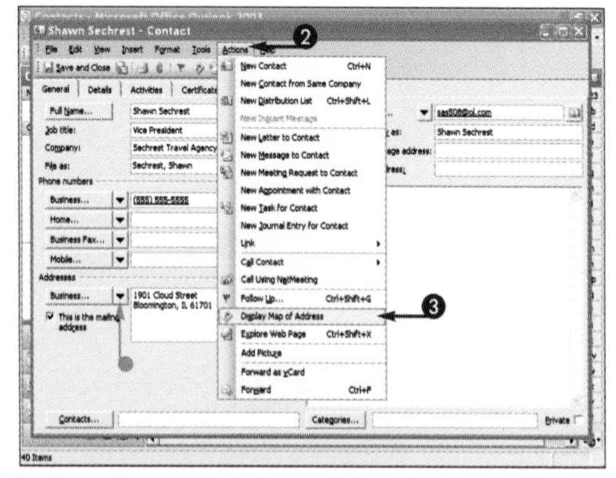

Note: *You may need to log on to your Internet connection before proceeding to step **3**.*

Your default Web browser opens and displays a map to the address.

- You can click your browser's Print button to print out a copy of the map.

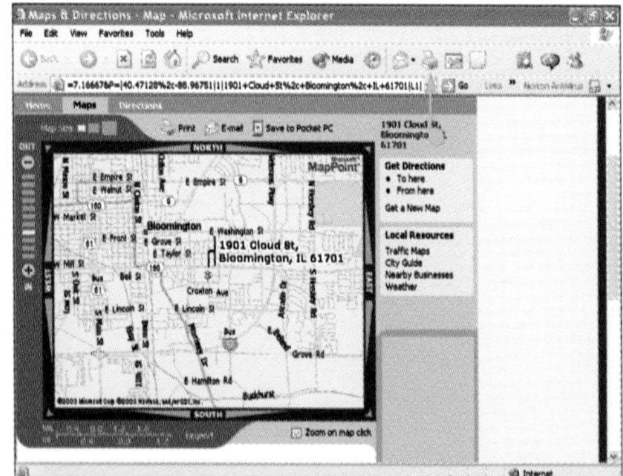

View a Calendar with Nonconsecutive Dates

Although the Outlook Calendar view shows consecutive dates by default, you may need to see several nonconsecutive days side by side. For example, you can compare your schedule with similar dates in previous months, or view all the days that you met with the same client. Viewing nonconsecutive dates allows you to access associated meeting summaries, attachments, and meeting attendees. Outlook can display up to 14 nonconsecutive days in your calendar.

This technique works best in Day view; in Work Week or Week view, Outlook displays the selected nonconsecutive date alongside the displayed week.

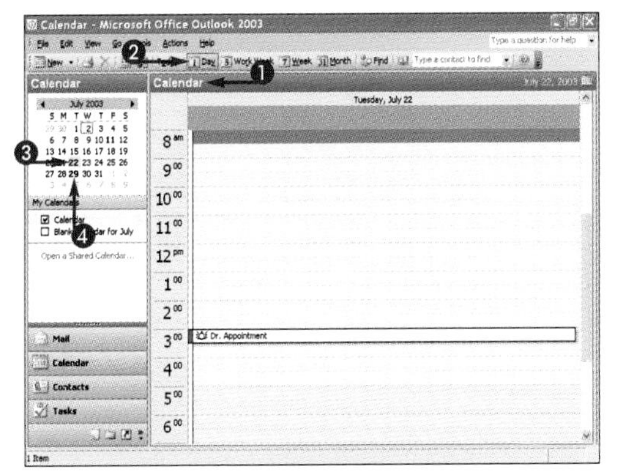

1. Switch to Calendar view.
2. Click the Day view button.
3. Click the first date you want to view.
4. Press and hold the Ctrl key and click the next nonconsecutive date you want to view.

Note: *If you accidentally click the wrong date while pressing the Ctrl key, you can click the same date again to deselect it.*

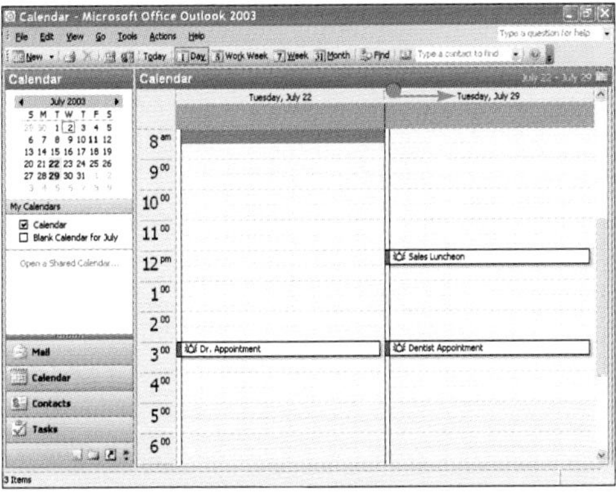

- Outlook displays the new date next to the first date you selected.

Repeat step **4** to select additional dates.

Note: *You can select up to 14 nonconsecutive dates to view in the calendar.*

Display Two Time Zones

You can tell Outlook to display two time zones in your calendar. This is particularly useful if your company works with offices across several states or around the globe.

When you add another time zone to your calendar, the hourly increments appear for both zones in the Day and Work Week calendar views. Adding another time zone to your calendar does not change the way your appointments and calendar notes appear. Office lists the hours for the extra time zone on the far left side of the calendar. You can also include a label for the newly added time zone so you can easily determine which zone is which. You can use a default label that describes the time zone, or you can create your own unique label for the zone.

1. Click Tools.
2. Click Options.

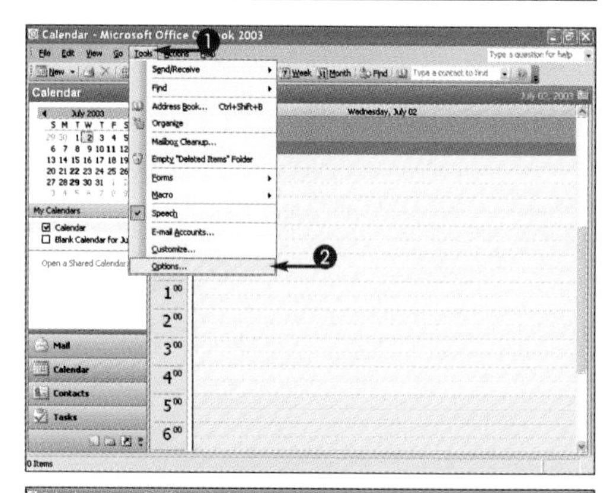

The Options dialog box appears.

3. Click the Preferences tab.
4. Click Calendar Options.

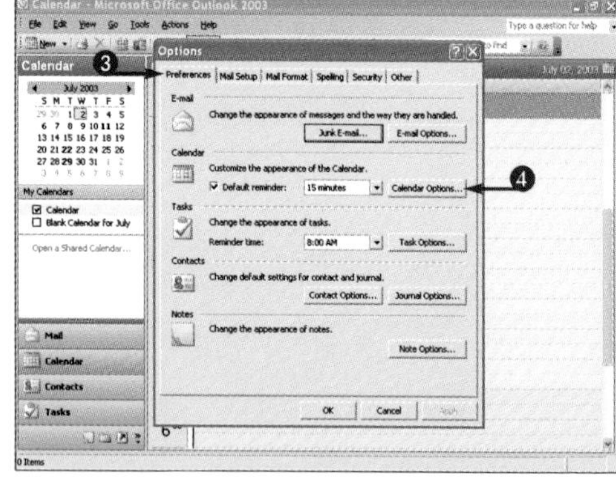

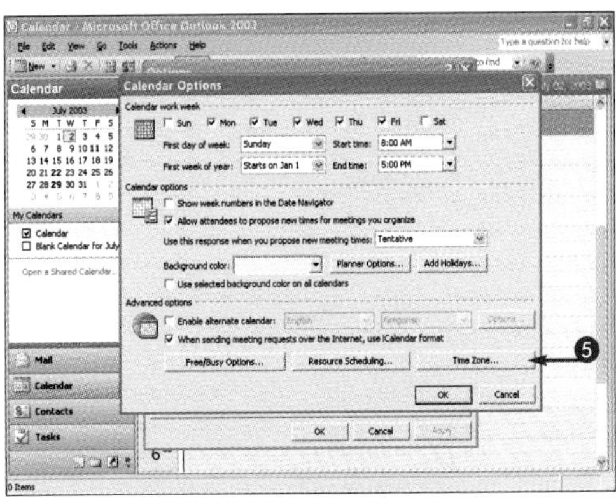

The Calendar Options dialog box opens.

5. Click Time Zone.

The Time Zone dialog box opens.

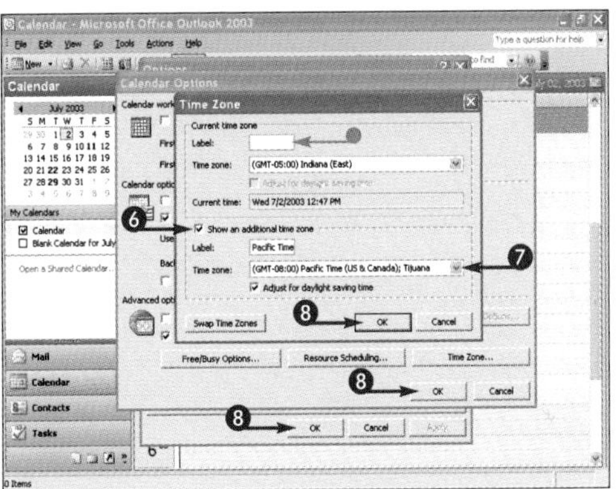

- You can type a brief label for the zone here.

6. Click the Show an additional time zone option.
7. Click here and select the time zone you want to include.
8. Click OK to close out of the Time Zone, Calendar Options, and Options dialog boxes.

Outlook displays two time zones in your calendar.

Did You Know?

To turn off the second time zone, follow the steps in this task, but deselect the Show an additional time zone option (☑ changes to ☐) in the Time Zone dialog box.

Chapter 6

Improve Your Database Productivity Using Access

Of all the Microsoft Office programs, Access has a well-deserved reputation for being the most challenging application to use. After all, building and maintaining a database is not a simple task. Access is a complex and powerful tool that allows you to organize and track many types of data. Because of the complexity of the application, the makers of Access have included a lot of useful wizards in the program to help users build individual components of a database. You should take advantage of these wizards whenever possible, as they can reduce the time it ordinarily takes to build database objects on your own.

Whether you are simply creating a database to track a home DVD collection, or using it to track purchases and orders for a corporation, this chapter offers you varied and unique techniques to make Access easier and more fun to use; some of the techniques even involve writing some simple programming code. For example, you can learn how to create your own splash screen that appears when you open your database file, open specific records automatically, add visual interest to forms by adding background pictures, and more. When it comes to customizing your database objects, Design View is the way to go. With Design View, you can quickly access various tools for controlling how an object looks and behaves. With the help of these tasks, you can find a few new ways to become more productive without needing to become a database professional.

Quick Tips

Personalize a Database with a Custom Splash Screen

You can create a custom splash screen that appears every time you open your Access database. Splash screens appear for just a moment as the database file opens. By default, a Microsoft Access splash screen appears when you start Access. The default splash screen displays the name of the program, the version number, product ID number, and copyright information.

You can create a custom splash screen that includes your name, your company name and logo, or a slogan. You can use a graphic file saved in the bitmap file format to create your own splash screen.

To see the custom splash screen, you must open the database file directly from the My Computer or My Documents folder, or from the desktop.

1. Open the Save As dialog box in the program in which you have created the splash screen image.

   This example uses the Windows Paint program.

2. Assign the bitmap object the same name, and to the same location, as the Access database file.
3. Click Save.
4. Close the program window.
5. Double-click the My Documents icon.

   The My Documents window appears.

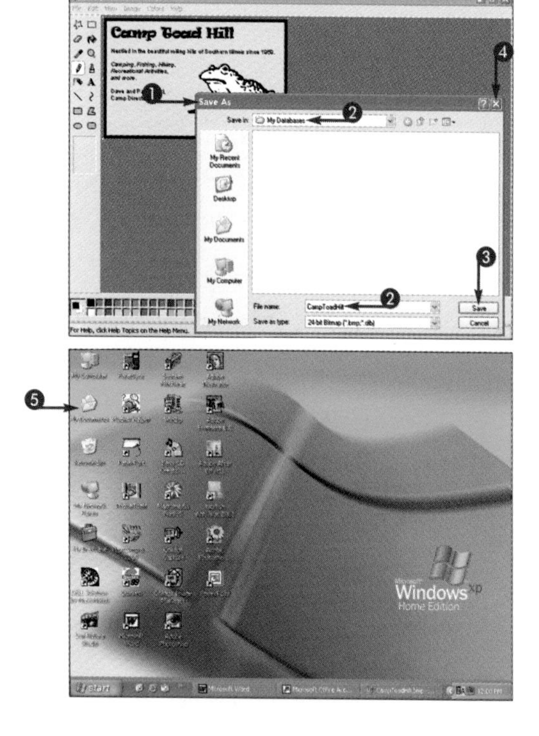

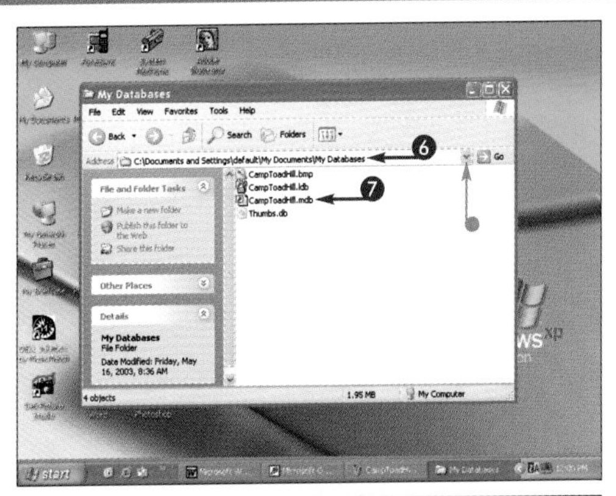

6. Open the folder containing your Access database file.
- You can click here to navigate to the drive and folder that contain the database and bitmap file.

7. Double-click the database filename.

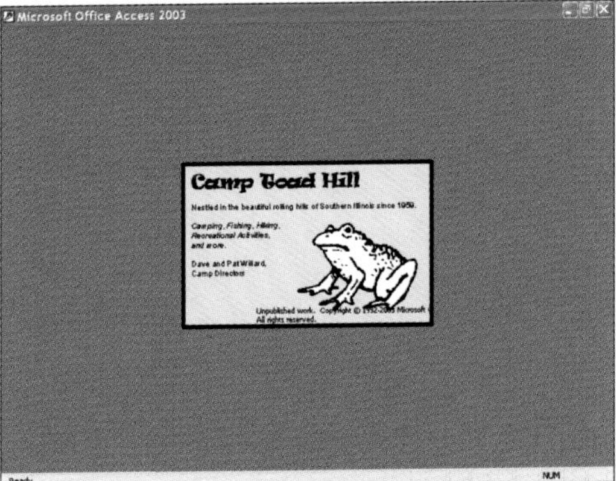

The Access program window opens and briefly displays your custom splash screen.

Did You Know?

If you have trouble finding your Access database file, consider storing it in a separate folder in the My Documents window. You must save database files with the .mdb file extension, as in MyDatabase.mdb.

Add Commonly Used Buttons to the Toolbox

When you switch to Design View in forms, reports or pages, the Toolbox appears. The Toolbox is a specialized toolbar for setting design controls for tables, forms, and reports. You can add buttons to the Toolbox for tasks you perform most often in Design View.

As a floating toolbar, you can move the toolbar by dragging the title bar to a new location on the screen, or resize it by dragging any edge of the toolbar. If you close the Toolbox toolbar, you can open it again by clicking the Toolbox button on the Database toolbar at the top of the program window.

1. Switch to Design View.

***Note:** Click the View button and then click Design View to open any object in Design View.*

2. Click here on the Toolbox title bar.
3. Click Add or Remove Buttons.
4. Click Customize.

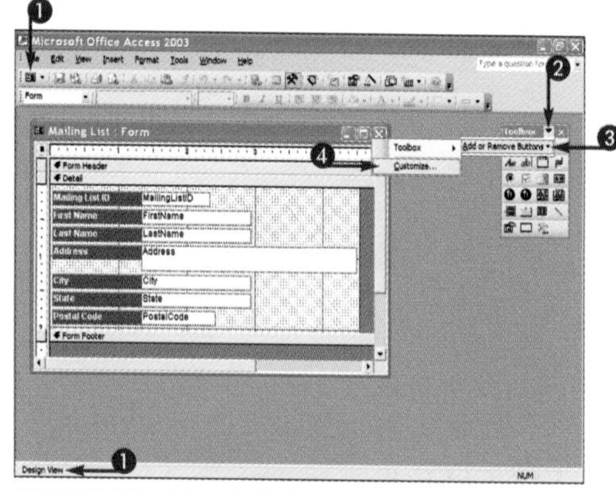

The Customize dialog box appears.

5. Select a command category.
   - This example selects the View category.
6. Select a command you want to add to the Toolbox toolbar.

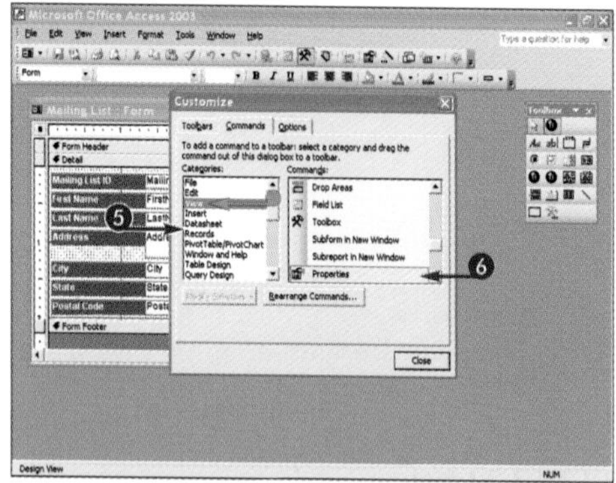

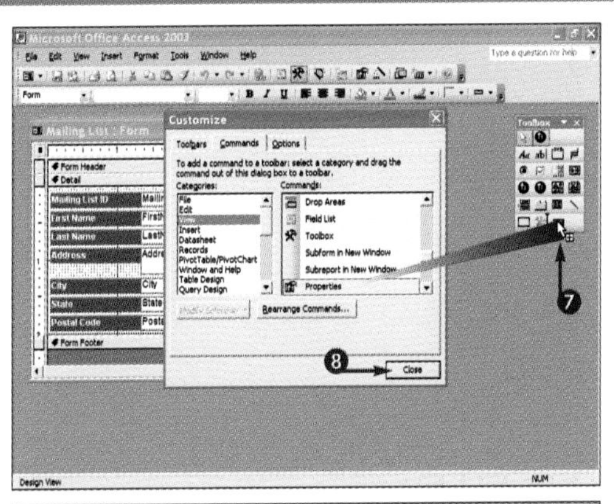

7. Click and drag the command from the Customize dialog box, and dropping it where you want it to appear on the toolbar.

   Access adds the button to the toolbar.

   This example adds the Properties button.

8. Click Close.

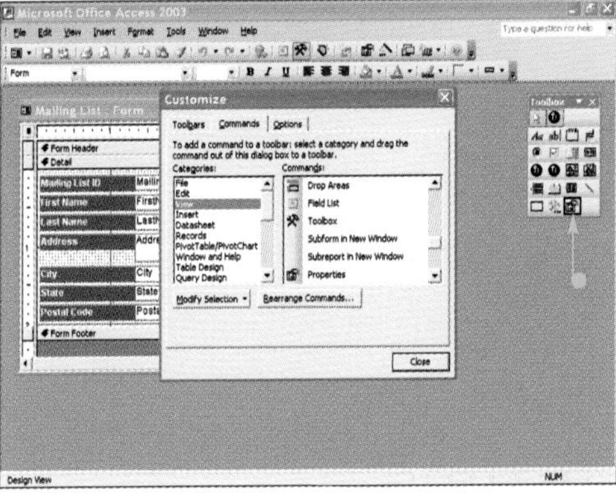

- You can now activate the command with a click of the toolbar button.

Apply It!

To remove a Toolbox toolbar button you no longer need, press and hold the Alt key while dragging the button off of the toolbar.

Open Access Objects with Disposable Toolbar Buttons

If you find yourself constantly switching back and forth between the same database objects in the Database window, you can use a shortcut technique to quickly open each object. This technique is particularly helpful for opening database objects that are not all the same type.

You cannot create buttons for module objects, but you can create them for all of the other database object types. You must remember to remove the buttons when you finish working on the database. Otherwise, you may end up creating confusion for yourself or other users when they open different database files in the Access program window.

CREATE A DISPOSABLE BUTTON

1. Display the object category for which you want to create a button.
2. Select the object.
3. Drag the object to the end of the Standard toolbar.

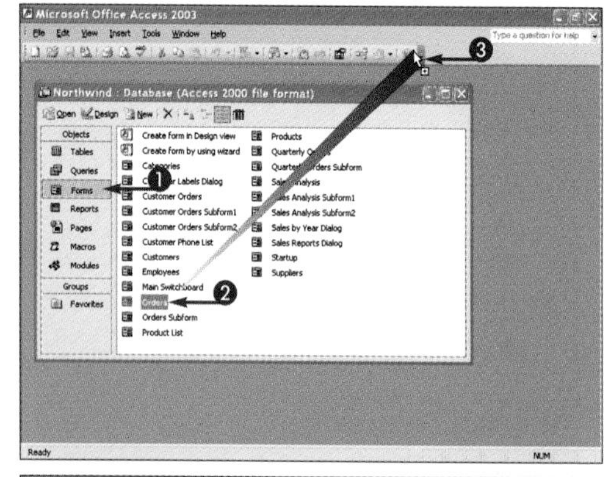

Access creates a button for the object.

4. Click the button to open the object.

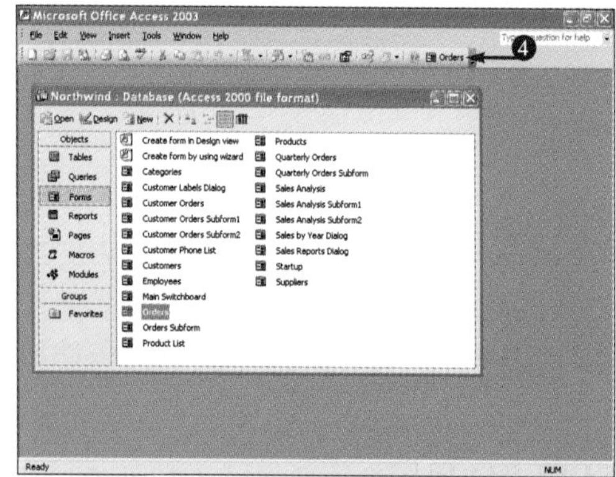

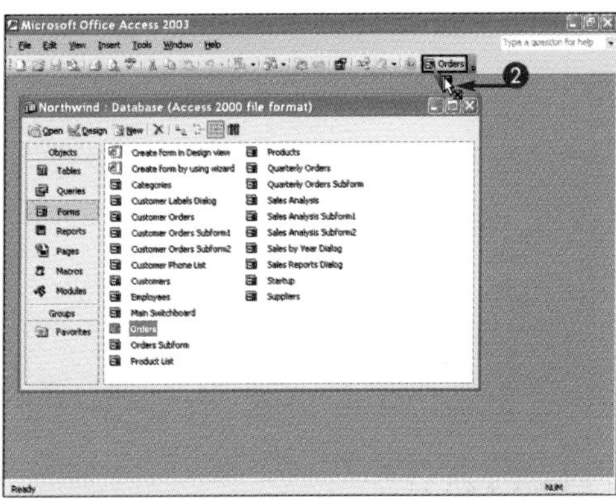

REMOVE A DISPOSABLE BUTTON

1. Press and hold the Alt key.
2. Drag the button off the toolbar.

- Access removes the button.

Did You Know?

You can create customized toolbars for all of the Microsoft Office programs. To learn more, see the task "Create a Customized Toolbar."

Make a Database Window Work Like a Web Browser

By default, the Database window in Access works like the My Computer or Explorer window. Objects appear as icons in the window, and to open an object, you simply double-click it. You can make your Database window work more like a Web browser by changing the way in which the objects appear. Rather than viewing objects as icons, you can turn them into links that, when clicked, open the object. You may find this environment faster and more intuitive to work with if you frequently use both your Web browser and your Access databases.

1. Click Tools.
2. Click Options.

The Options dialog box appears.

3. Click the View tab.
4. Click the Single-click open option.
5. Click OK.

- Database window objects now appear as links.

  Move your mouse pointer over a link to select it, and click to open it.

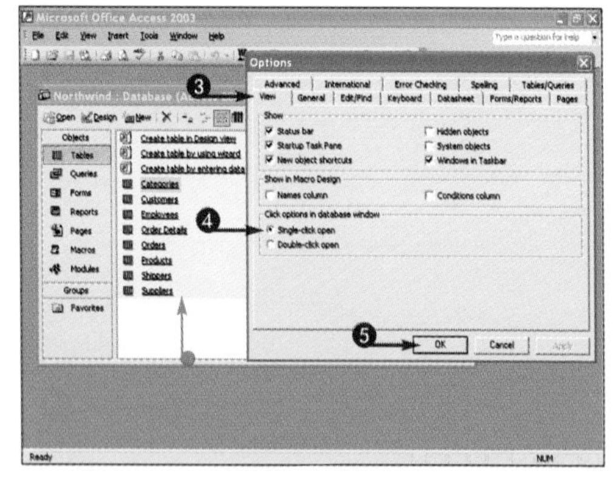

Zoom Entries for Easy Editing

Databases often contain vast amounts of data, but to display all of the data, the entry fields are often small and limited in space. You can edit your entries directly. However, you often cannot see the entire entry, or the text size for the entry appears too small to view comfortably.

You can use the Zoom dialog box to increase the magnification of an entry to more easily view and edit your field, text box, or property settings. After you make your edits and close the dialog box, the changes to the field, text box, or property setting immediately take effect.

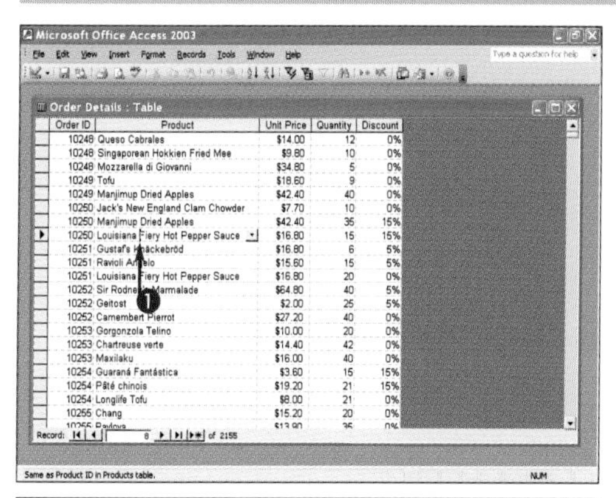

1. Click in the field, text box, or property setting you want to view.
2. Press Shift+F2.

The Zoom dialog box appears.

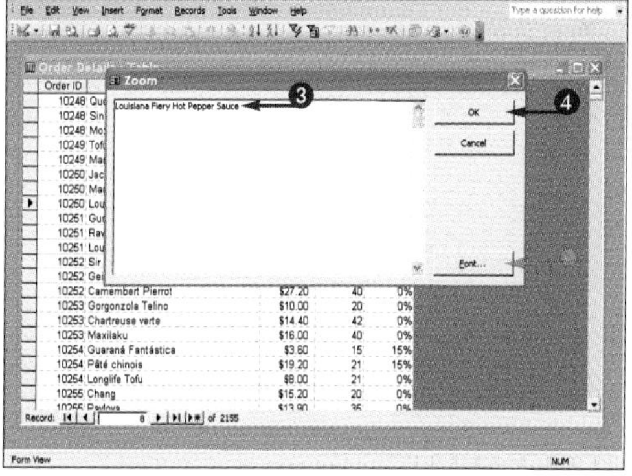

3. Make any edits you want to the entry.

- To change the font to a more legible size, click the Font button to open the Font dialog box and change the settings.

4. Click OK.

The Zoom dialog box closes.

Automatically Open a Form at Startup

If you frequently work with the same database in Access, you can instruct the program to automatically open the form you use most often.

You can specify a startup form in the Startup dialog box. The Startup dialog box is unique to Access and includes several options for controlling how a database behaves when you open it. Any options you select in the Startup dialog box apply only to the current database.

1. Click Tools.
2. Click Startup.

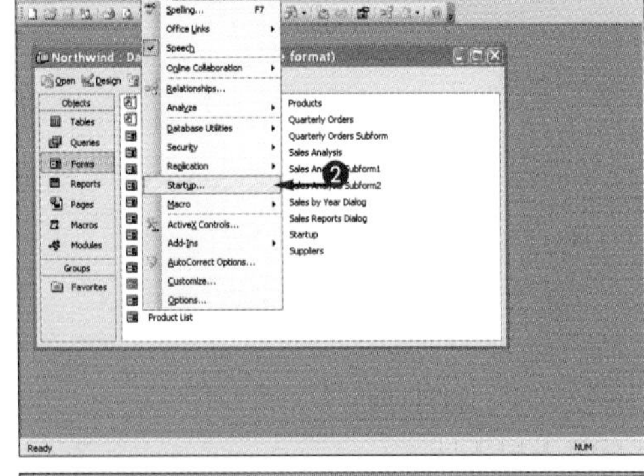

The Startup dialog box appears.

3. Click here and click the name of the form you want to open.
4. Click OK.

The next time you open the database file, the form you specify opens automatically.

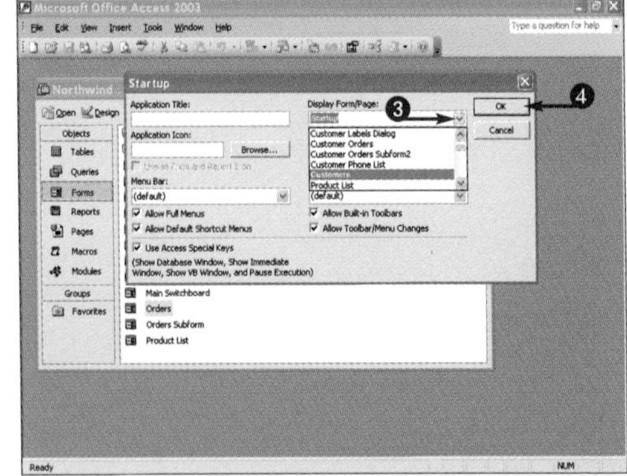

Change a Form's Tab Order

Most users press the Tab key to move from one field to the next in an Access form. You can control the direction in which the Tab key takes the user by specifying a tab order. By default, Access sets the tab order from left to right and from top to bottom.

To change the tab order, you must view the form in Design View. You can use the Tab Order dialog box to reorder the fields for tabbing. To return a custom tab order back into the left-to-right and top-to-bottom order, you can click the Auto Order button.

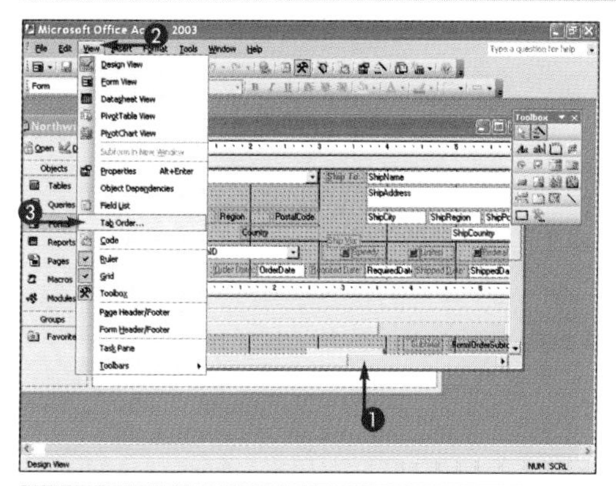

1. Open the form in Design View.

***Note:** Click the View button and then click Design View to open any object in Design View.*

2. Click View.
3. Click Tab Order.

***Note:** The Tab Order command is only available in Design View.*

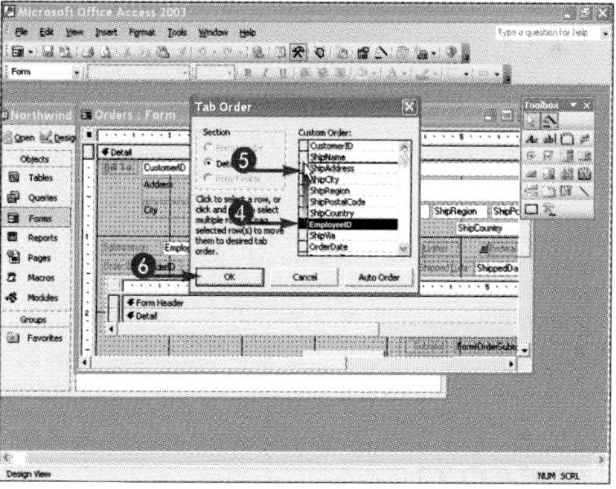

The Tab Order dialog box appears.

4. Click the field you want to change in the Custom Order list.
5. Drag the field up or down in the list.
6. Repeat steps **4** and **5** to reorder any other fields you want.
7. Click OK.

Access assigns the new tab order to the form.

Make a Form Interesting by Adding a Picture

Forms offer an easy way to enter data into your table, but are not very interesting on their own. If other people use your database, you may want to add an image or graphic to make your form more visually appealing.

You can add pictures to your Access forms using Design View. Design View lets you resize the form to accommodate a picture or graphic object. Using the Image tool, you can determine the size and the placement of the image that you want to appear on the form. After defining the picture parameters, you can select the file you want to insert.

1. Open the form to which you want to add a graphic in Design View.

***Note:** Click the View button and then click Design View to open any object in Design View.*

2. Click and drag a corner or edge of the form to make room for the graphic object.

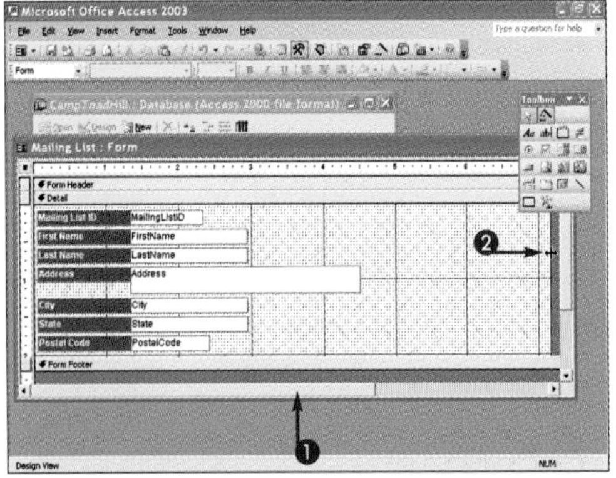

3. Click the Image button on the Toolbox toolbar.

***Note:** If the Toolbox is not open, click View, and then click Toolbox.*

4. Click and drag on the form to create a placeholder for the graphic object.

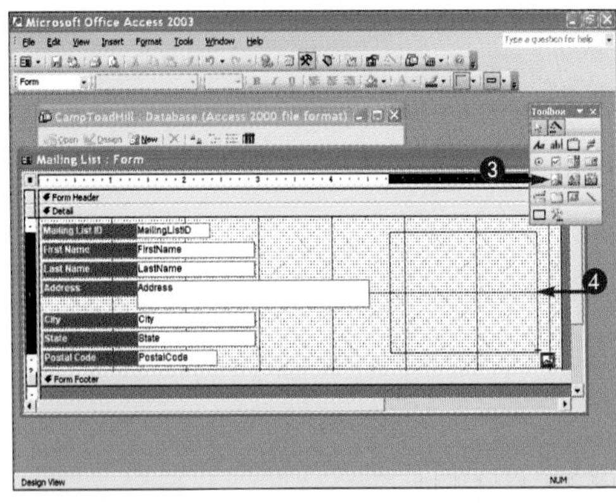

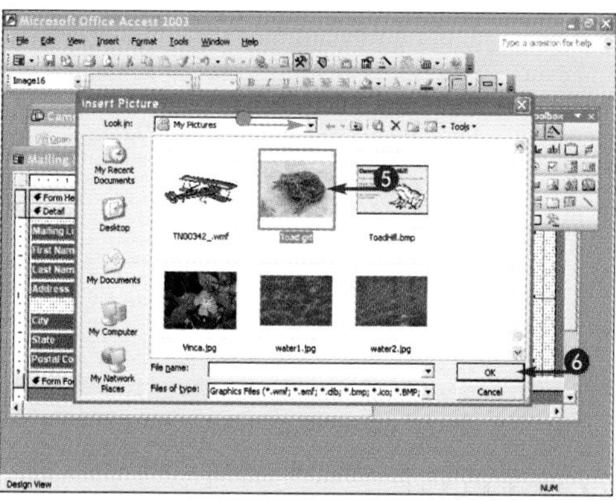

The Insert Picture dialog box appears.

5. Click the image file you want to insert.

- You can click here to navigate to the folder or drive containing the graphic.

6. Click OK.

Note: *If you are adding a picture to a data access page, you click Insert instead of OK.*

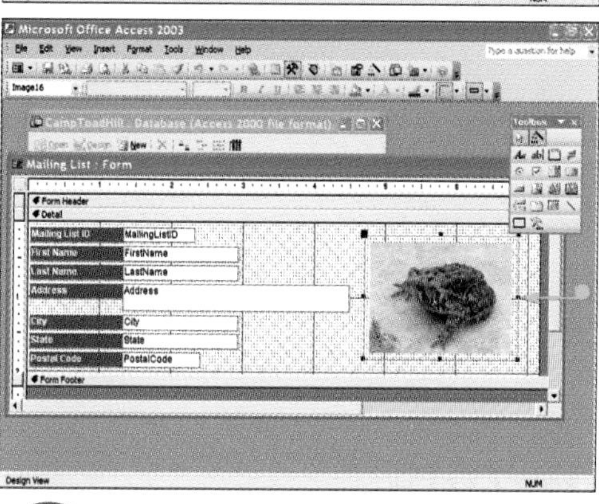

- The image appears on the form.

When you switch to Form View, you may need to resize the Form window to see the image that you add.

Did You Know?

You can apply formatting to an image object. Select the image in Design View and right-click over the image. A shortcut menu appears with formatting controls, including commands for changing the fill or background color, and adding a stylized effect. For more image-formatting options, you can open the image's properties sheet, or you can open the Properties dialog box by right clicking over the image and then clicking Properties.

Automatically Open a Specific Record

You can instruct Access to open a specific record in a form automatically when you open the form. By default, Access displays the first record in the underlying record set when you open a form.

You can use the `GoToRecord` VBA method in the form's `Open` event to open a specific record the next time you open the form. To use this technique, you must type some code in the control object's `On Open` event. You can enter VBA code using the Code Builder window. When entering the code, you must substitute the name of your own form and make sure you know which record number you want to display automatically.

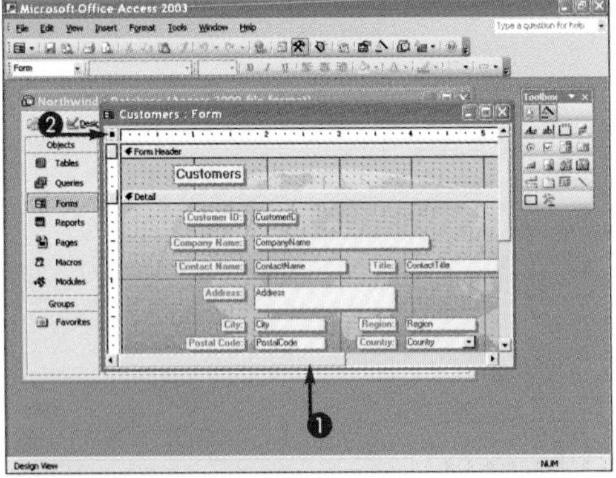

1. Open the form you want to edit in Design View.

***Note:** Click the View button and then click Design View to open any object in Design View.*

2. Double-click the selector box for the form.

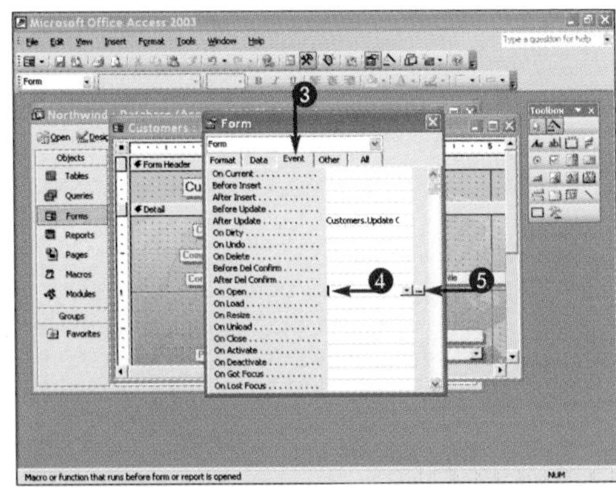

The properties sheet appears for the object.

3. Click the Event tab.
4. Click the `On Open` event field.
5. Click the Build button.

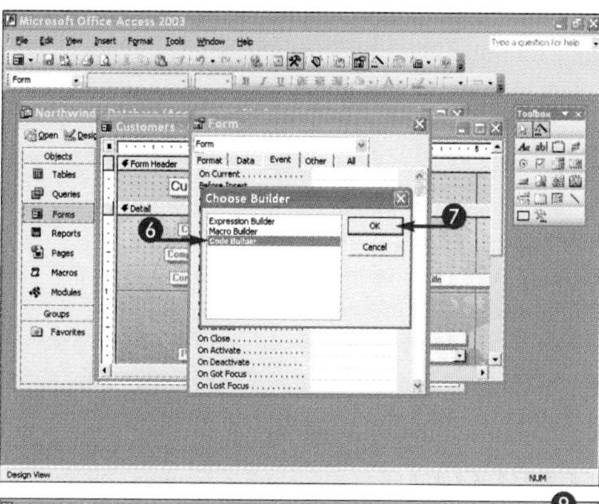

The Choose Builder dialog box appears.

6. Click Code Builder.
7. Click OK.

The Visual Basic window appears.

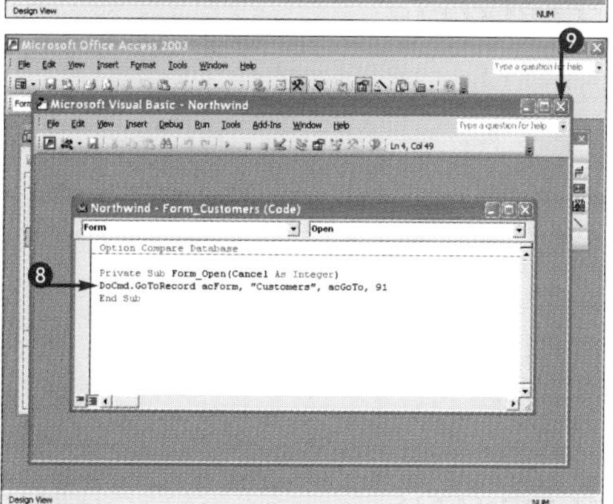

8. Type the code **DoCmd.GoToRecord acForm, "?", acGoTo, #**, replacing ? with your own form name, and **#** with the number of the record you want to display.
9. Click the Visual Basic window's Close button.
10. Close the form and save your changes.

You can now test your code by reopening the form in Form View.

Did You Know?

If you make a mistake with your VBA code, Access cannot display the record automatically. Instead, a prompt window appears, warning you of the error. Click Debug to reopen the Code Builder window, and examine your code for errors. In most instances, errors result from mistyping the code or specifying the wrong form name. After making your corrections, close the code window, save your changes, and try opening it again.

Set Up Forms to Close Automatically

You can have a frequently used form automatically close after a specific amount of time. To set an automatic close, switch to the Design View mode for your form and make changes to the form's properties sheet. You set a time interval using the `Timer Interval` property in the form's properties. The value for seconds is measured in thousands, so an entry of 3,000 equals 3 seconds.

After establishing a time value, you must add a string of VBA code into the `On Timer` property, using the Visual Basic code window. After adding the code string, you can return to the form's Design View and save the form.

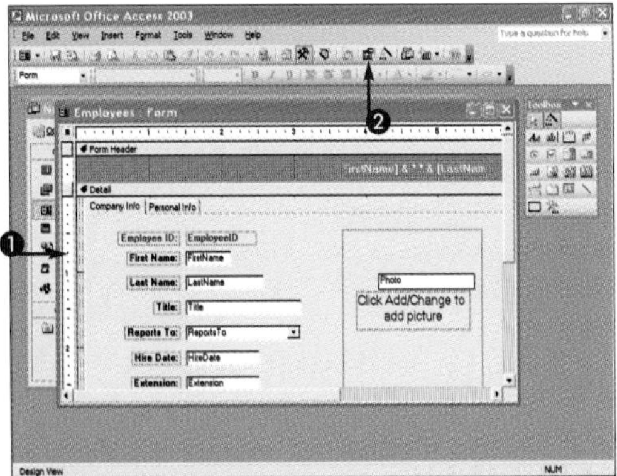

1. Open the form in Design View.

   Note: *Click the View button and then click Design View to open any object in Design View.*

2. Click the Properties button.

   The form's properties sheet appears.

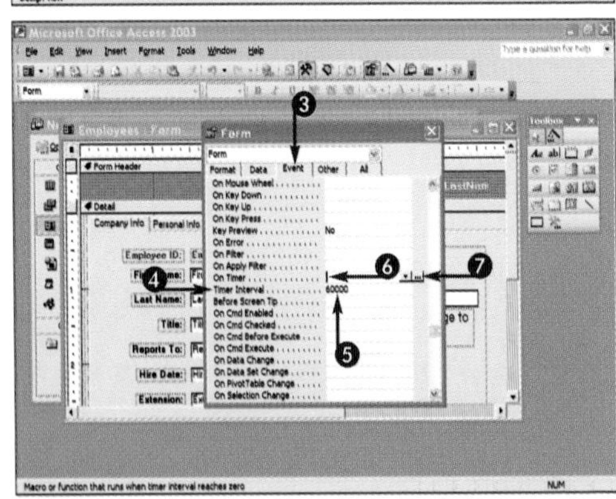

3. Click the Event tab.
4. Scroll down the property list and click `Timer Interval` property.
5. Set the number of seconds you want to leave the form open.

   In this example, the value 60000 leaves the form open for 60 seconds.

6. Click the `On Timer` property.
7. Click the Builder button.

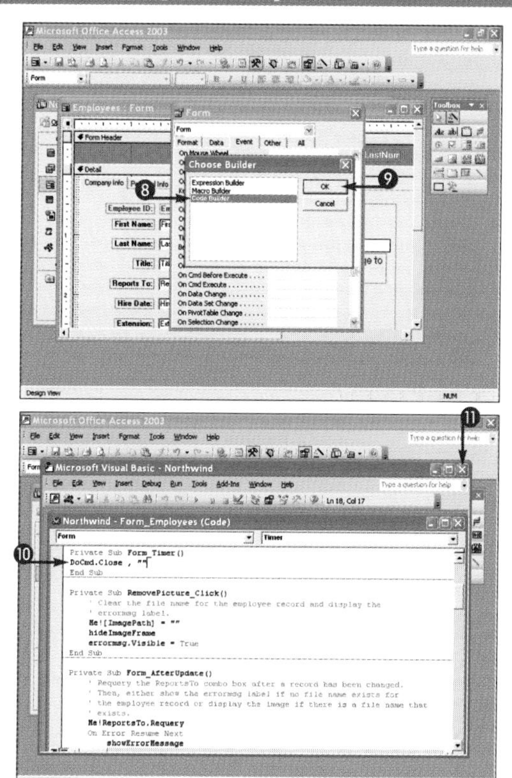

The Choose Builder dialog box appears.

8. Click Code Builder.
9. Click OK.

The Visual Basic window appears.

10. Type **DoCmd.Close,""**.
11. Click the Visual Basic window's Close button.
12. Close the form and save your changes.

You can reopen the form in Form View to test the timer.

Apply It!

To remove a timer interval you assign to a form, reopen the form in Design View and display the form's properties sheet. Click the Event tab and clear the `On Timer` and `Timer Interval` properties.

Add Ampersands to Caption Labels

If you try to type an ampersand character (&) in a caption label property of a control, Access displays another character in the label instead. For example, if you type the name **Electric Power & Light**, Access displays the name as Electric Power_Light. Access interprets the ampersand as a shortcut method to selecting the control. To remedy this problem, you must specify two ampersands in the label instead of one.

1. Open the form you want to edit in Design View.

Note: *Click the View button and then click Design View to open any object in Design View.*

2. Click the Label button on the Toolbox.

   Draw the label box on the form.

4. Type the label text, using two ampersand symbols instead of one.

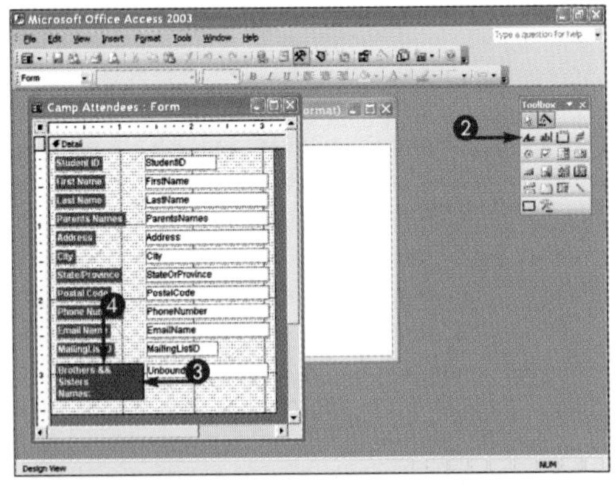

5. Click anywhere outside the label box.

- Access displays a single ampersand in the caption label.

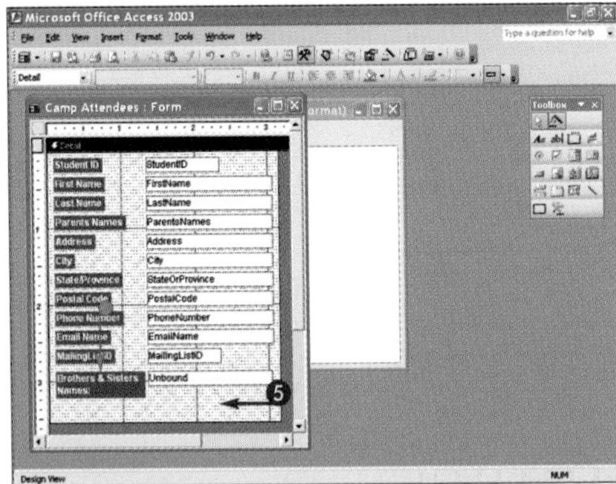

Save Time with Default Table Values

When you build a table in Microsoft Access, you can have some field values display default values to make the table more convenient to use. You can specify a value that appears in the field by default, until the user changes it to another value. For example, perhaps you have an order-processing table that includes a field for specifying delivery type. Delivery type choices may include Standard Post, Express, or Next Day. If the majority of the time the delivery type is Standard Post, you can make Standard Post the default value that appears in the field automatically.

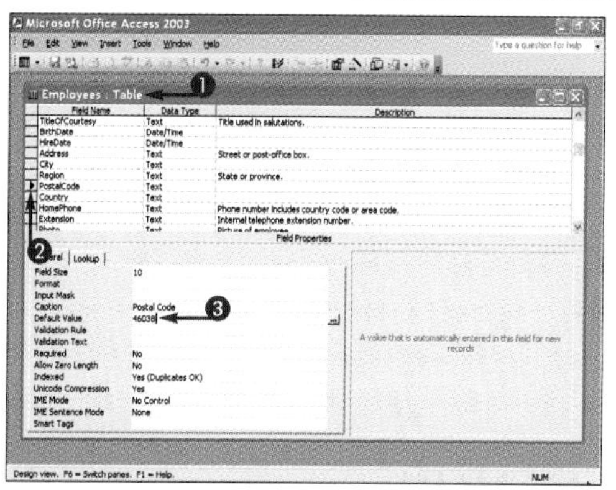

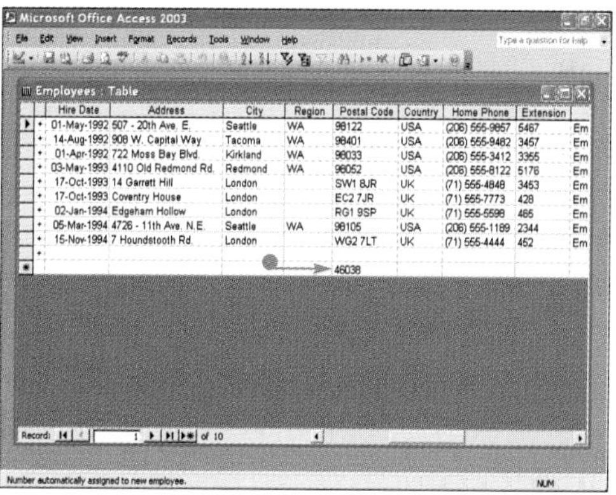

1. Open the table in Design View.

Note: *Click the View button and then click Design View to open any object in Design View.*

2. Click the field you want to edit.

3. Type a default value in the Default Value property field.

   Access applies the new value to any new records you create.

- When you save and close the table, Access applies the new default value to any new records you add in Datasheet view.

Hide Existing Records in a Table

The more records you enter in a table, the longer the table becomes. If you want to enter table data in Datasheet View rather than in a form, you can hide the existing records to keep them out of the way as you type new records. Hiding the existing records allows you to concentrate on the blank record on which you are working. Any new records that you add after hiding the existing records remain visible in the datasheet.

1. Open the table to which you want to add records in Datasheet View.
2. Click Records.
3. Click Data Entry.

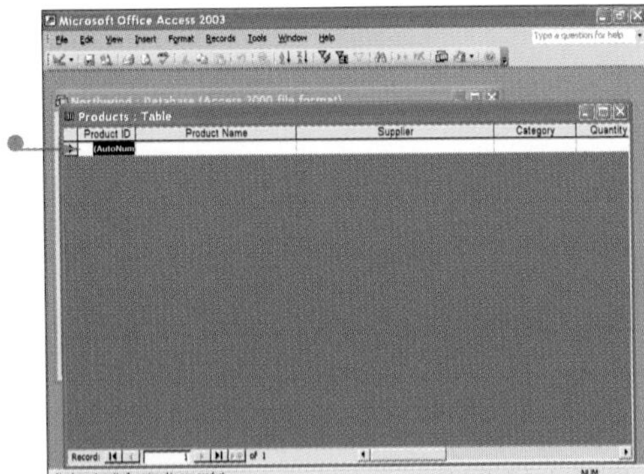

- Access immediately hides all the records, leaving only the blank record onscreen.

Copy a Previous Record into a New Record

If you are repeatedly entering the same value in the same field in a table or form, you can use a shortcut technique to copy the value of the previous record. Rather than retype it, you can press a keyboard shortcut instead. This can reduce the time you spend entering records into tables or forms.

To make the best use of this shortcut technique, you can type your record data in table form using Datasheet View. This allows you to see the values that you typed into the same field for a previous record.

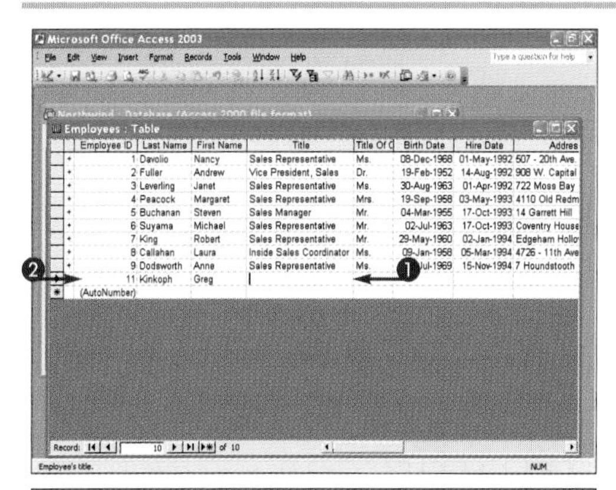

1. Open or start a blank record.
2. Click the field in which you want to copy a value.
3. Press Ctrl+'

- Access immediately copies the value from the previous field.

Print a Table Relationships Map

Understanding the relationships between tables is an important part of building a successful database. Good database designers always evaluate the relationships between database tables.

Ordinarily, you can view table relationships using the Relationships window. To help you analyze the connections between tables, you can print out a copy of the map of table relationships.

When you activate the Print Relationships command, Access automatically generates a report of the table relationships and switches you to Print Layout view. You can use this view mode to see the map layout and to activate the Print command.

1. Click Tools.
2. Click Relationships.

The Relationships Print Layout view.

3. Click File.
4. Click Print Relationships.

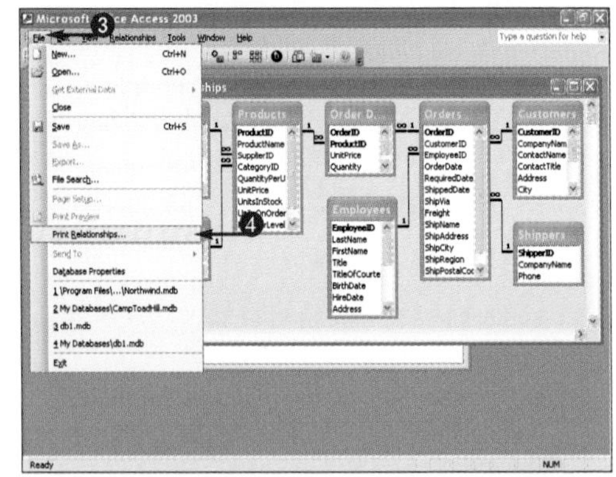

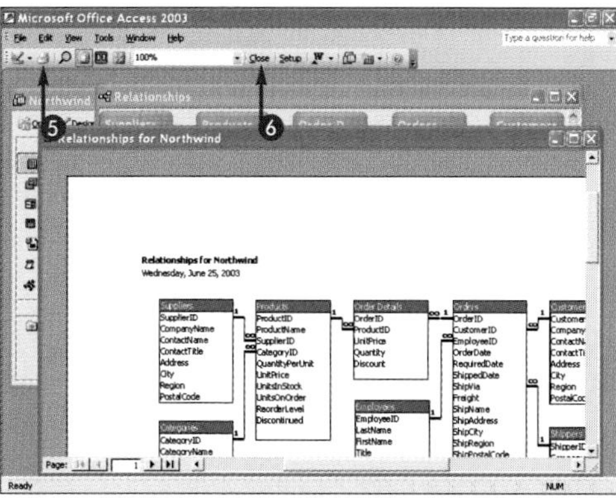

Access creates a report of the table relationships and opens the report in Print Preview mode.

5. Click the Print button.
6. Click Close.

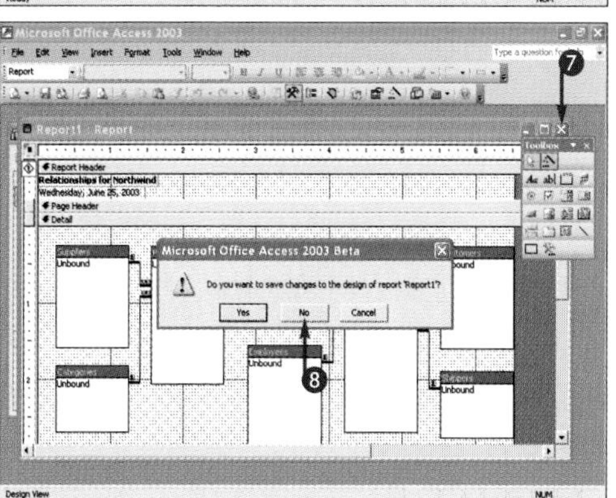

7. Click the Report window's Close button to close the report.

   A prompt window appears, asking whether you want to save the report.

8. Click No to exit the report window without saving the report.

Did You Know?

Both Print Layout and Layout Preview view modes let you see how your report looks when you print it. However, Layout Preview mode does not first load any underlying queries, using sample data from your report instead. To learn more about Layout Preview mode, see the task "Using Layout Preview to Quickly View a Report Layout."

Using the Database Window to Append Records

Ordinarily, you use queries to append or make changes to data in your database. An *append query* lets you copy records from one table to the end of another table, thus avoiding the duplication of pre-existing records.

The Paste Table As dialog box offers three choices for the data to copy. To append data, you type the name of the table to which you are appending data, and then activate the Append Data To Existing Table option. To paste the table structure without the table contents, you select the Structure Only option. To paste the structure and the data, you activate the Structure & Data option.

1. Right-click the table that contains the records that you want to copy to another table.
2. Click Copy.

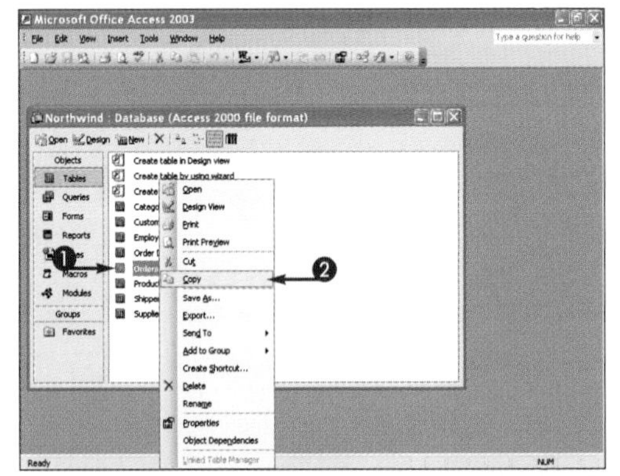

3. Right-click an empty background area of the Database window.
4. Click Paste.
5. In the Paste Table As dialog box that appears, type the name of the table to which you want to append data.
6. Click the Append Data to Existing Table option.
7. Click OK.

   Access appends the records.

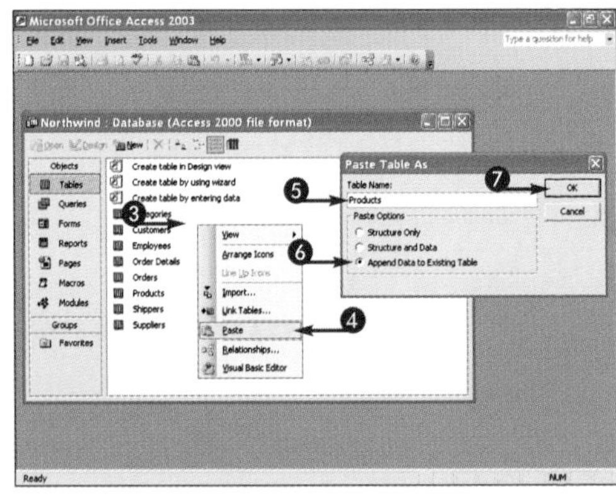

Optimize Performance by Reducing Detabase Size

To keep your database file running efficiently, you can compact the database. Compacting is a periodic maintenance task that allows you to recover wasted disk space.

You can use the Compact feature to reclaim space left by deleted records and data. If you work every day with a database, it is a good idea to compact it at least once a week to keep the database file running efficiently.

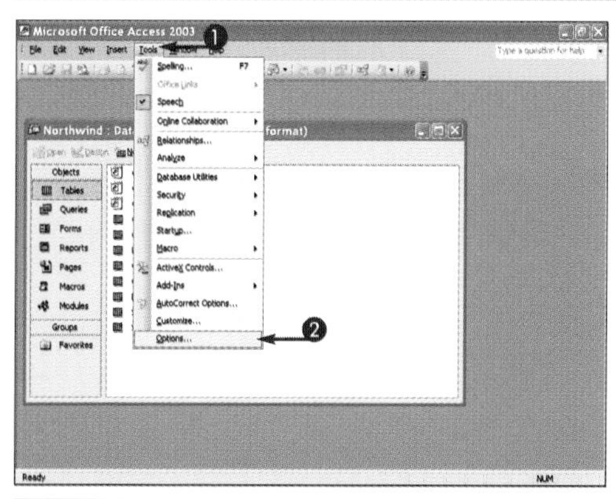

1. Click Tools.
2. Click Options.

The Options dialog box appears.

3. Click the General tab.
4. Click the Compact on Close option.
5. Click OK.

When you close the file, Access compacts the database.

Using Input Masks to Control Users' Table Data Entry

You can use input masks, also called field templates, to control how users enter data into a table field.

Input masks can control separator characters for entries. Input masks can also control which characters are mandatory or optional for the entry.

You can use the Input Mask Wizard to define an input mask for a table entry.

Using the Input Mask Wizard is much easier than entering the input mask expression. The Input Mask Wizard includes a list of pre-defined masks for common database fields. You can also revise any of the pre-defined masks to customize them for your own table data entries.

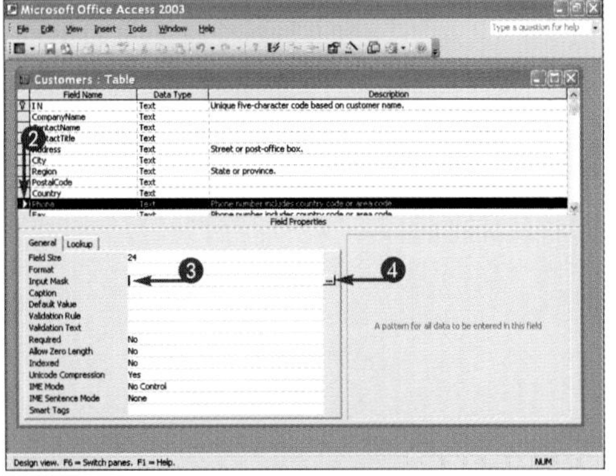

1. Open the table in Design View.

***Note:** Click the View button and then click Design View to open any object in Design View.*

2. Click the field you want to edit.
3. Click the Input Mask field property.
4. Click the Build button.

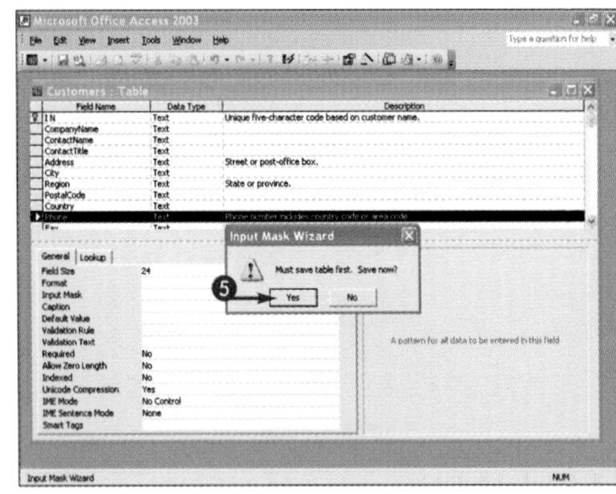

An Input Mask Wizard prompt window appears, asking you to save the table.

5. Click Yes.

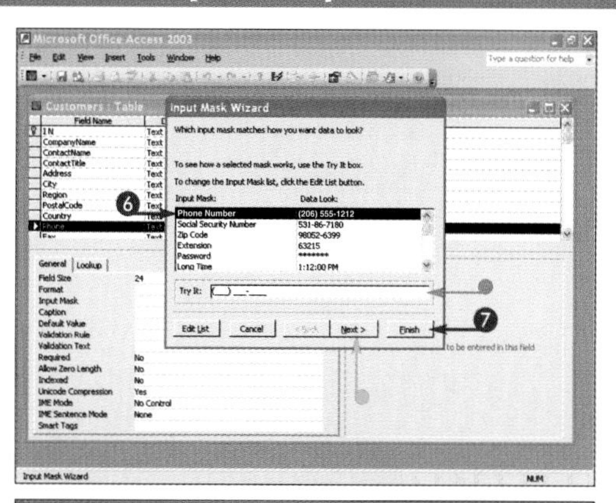

The Input Mask Wizard dialog box appears.

6. Click the input mask you want to assign.

- Click inside the Try It field if you want to test the data entry.
- To further define the input mask, you can click Next and continue with the Input Mask Wizard process.

7. Click Finish.

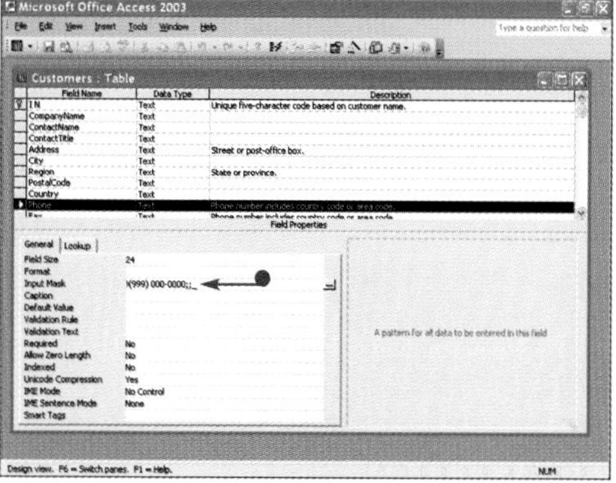

- Access assigns the Input Mask field property.

Any future values that you type must meet the criteria you define.

Did You Know?

You can click the Edit List button in the Input Mask Wizard dialog box to make edits to the pre-defined input masks.

Using Layout Preview to Quickly View a Report Layout

Because of the popularity of the Print Preview function among the Microsoft Office programs, many users automatically use the Print Preview feature to see how an Access document looks before they print it out.

The Layout Preview feature uses a sample of the data to give you an idea of what the report looks like when you print it out. The Layout Preview mode automatically ignores any underlying queries, and can also ignore parameter values if you want.

Layout Preview mode displays the same toolbar buttons as Print Preview mode, including buttons for viewing multiple pages and changing your view magnification.

1. Open a report that you want to view in Design View.

Note: *Click the View button and then click Design View to open any object in Design View.*

2. Click View.
3. Click Layout Preview.

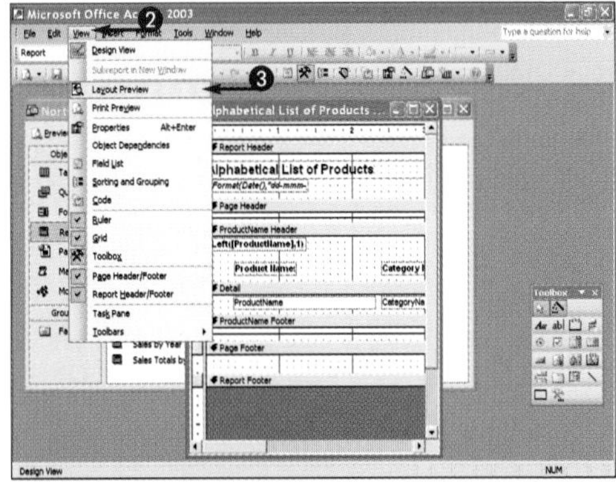

Access displays the report in Layout Preview mode.

- You can click here to zoom in for a closer look.
- Click the Close button to exit Layout Preview mode.

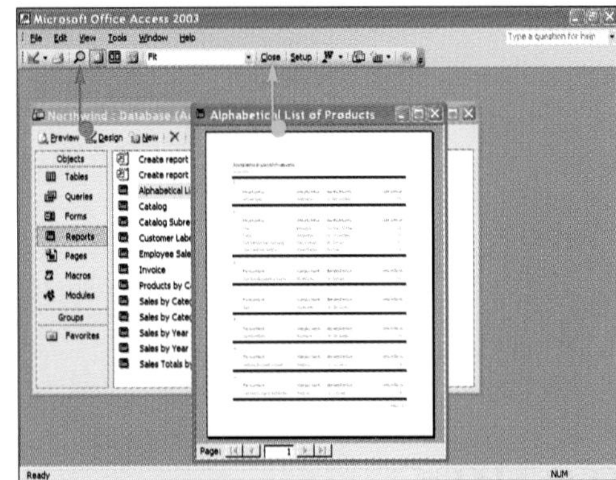

View a Query or Report in Word or Excel

When most users export data from Access to view in another Microsoft Office program, they commonly export the data using the Export command on the File menu. This procedure involves opening the Export dialog box, specifying a folder to which you want to export the data, and activating the Export command. To view the query or report, you must then open the program to which you export the data.

You can copy data more quickly and easily to Microsoft Word or Excel using the Office Links commands.

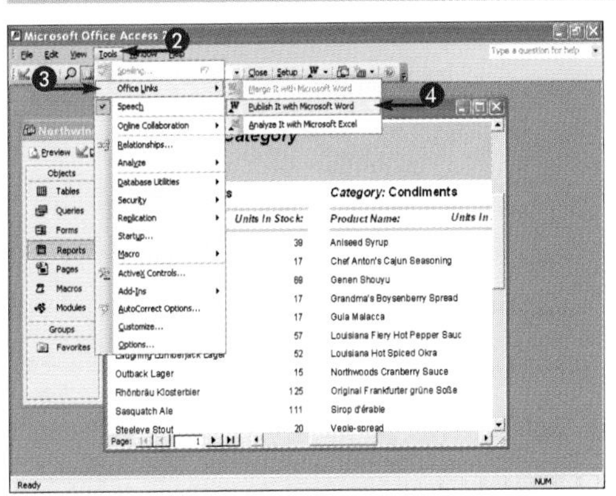

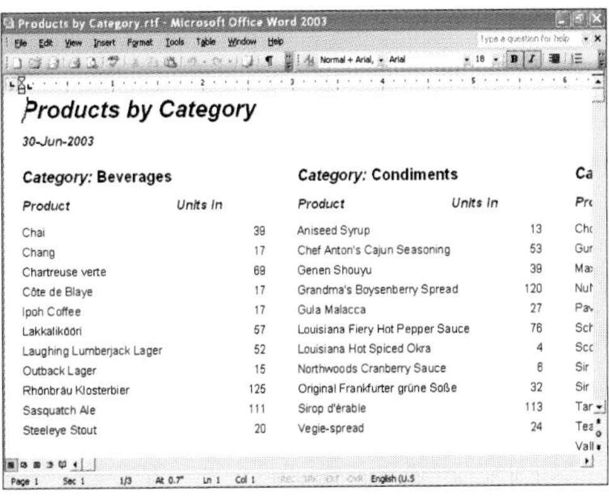

1. Open the query or report you want to view.
2. Click Tools.
3. Click Office Links.
4. Click a program.

   Select Publish It with Microsoft Word to view the query or report in Word.

   Select Analyze It with Microsoft Excel to view the query or report in Excel.

- Access copies the query or report and opens the window of the program you specify.

  This example views the report in Word.

Convert Forms and Reports into Web Pages

With more recent versions of Access, including Access 11, you can select any form or report in the Database window and quickly convert it into a data access page for posting on the Web.

Using this shortcut technique, you can open the Save As dialog box and specify how you want to save the form or report, after which you can use the New Data Access Page dialog box to save the page to a specific folder. After saving the page, Access opens it as a data access page.

1. Select the form or report you want to convert into a Web page in the Database window.
2. Click File.
3. Click Save As.

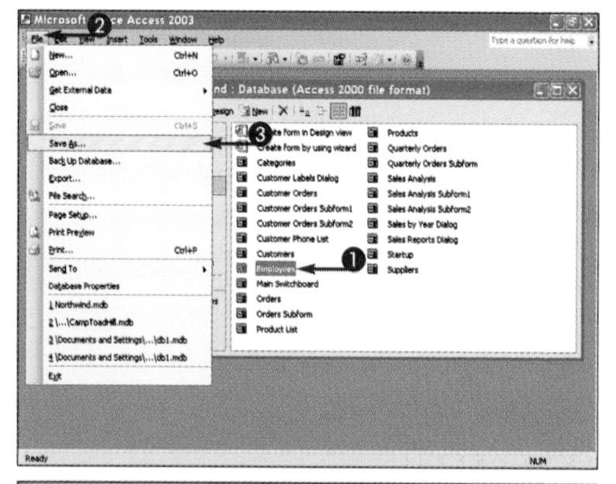

The Save As dialog box appears.

4. Type a unique name for the page.
5. Click here and then click Data Access Page.
6. Click OK.

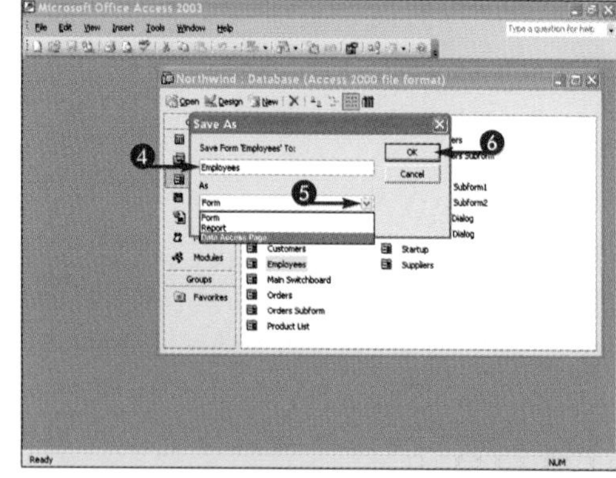

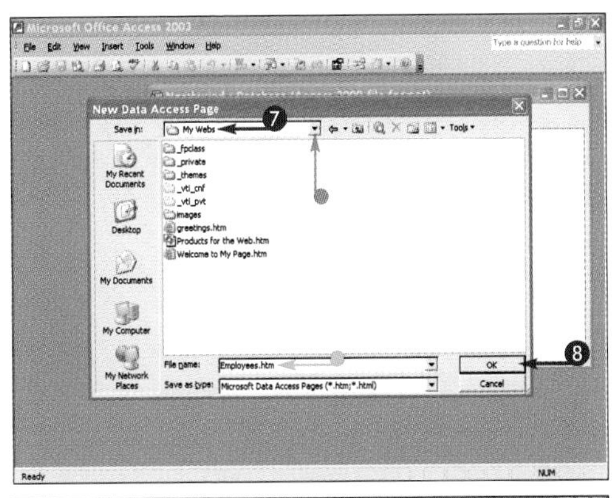

The New Data Access Page dialog box appears.

7. Open the folder in which you want to store the page.

- You can click here to navigate to the folder you want.

- If you did not name the file in step **4**, you can do so now in the File name box.

8. Click OK.

Access saves the form or report as a data access page, ready for posting on the Web.

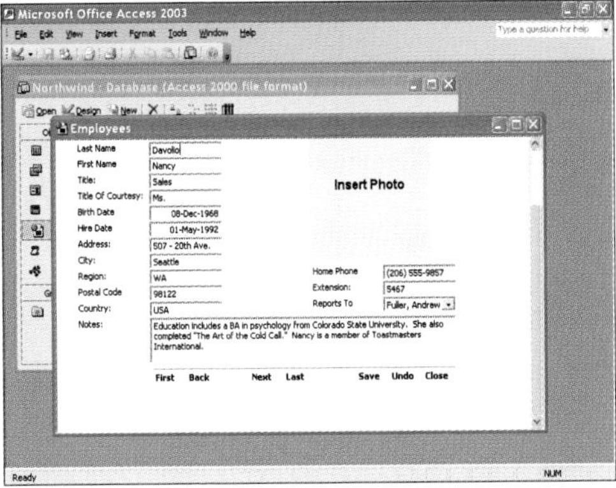

Did You Know?

If you use Microsoft Internet Explorer, you can display a Web page on a form. Open the form in Design View and click the More Controls button on the Toolbox. Click Microsoft Web Browser in the list of ActiveX controls, and click on the form where you want the control object to appear. You can now move and resize the object.

Appendix A

General Office Shortcuts

Action	*Shortcut Key*
Cut	Ctrl+X
Copy	Ctrl+C
Paste	Ctrl+V
Open	Ctrl+O
Cycle between open windows	Alt+Tab
Close a document	Ctrl+W
Close the program window	Alt+F4
Save	Ctrl+S
Open the Save As dialog box	F12
New document	Ctrl+N
Print	Ctrl+P
Select All	Ctrl+A
Find	Ctrl+F
Replace	Ctrl+H
Go To	Ctrl+G
Task pane	Ctrl+F1
Help	F1
Spelling	F7
Undo	Ctrl+Z
Redo	Ctrl+Y
Bold	Ctrl+B
Italics	Ctrl+I
Underline	Ctrl+U
Subscript	Ctrl+=
Superscript	Ctrl+Shift++
Cycles through upper, lower, and title case	Shift+F3

Action	Shortcut Key
Insert a hyperlink	Ctrl+K
Copy a picture of the screen to the Clipboard	PrtScn
Move to the end of a text line	End
Move to the beginning of a text line	Home
Display Properties dialog box	Alt+Enter

Word Shortcuts

Action	Shortcut Key
Select an entire word	Double-click anywhere in the word
Select an entire sentence	Press Ctrl while clicking in the sentence
Select an entire paragraph	Triple-click anywhere in the paragraph
Move to the beginning of the current word	Ctrl+Left Arrow
Move to the beginning of the next word	Ctrl+Right Arrow
Move to the beginning of a paragraph	Ctrl+Up Arrow
Move to the beginning of the next paragraph	Ctrl+Down Arrow
Indent a paragraph	Ctrl+M
Remove an indent	Ctrl+Shift+M
Hanging indent	Ctrl+T
Remove a hanging indent	Ctrl+Shift+T
Center a paragraph	Ctrl+E
Left-align a paragraph	Ctrl+L
Right-align a paragraph	Ctrl+R
Justify a paragraph	Ctrl+J
Create a non-breaking space	Ctrl+Shift+Spacebar

continued

Word Shortcuts *(continued)*

Action	*Shortcut Key*
Create a page break	Ctrl+Enter
Create a line break	Shift+Enter
Remove all formatting	Ctrl+Shift+N
Open the Page Setup dialog box	Double-click the ruler margin
Open the Paragraph dialog box	Double-click an indent marker
Open the Tab dialog box	Double-click a tab marker
Insert the current date	Alt+Shift+D
Insert the current time	Alt+Shift+T
Set single-space line spacing	Ctrl+1
Set double-space line spacing	Ctrl+2
Set 1.5-line spacing	Ctrl+5
Open the Macros dialog box	Alt+F8
Open the Thesaurus	Shift+F7
Open the Word Count dialog box	Ctrl+Shift+G
Recalculate word count on the Word Count toolbar	Alt+C

Excel Shortcuts

Action	*Shortcut Key*
Edit cells	F2
Delete cells entirely	Ctrl+-
Move between open workbooks	Ctrl+Tab
Move to the next sheet	Ctrl+PgDn
Move to the previous sheet	Ctrl+PgUp
Insert a new worksheet	Shift+F11
Select the current sheet and the next sheet	Shift+Ctrl+PgDn

Action	*Shortcut Key*
Select the current sheet and the previous sheet	Shift+Ctrl+PgUp
Select the entire column	Ctrl+Spacebar
Select the entire row	Shift+Spacebar
Display the Format Cells dialog box	Ctrl+1
Select a range of cells	Ctrl+Shift+*
Enter a line break within a cell	Alt+Enter
Toggle between absolute and relative cell references	F4
Toggle between viewing values and formulas in cells	Ctrl+`
Delete the selected cells	Ctrl+-
Insert blank cells	Ctrl+Shift++
Hide the selected rows	Ctrl+9
Unhide any hidden rows in the selection	Ctrl+Shift+(
Hide the selected columns	Ctrl+0
Unhide any hidden columns in the selection	Ctrl+Shift+)
Apply an outline border to the selected cells	Ctrl+Shift+&
Remove the outline border	Ctrl+Shift+_
Open the Visual Basic Editor	Alt+F11
Insert the current date	Ctrl+;
Insert the current time	Ctrl+Shift+;
Insert the current date and time	Ctrl+;+Spacebar then Ctrl+Shift+;
Create a chart	F11
Repeat the last action	F4
Define a range name	Ctrl+F3
Fill a range to the right	Ctrl+R
Fill a range down	Ctrl+D
Enter the cent character	Alt+0162

continued

Excel Shortcuts *(continued)*	
Action	***Shortcut Key***
Enter the pound sterling character	Alt+0163
Enter the yen symbol	Alt+0165
Enter the euro symbol	Alt+0128
Display the Insert Function dialog box	Shift+F3
Copy the value from the cell above	Ctrl+Shift+"
Copy the formula from the cell above	Ctrl+'
Edit a cell comment	Shift+F2
Apply the currency format	Ctrl+Shift+$
Apply the percentage format	Ctrl+Shift+%
Apply the exponential number format	Ctrl+Shift+^
Apply the number format with two decimals	Ctrl+Shift+!
Apply the general number format	Ctrl+Shift+~
Display the Style dialog box	Alt+'

PowerPoint Shortcuts	
Action	***Shortcut Key***
Switch between Outline and Slide view	Ctrl+Shift+Tab
Insert a new slide	Ctrl+M
Duplicate the current slide	Ctrl+D
Increase font size	Ctrl+Shift+>
Decrease font size	Ctrl+Shift+<
Display the Font dialog box	Ctrl+T
Open the properties for an object	Double-click the object
Promote a paragraph in an outline	Alt+Shift+Left Arrow
Demote a paragraph in an outline	Alt+Shift+Right Arrow
Move selected outline paragraphs up	Alt+Shift+Up Arrow

Action	*Shortcut Key*
Move selected outline paragraphs down	Alt+Shift+Down Arrow
Display outline heading level	Alt+Shift+1
Expand outline text below a heading	Alt+Shift++
Collapse outline text below a heading	Alt+Shift+-
Collapse or show all text or headings	Alt+Shift+A
Show or hide the grid	Shift+F9
Show or hide guides	Alt+F9
Change grid and guide settings	Ctrl+G
Run a slide show	F5
Activate the Pen tool during a show	Ctrl+P
Erase Pen tool drawings during a show	E
Turn off the Pen tool	Esc
Change the pen to a pointer	Ctrl+A
Hide the pointer or pen	Ctrl+H
Move to the next hyperlink	Tab
Make the screen go black during a show	B
Make the screen go white during a show	W
Stop or restart a show	S
Return to the first slide	1+Enter

Outlook Shortcuts

Action	*Shortcut Key*
Switch to Mail	Ctrl+1
Switch to Calendar	Ctrl+2
Switch to Contacts	Ctrl+3
Switch to Tasks	Ctrl+4

continued

Outlook Shortcuts *(continued)*	
Action	***Shortcut Key***
Switch to Notes	Ctrl+5
Switch to Folder List in the Navigation pane	Ctrl+6
Next item	Ctrl+,
Previous item	Ctrl+.
Create a new appointment	Ctrl+Shift+A
Create a new contact	Ctrl+Shift+C
Create a new distribution list	Ctrl+Shift+L
Create a new journal entry	Ctrl+Shift+J
Create a new task	Ctrl+Shift+K
Create a new note	Ctrl+Shift+N
Create a new fax	Ctrl+Shift+X
Create a new e-mail message	Ctrl+Shift+M
Flag a message for follow-up	Ctrl+Shift+G
Forward a message	Ctrl+F
Send a message	Ctrl+Enter
Reply to a message	Ctrl+R
Reply All to a message	Ctrl+Shift+R
Check for new e-mail	Ctrl+M or F9
Open a received message	Ctrl+O
Mark a message as read	Ctrl+Q
Dial a contact phone number	Ctrl+Shift+D
Create a new folder	Ctrl+Shift+E
Display the current week in Calendar view	Alt+-
Display the current month in Calendar view	Alt+=
Change the number of Calendar days that display	Alt+(any number from 1-10)
Find a contact	F11

Access Shortcuts

Action	*Shortcut Key*
Select the current column containing the selected cell in Datasheet view	Ctrl+Spacebar
Select the column to the right of the current column	Shift+Right Arrow
Select the column to the left of the current column	Shift+Left Arrow
Undo changes for the current field	Press Esc Once
Undo changes for the current record	Press Esc Twice
Insert the current date	Ctrl+;
Insert the current time	Ctrl+:
Insert the current date and time	Ctrl+;+Spacebar then Ctrl+Shift+;
Insert the default field value	Ctrl+Alt+Spacebar
Insert the value of the previous record	Ctrl+'
Add a new record	Ctrl++
Delete the current record	Ctrl+-
Save changes to the current record	Shift+Enter
Recalculate the fields	F9
Requery	Shift+F9
Open a combo box	Alt+Down Arrow
Review a referenced code	Shift+F2
Display the property sheet in Design View	F4
Switch to Form View from Design View	F5
Open the property sheet for a selected object	Shift+V+P
Switch to the Code Builder window from Design View	F7
Return to Design view from the VB Editor window	Shift+F7
Switch between upper and lower window portions	F6
Bring the Database window to the front	F11

continued

Access Shortcuts *(continued)*	
Action	***Shortcut Key***
Cycle between open windows	Ctrl+F6
Open the Zoom box	Shift+F2
Rename a selected object in the Database window	F2
Create a new object in the Database window	Alt+N
Refresh the Database window	F5
Open the selected object in the Database window	Ctrl+Enter

Index

D

Index

E

F

G

H

I

J

K

L

Index

Q

R

S

Index

T

U

V

W

X

Index

Z